My Soul Lives in These Mountains

A collection of stories, poems and paintings of the Chilliwack Cascades

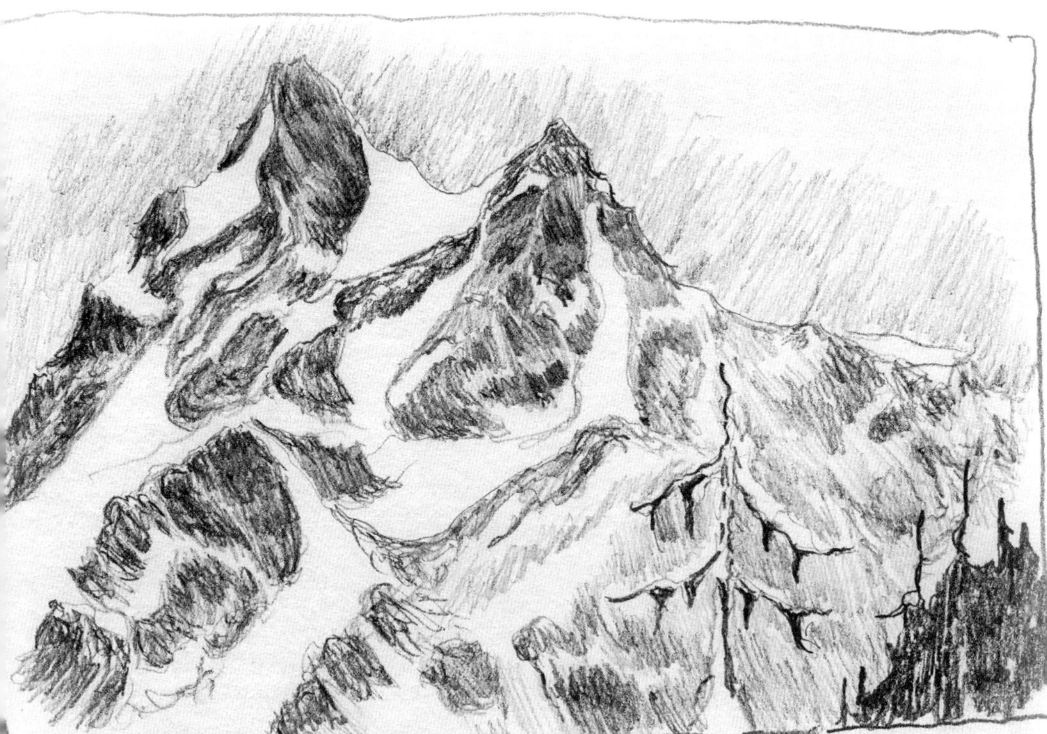

Peter D. Scott

I0894406

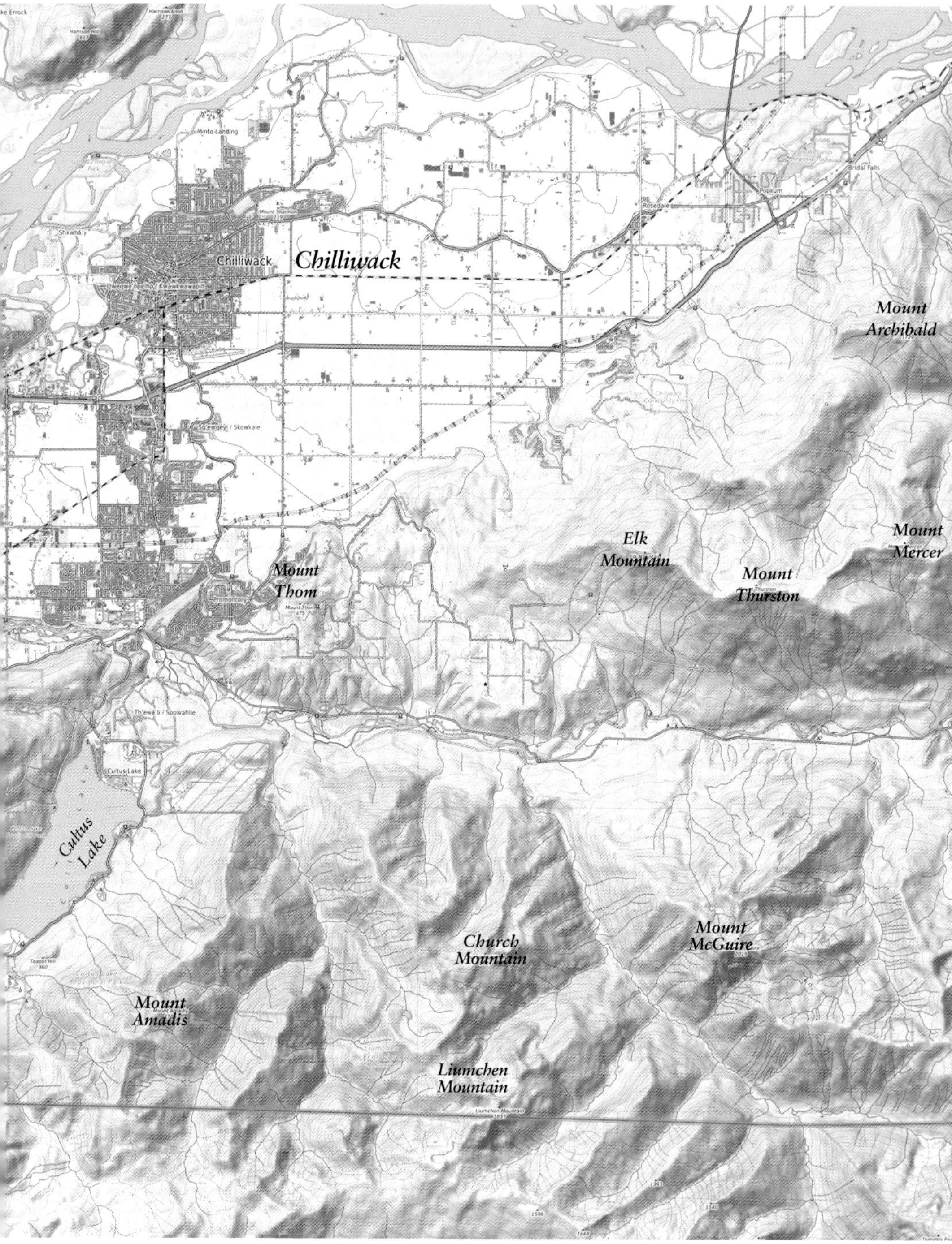
Chilliwack
Mount Archibald
Elk Mountain
Mount Mercer
Mount Thom
Mount Thurston
Cultus Lake
Church Mountain
Mount McGuire
Mount Amadis
Liumchen Mountain

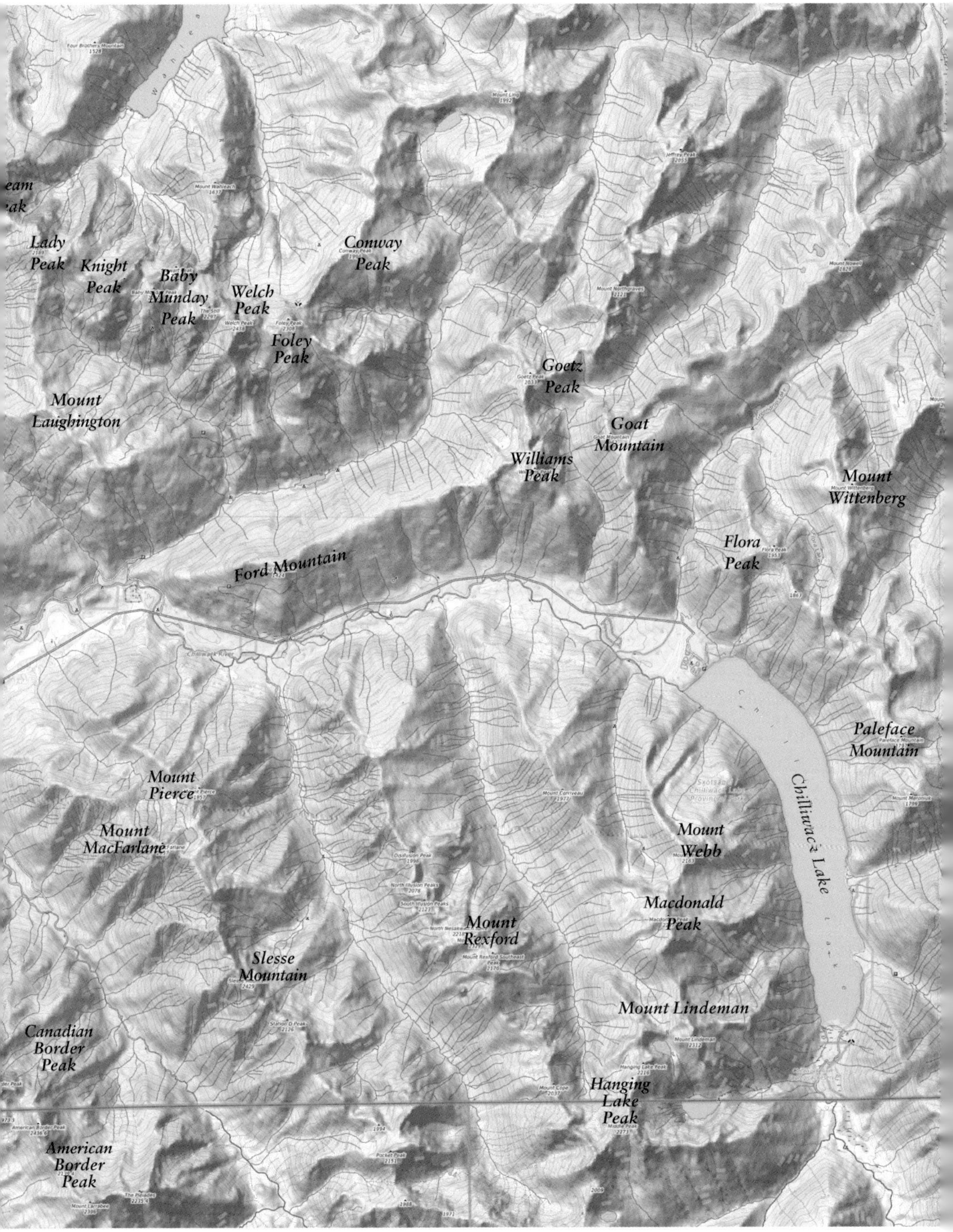
Lady Peak
Knight Peak
Baby Munday Peak
Welch Peak
Conway Peak
Foley Peak
Goetz Peak
Mount Laughington
Goat Mountain
Williams Peak
Mount Wittenberg
Flora Peak
Ford Mountain
Paleface Mountain
Chilliwack Lake
Mount Pierce
Mount MacFarlane
Mount Webb
Macdonald Peak
Mount Rexford
Slesse Mountain
Mount Lindeman
Canadian Border Peak
Hanging Lake Peak
American Border Peak

Cataloguing data available from Library and Archives Canada
978-0-88839-788-1 [paperback]

978-0-88839-798-8 [epub]

Printed in Korea

Cover Art: Peter Scott
Editor: D. Martens
Design & Layout: J. Rade, M. Lamont, E. Morton

We acknowledge the support of the Government of Canada through the Canada Book Fund and the Canada Council for the Arts, and of the Province of British Columbia through the British Columbia Arts Council and the Book Publishing Tax Credit.

Canada
BRITISH COLUMBIA ARTS COUNCIL
BRITISH COLUMBIA
Supported by the Province of British Columbia

Published simultaneously in Canada and the United States by

hancock house

HANCOCK HOUSE PUBLISHERS LTD.
19313 Zero Avenue, Surrey, B.C. Canada V3Z 9R9
#104-4550 Birch Bay-Lynden Rd, Blaine, WA, U.S.A. 98230-9436
(800) 938-1114 Fax (800) 983-2262
www.hancockhouse.com | info@hancockhouse.com

Hancock House gratefully acknowledges the Halkomelem Speaking Peoples whose unceded, shared and asserted traditional territories our offices reside upon.

This is for my parents Vern and Aileen Scott.
Thank-you for allowing me the freedom to explore.

To my Grandfather M.S. Demerse for
teaching me how to tell a good story...

Land Acknowledgment

In writing this book I acknowledge the Stó:lō community, as all the events that transpired in these stories took place on the traditional and unceded territory of the Stó:lō and Ts'elxwéyeqw peoples.

These cultures have existed in the Chilliwack region for thousands of years longer than the "ancient" civilizations of Greece, Egypt, and the mighty Roman Empire. For millennia, the Fraser Valley and Chilliwack River Valley have been their home and they the caretakers of this beautiful area.

The lakes, streams, rivers, and massive monuments of granite known as the Chilliwack Cascades exist to put into perspective the history of this remarkable, irreplaceable, mystical and special locale on this planet Earth.

We are each to cherish, appreciate and protect this sacred place for eternity. Thank you to the original inhabitants of this land for preserving it. We, the visitors to your land, are forever in your debt.

Peter D. Scott

Table of Contents

Foreword

I have known Pete Scott since shortly after I was born. Seriously—we were born two months apart (me first); our mothers were sisters, so we spent a lot of time together. Officially we're cousins, but for over 67 years we have been best friends, schoolmates, roommates, guitar mates, and co-conspirators.

Pete's love of the local Chilliwack Cascade Mountains started at a very early age. As kids, the forests and mountains surrounding Pete's Sardis, B.C., home was our playground. We had many adventures in the woods and only got in serious trouble twice. Once we needed rescuing when the "raft" we built out of an old door for the local quiet stream somehow ended up barrelling down the fast-moving Chilliwack River with two skinny 10-year-olds on board. The second time trouble found us in the bush is a story for another book.

Pete's love and knowledge of the Chilliwack Mountains went into hyperdrive when he landed his dream job in 1978.

At that time, the Chilliwack Search and Rescue and local RCMP needed detailed knowledge of the mountains and valley in order to have the fastest, safest routes to an emergency. They were looking for someone to lead a 14-member team charged with surveying, mapping, repairing and building trails and slashing new routes in the mountain forests. Pete's extensive knowledge of the mountains, plus his training in geography and cartography, made him the obvious choice for project manager. Pete and his crew were basically getting paid to explore the massive Chilliwack River Valley and surrounding mountains, finding routes. How sweet is that, for a mountain-loving guy!

Throughout his life Pete continued to soak up knowledge about the mountains anywhere he could, from colleagues, SAR, research, relatives, First Nations friends and family.

I watched with pride as Pete pursued not one, but two successful careers as a result of his love and knowledge of the Chilliwack Cascade Mountains. First as an acclaimed artist mentored by Gordon Appelbe Smith, famous Canadian artist, and influenced by Emily Carr and Toni Onley. Secondly, as a well- loved art educator never afraid to bend a few rules to inspire his students.

All the while, the mountains kept calling. Pete has had many nicknames over the years. I like "The One Who Never Sleeps," which is an apt testament to his habit of painting and writing late into the night.

So lace up your reading boots, enjoy the artwork, stories, and poems, and discover why Pete's soul lives in the Chilliwack Cascade Mountains.
Andrew Bitcon

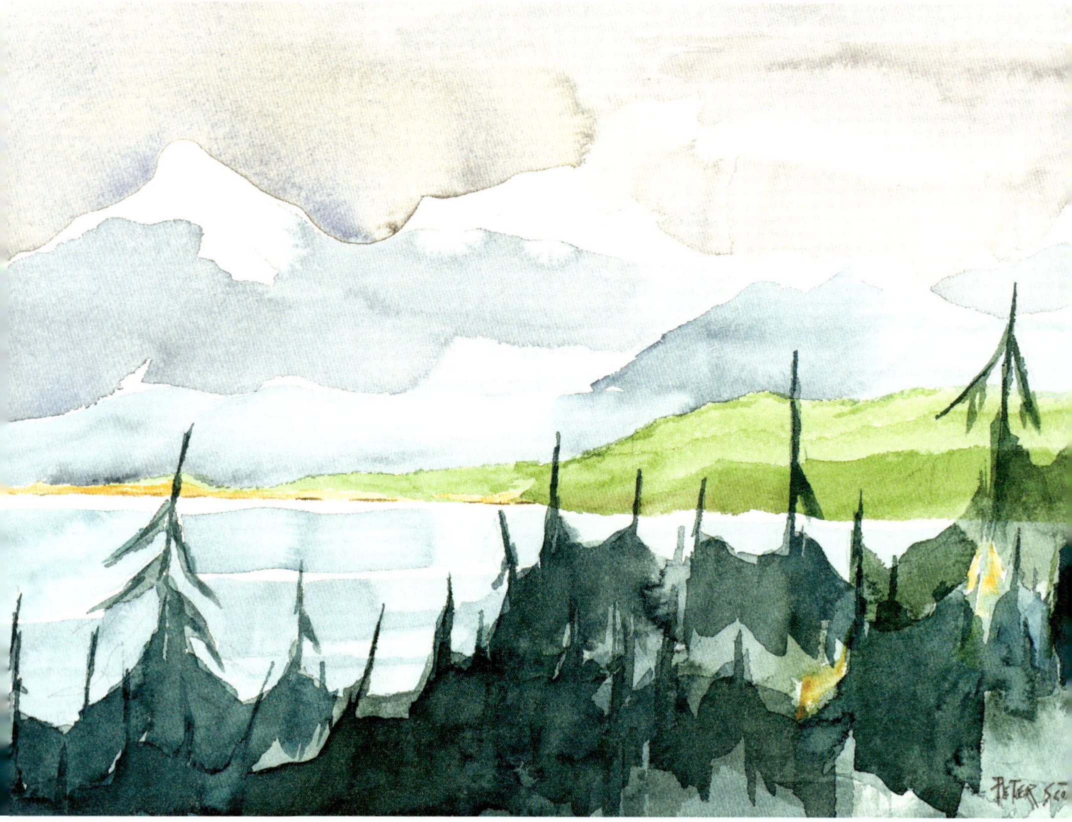

The Cheam Range

Introduction

The Chilliwack River Valley is a magical, mystical place, steeped in legend and lore, from the Ts'elxwéyeqw people to the fur traders, prospectors and European settlers that came to the area.

The valley is surrounded by dramatic mountains. The streams that run down them flow into the beautiful Chilliwack River as it makes its way to Vedder Crossing, where it becomes the Vedder River and eventually empties into the mighty Fraser River.

For thousands of years, the valley was home to the Ts'elxwéyeqws. Their stories of these mountains make the valley an enchanted place.

Growing up in Sardis, I was unfortunately unaware of what a culturally rich place the Chilliwack region is. I was, however, aware of the beautiful scenery and surrounding mountain peaks. I was proud to call this place home.

My maternal grandfather worked in the hop yard at Sardis from the 1920s, and my paternal grandfather worked in the sawmill. My father and uncle worked on their tugboat on the Fraser River.

One of my uncles was of Stó:lō heritage. His family had lived on the great river for thousands of years. From him, I learned the traditional names and stories of the Cascade Mountains and of the "STAW-Lo" River. I am not aboriginal, however several of my relatives are. I admire and respect the First Nations culture.

My reason for writing this book is to share my love of the Chilliwack Cascades and to relate my experiences of working in and exploring them.

These mountains have inspired me to hike and paint them. For decades, I have tried to capture their spirit on canvas. I hope I have succeeded.

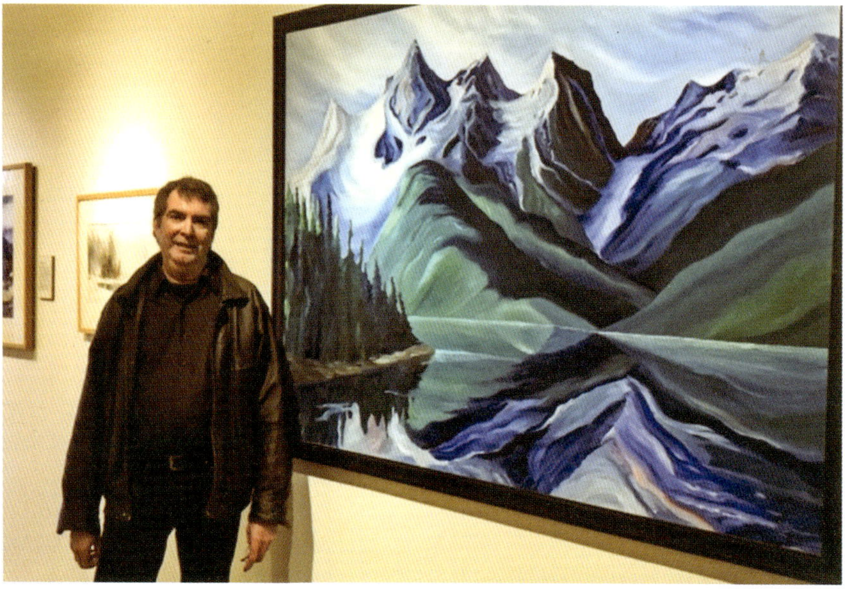

Author with "Lucky Four" painting at the Quesnel Art Gallery

Peter Scott Biography

Book biography

Peter Scott was born in Chilliwack in 1956 and raised in Sardis. He grew up in the shadow of the Chilliwack Cascade Mountains, where he spent much of his youth hiking, camping, sketching and painting.

In 1977, he entered the faculty of education at the University of British Columbia and majored in art with a minor in geography. Peter studied art under the mentorship of the prominent Canadian painter Gordon Appelbe Smith, who helped Peter refine his impressionist style of landscape painting.

In 1978, the Chilliwack Search and Rescue, under the leadership of local mountaineer Neil Grainger and in partnership with the local RCMP detachment, applied for and received a government grant to fund a project that would update all the Forest Service maps of the Chilliwack River Valley. Peter was hired as project manager, and for two summers he and his crews slashed routes to remote areas and built and repaired, surveyed, marked and mapped popular hiking trails throughout the Cheam Range and mountains of that area. The inspiration for his artwork came from the glaciers, forests, and mountains of that region.

In 1983, Peter relocated to Quesnel, B.C., where he began a 30-year career as a secondary school art educator. Peter also spent these years raising a family, coaching a variety of sports, camping, hiking, canoeing and painting vistas of the beautiful Cariboo region of British Columbia.

In 2012, Peter relocated to Osoyoos, in Canada's only desert, and began painting the beautiful lakes, desert landscapes and skies of the Okanagan. There he met a group of local painters known as The Artists on Main. Support and leadership from legendary local artists Helen Fisher, Sandra Albo and others helped him make the transition from high school art educator to full-time working artist.

For the past 46 years, Peter has been painting and selling his artwork professionally. His paintings reflect the vast and varied landscape of his home province, primarily the awe-inspiring Cascade Mountains of Chilliwack. Peter continues to show his work in various galleries, group and one-man shows, and sells to private collectors.

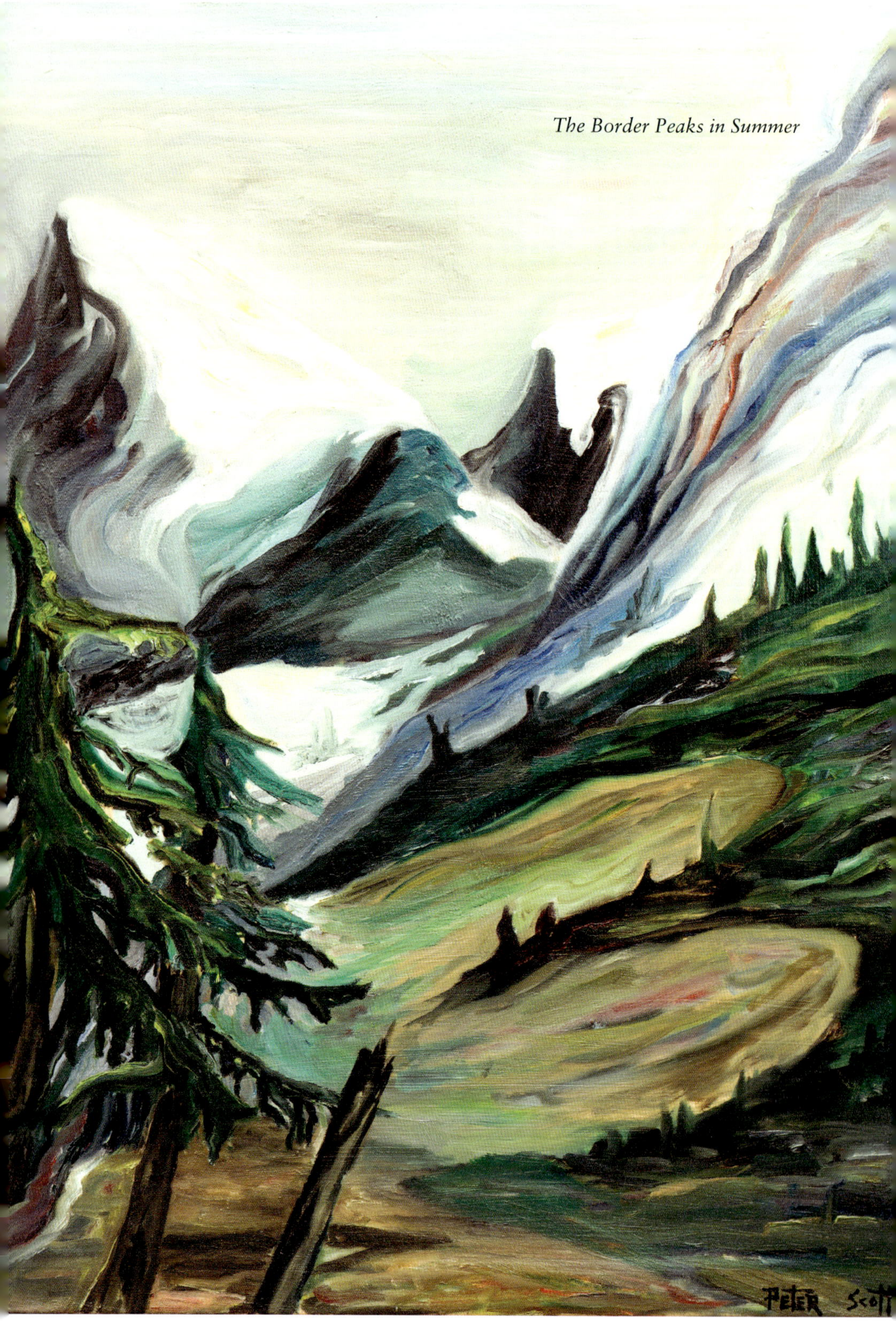

The Border Peaks in Summer

Chapter One

Meeting These Mountains — And Emily Carr

A long time ago, in the shadow of the Chilliwack Cascade Mountains, I was born. I didn't realize at the time that these mountains would have a major influence on my life and serve as the inspiration for my career as an artist. Growing up, I discovered that each of these mountains had personalities and a soul of their own. They were tall, strong and impressive. As a child I saw images of animals in the snow patches on their slopes. They told me stories.

One of my uncles was of Stó:lō heritage and told me the original, traditional names of these peaks, and this made them alive to me.

One of my earliest memories goes back to when I was one year old. I was too young to walk but was able to stand in my crib and support myself with the side rails. My vocabulary consisted of few words. But I have a photographic memory; I remember events as pictures in my mind, and memories replay like vintage movies. I recall this moment clearly because it was when I first became aware of our surrounding mountains. It was early in the morning, and I was standing in my crib, next to the window in my parents' bedroom. I leaned over the railing to pick up a toy tractor with a farmer sitting on the tractor's seat. The toy was soft rubber, and I remember biting the farmer's head off. I still have that childhood toy; it sits on the art table in my studio.

After beheading the farmer, I turned and looked out the window and saw the mountains. Halfway down the slope from Lady Peak's head was a patch of snow. I screamed! I saw a monster's face, and it terrified me. My parents woke and came running to my crib to pacify me. I was frozen in fear. My parents, who also remember that event, say I was pointing to the mountain, screaming "The man! The man!" Confused by my erratic behavior, they couldn't get me to calm down. I screamed and cried and trembled in fear for a long time, despite their efforts to console me. That was the first time my imagination created faces, figures, and animals out of the snowy shapes on the sides of those mountains.

I still see that face on Lady Peak Mountain, the face of a terrifying Sasquatch. For many years I feared Lady Peak, but as I grew older my fear of the "Sasquatch" eventually faded and I came to recognize Lady Peak, Sqwema:y, as the head of a dog, Mount Cheam's faithful companion, and I ceased to fear her. Gradually, I learned to know these mountains more intimately, and they became my friends. As I aged, they all became familiar to me and I soon learned their names: Mount Cheam, Lady Peak, Slesse, Welch Peak, Mount Foley, Elk, Mount Tomyhoi, and the Border Peaks. I was a happy child, surrounded by these impressive, massive monuments of Mother Nature.

When I was a teenager, a friend and I began going on camping trips to the great outdoors. We would load our backpacks with the basics—pup tent, sleeping bag, hatchet, jar of peanut butter, loaf of bread—and then mount our bicycles and make the long ride from Sardis to the Chilliwack River and up the long, winding, hilly Chilliwack Lake Road. Our usual destination was the Slesse Creek Valley. Our favourite camping spot was halfway up the valley, in a sheltered grove of cedars next to Slesse Creek. We would set up our old orange pup tent, start a campfire, and take in the view.

Looming high above us were the Border Peaks, two massive columns of granite. One was on the American side of the border, the other on our side, the Canadian Border Peak. To me, they looked like twin brothers: tall, powerful, and strong. They were our protectors. I never feared the wildlife that roamed the woods—black bears, wolves, cougars. Our Border Peak brothers protected us from harm.

Mount Cheam is the most recognizable and loved mountain in the Chilliwack Cascades. My favourite, however, is Mount Slesse. She stands at the far end of the valley, dominating the skyline. She has a dark history—the killer of 62 souls on the ill-fated Trans-Canada Air Lines flight 810 on Dec. 9, 1956. Her name means Fang in the Halq'emeylem language. To me she is the Madonna, a mother bathed in white, holding her son in her arms. She always looks to me like Michaelangelo's famous sculpture, the Pieta. She impresses me. Mount Slesse is strong, quiet, stoic, and peaceful. A mother figure, tall and alone, standing proud among her brothers and sisters of the Cascade Range.

When I was 19, I moved to Vancouver to major in art at the University of British Columbia. I was fortunate to have one of Canada's prominent painters as my mentor. Gordon Appelbe Smith was a major force in the Canadian art world. He had been a friend of Lawren Harris, the legendary leader of the famous Group of Seven impressionist landscape painters. Through Gordon, I learned several of Lawren Harris's painting techniques, which helped shape my painting style.

When I began studying, Gordon taught us how to stretch a canvas, gave us basic colour theory, and told us to create a painting. I was a duck out of water. I was a kid from the country living in the city. I needed to paint trees, so I headed to a large grove of cedars on the campus, located at the anthropology museum. Bill Reid, the First Nations carver, had just completed a mortuary pole, and it had been erected in front of a longhouse. I sketched the scene, then returned to the studio and painted a large three-by-three-foot oil of the longhouse and totem pole. Gordon told me I painted like Emily Carr. I told him maybe she painted like me. He laughed and told me she was a famous B.C. artist. He then took me to the Vancouver Art Gallery and introduced me to their permanent Emily Carr collection. I had never seen anything like it. Each of those paintings emanated a force of energy. I was hooked. Emily Carr became my favourite artist, and her work changed my life.

Gordon instructed me to visit the gallery twice a week and sketch from her paintings. This procedure shaped my style and taught me how to paint trees. When I returned to the classroom to finish my totem painting, a man in a suit visited our class and came over to look at my painting. He was captivated and asked if he could buy it. Being a starving artist, I quickly said yes, and for three hundred dollars it could be his. Three hundred dollars would buy a lot of peanut butter and paint. I told him I had a few finishing touches to complete and asked him to return the next day. He agreed. When I returned to the studio the following day, I discovered my painting was missing.

When the businessman arrived to get his painting, I told him it was gone. My first artistic work, and someone had stolen it. He was disappointed. I was devastated. Gordon came over and told me having a painting stolen was the highest form of flattery. Great. I wanted the three hundred dollars so I could eat.

BORDER PEAKS

Guardians of a boundary
that separate our lands,
mighty, strong, majestic,
powerful and grand.

Together stand like brothers,
protecting all the land.
Existing for a thousand
years, hovering over man.

Granite, quartz and feldspar,
solid to the core.
To the sky, they speak and
try, tall their summits soar.

Man has tried to own them,
feeble efforts all,
to stand upon their peaks so
high, daring not to fall.

For an eternity,
they will stand their ground,
looming o'er the valley, they
are timeless bound.

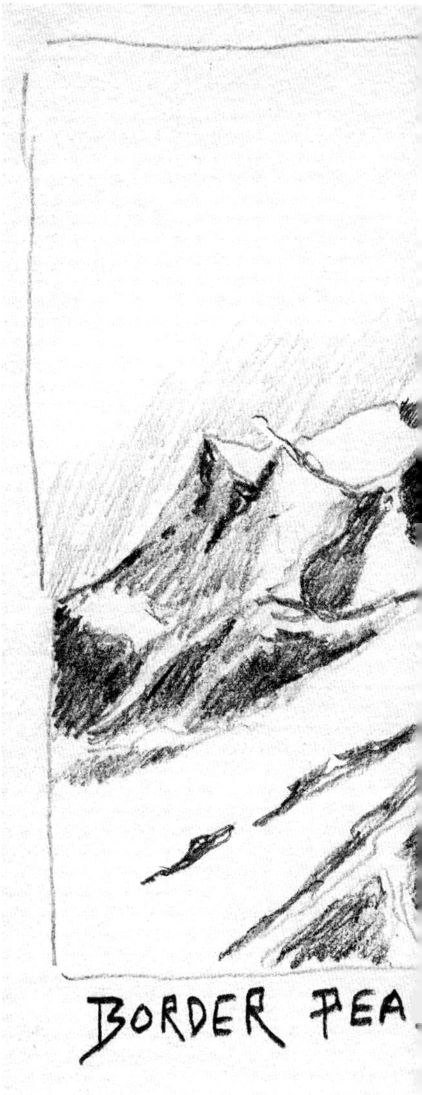

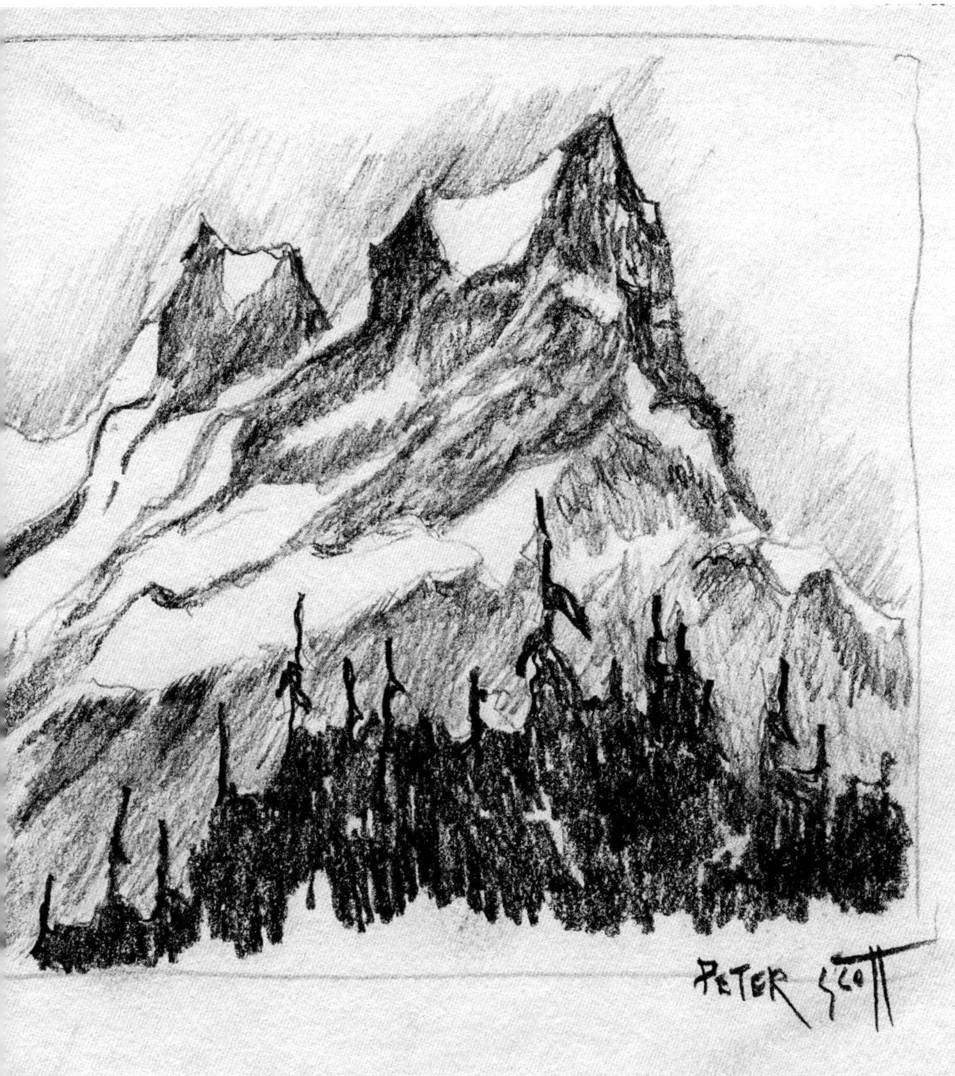

Sketch of the Border Peaks

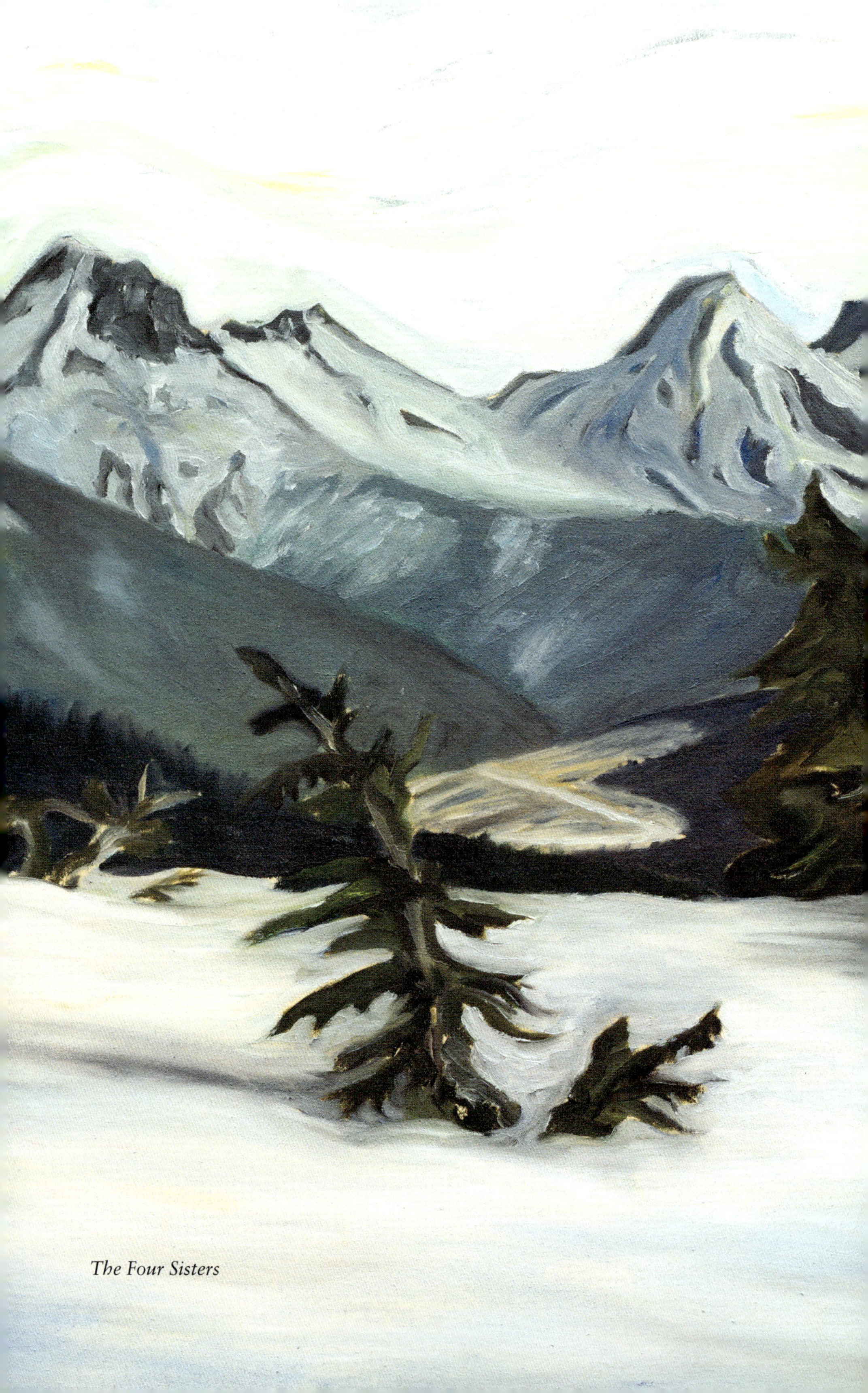

The Four Sisters

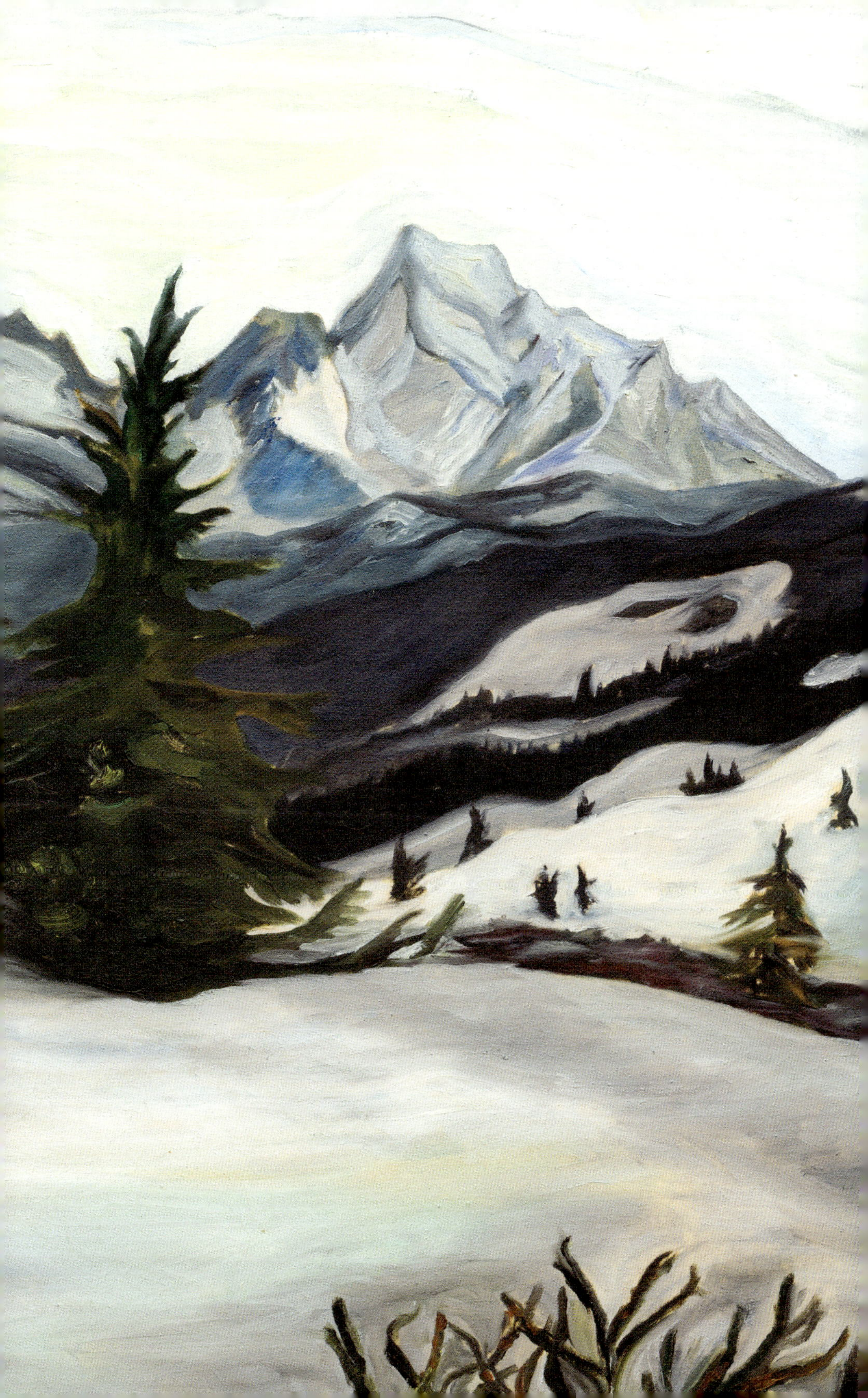

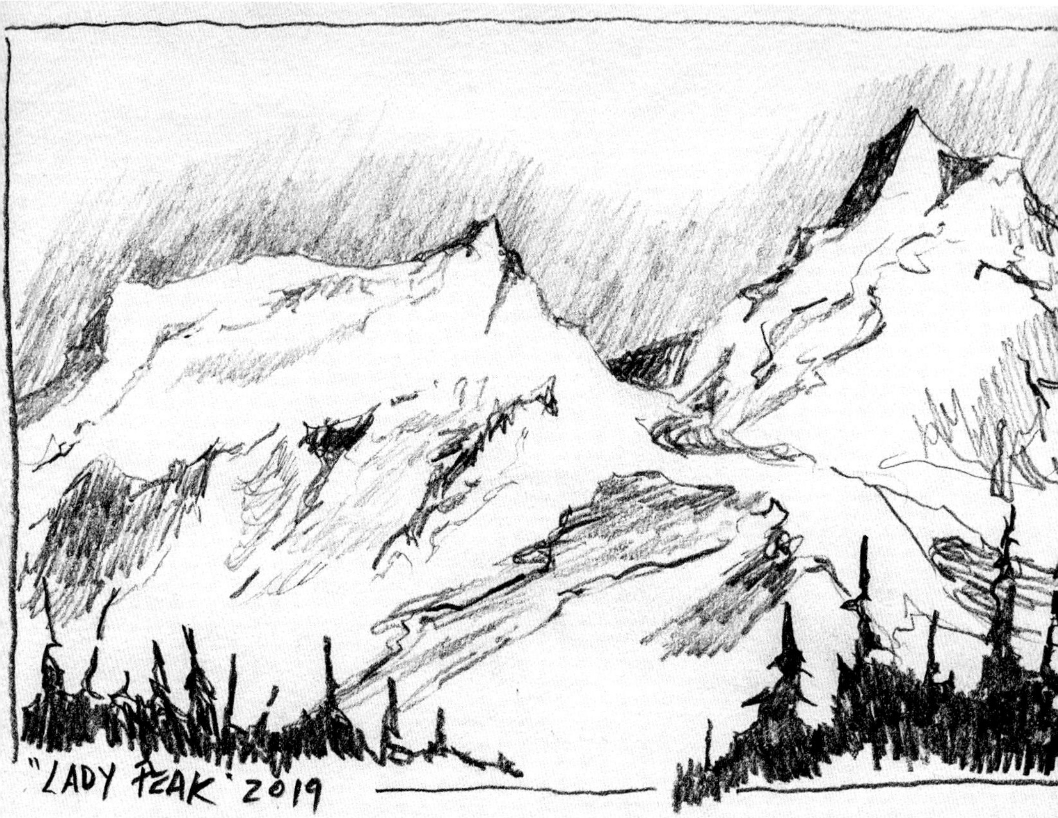

Lady Peak

Chapter Two

Where Did These Mountains Come From?

The Cascade Range is a great mountain range in North America. It spans all the way from southern British Columbia, Canada, to Northern California in the United States, and is nearly 700 miles (1100 km) long.

The Cascade Range was formed when the Juan De Fuca Plate (part of the oceanic crust) dove under the North American Plate (the continental crust). The collision of these plates caused an uplift in the Earth's crust and resulted in the formation of the Cascade Mountains.

The Cascade Range has been volcanically active for several million years. The mountains lie within the Pacific Ring of Fire and are part of the Pemberton Volcanic Belt. The large Chilliwack Batholith forms much of the North Cascades and Washington State. Formed from cooled magma deep in the Earth's crust, it ranges from 26 million to 29 million years old. In Greek, bathos means "depth" and lithos means "rock." A batholith is always composed of rock such as granite, quartz and feldspar.

Some 10,000 years ago, the Chilliwack River Valley was covered, or partially covered, in massive glaciers and lakes. This geological activity carved the landscape that is known today.

The Chilliwack Batholith is responsible for the rugged peaks of Mount Rexford, Mount Slesse and the Border Peaks. There are also extensive areas of ancient volcanic and sedimentary rocks. The limestones of the Borden-Slesse Creeks area in the Chilliwack Valley here and there reveal fossil crinoids, starfish-like animals that flourished in warm seas over 200 million years ago. In 1978, my crew and I came across an area full of these fossils on Mount McGuire.

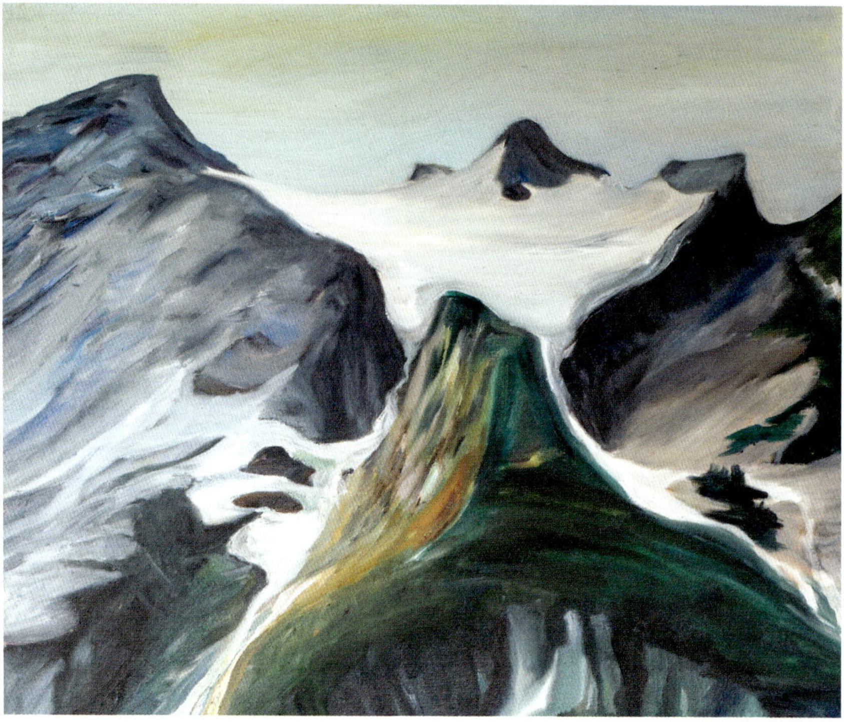

Mount Tomyhoi

Over the past million years, there have been at least four ice ages, during which continental ice sheets overrode the land. Since those days, smaller alpine glaciers, some of them still in existence, have altered the mountains further.

The North Cascades feature some of the most rugged topography in the Cascade Range. The four western mountain peaks, Mount Cheam, Lady Peak, Baby Munday, and the Still, are known as the "Four Sisters."

The eastern peaks, at the south end of Waleach Lake, are known as the "Lucky Four." They consist of Welch Peak, Mount Foley, Knight Peak and Stewart Peak. Foley, Welch and Stewart are named for the three partners who founded the abandoned Lucky Four Mine, located on the ridge above Waleach Lake near the cirque formed by Welch Peak and Foley Mountain. Within the cirque lies the Lucky Four Glacier.

The view of these massive peaks is spectacular from Waleach Lake and has inspired many of my paintings over the years.

PROMINENT MOUNTAINS WITHIN THE CHILLIWACK RIVER VALLEY

MOUNT CHEAM – Protector of the Stó:lō people and one of the Four Sisters group of the Cheam Range. Mount Cheam overlooks the city of Chilliwack at an elevation of 6,903 feet (2104 metres).

When I was a teen-ager I knew a prominent Stó:lō Elder, Mrs. Amy Cooper. I used to visit her and her husband Albert every Thursday afternoon at their little house in the Chilliwack River Valley down near the River. She always told me stories of the local mountains. One of her stories was of Mount Cheam. Mrs. Cooper told me that Cheam was a Halq'emeÿlem word pronounced "Chiyo:m" which means "always wild strawberries" or "wild strawberries place' referring to the lowland below.

She also told me the Stó:lō name for the mountain is "Lhilheqey", pronounced "Theeth-uhl-kay" and that Lhiheqey is from the word "Lhelqey" which means "glacier". It also means "to soak dried berries, meat and fish" in the little lakes on top of Mount Cheam to rehydrate their food while they were on hunting trips in the Cheam Range. Mrs. Cooper told me

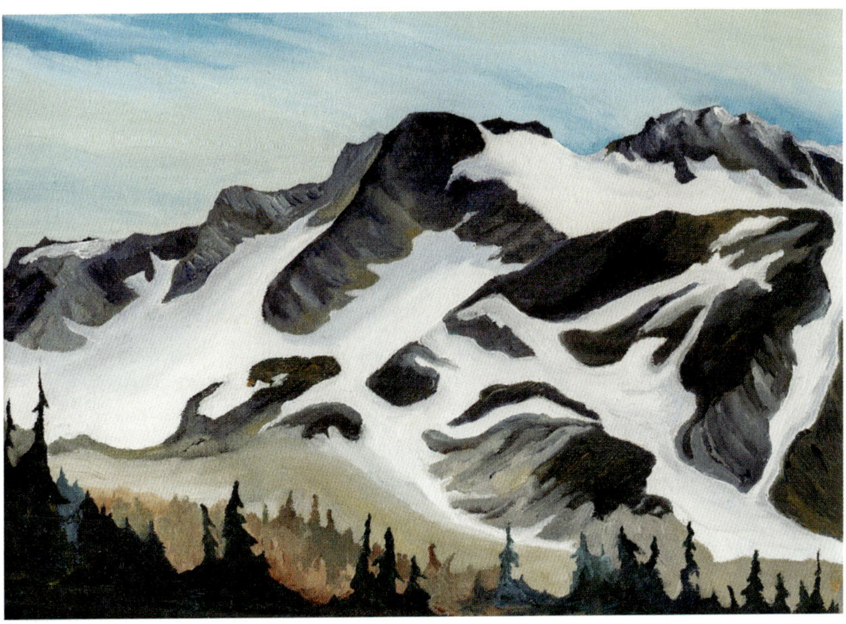

The Still

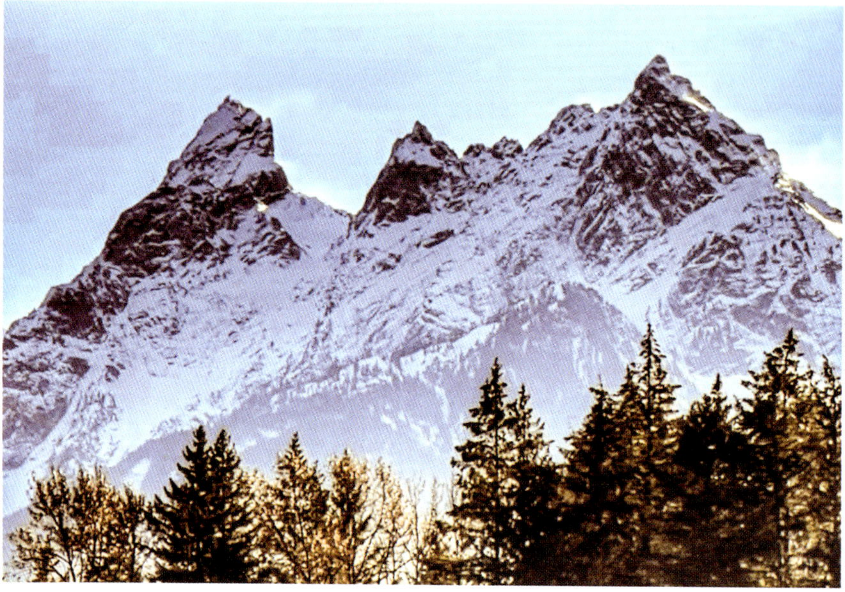

The Border Peaks. Photo by Skipper Fisher.

Lhilheqey refers to the west ridge of the mountain's peak.

There is an angel-shaped snow patch on Mount Cheam that looks out over the valley and is best seen from the towns of Agassiz and Harrison. The angel is formed when snow melts off Cheam in the summer. Some locals say she protects the valley from flooding, while others believe she is an indication of whether there will be a shortage of fish this season.

Mount Cheam is the most famous and recognizable mountain of the region and is a very popular hike for Lower Mainland residents.

LADY PEAK is located north of the Chilliwack River, and Foley Creek, next to Mount Cheam, is another of the Four Sisters. Called Squema:y in Stó:lō, she is, according to Stó:lō legend, Mount Cheam's dog, rising to an elevation of 7,146 feet (2178 metres).

BABY MUNDAY PEAK, located north of Foley Creek, was named after well-known alpinist Phyllis

Munday, in honour of her mountaineering experience. Elevation 7,382 feet (2250 metres). This is another of Mount Cheam's sisters.

STEWART PEAK, one of the Lucky Four, stands north of the Chilliwack River and Foley Creek, east of Mount Cheam. It was named after Major General John William Stewart, one of the partners of the engineering firm Foley, Welch and Stewart who built the Lucky Four Mine located above Waleach (Jones Lake). Elevation 7,343 feet (2238 metres).

MOUNT FOLEY, another of the Lucky Four, is east of Mount Cheam and north of the Chilliwack River. Named after one of the owners of the Lucky Four Mine, elevation 7,572 feet (2308 metres).

WELCH PEAK, located between Wahleach Lake and the Chilliwack River east of Mount Cheam, is the third of the Lucky Four group. Named after Patrick Welch, also one of the owners of the Lucky Four Mine, it rises to elevation 7,976 feet (2431 metres), the tallest peak of the Cheam Range.

KNIGHT PEAK, located near Mount Welch and Foley Peak, is the last of the Lucky Four group. It was named after E.R. Knight, a leading Chilliwack mountaineering guide. An acknowledged authority on climbing Mount Cheam, Knight led more than 150 Cheam expeditions, and owned and operated a sawmill at Popkum. Elevation 7,333 feet (2235 metres).

THE STILL, north of the Chilliwack River and Foley Creek, is named for the vapour that steams up from gullies on its north face.

MOUNT LINDEMAN stands tall at the south end of Chilliwack Lake, taking its name from Charles Lindeman, who spent many years in the Chilliwack Valley as a pioneer, trapper and prospector. Elevation 7,585 feet (2312 metres).

MOUNT REXFORD, located between Nesakwatch and Center Creeks, south of the Chilliwack River, was named Siyameteq by the Stó:lō. Elevation 7,641 feet (2329 metres).

ILLUSION PEAKS, between Nesakwatch and Center Creeks, west of Chilliwack Lake on the south side of Chilliwack River, were named so by the first ascent party in 1962, who thought the peaks looked easy to climb but were quickly disillusioned. Elevation 6,824 feet (2080 metres).

MOUNT SLESSE, between Nesakwatch and Slesse Creeks, south of the Chilliwack River, was named Silisi, (Suh-LEE-see) by the Stó:lō; it means Fang in the Halq'eméylem language. An impressive, famous mountain in the Chilliwack Cascades and a favorite challenge for local climbers, it rises to 8,002 feet (2439 metres).

CROSS OVER PEAK, northwest of Slesse Mountain, was so named because it's a very popular cross-over hike from the Pierce Lake trail to the Slesse trail. Elevation 7,136 feet (2175 metres).

MOUNT PIERCE stands on the south side of the Chilliwack River, east of Slesse Creek and north of Mount MacFarlane. Named after gold prospector G.O. Pierce, who prospected the mountain in the early 1900s, its peak is at 6,381 feet (1945 metres).

CANADIAN BORDER PEAK, an impressive granite peak located along the British Columbia and Washington State border at the head of Slesse Creek, stands at 7,516 feet (2291 metres).

MOUNT McGUIRE, south of the Chilliwack River, east of Tamahi Creek, was called T'amiyehō:y Mountain by the Stó:lō. In the Halq'eméylem language, this means deformed. Elevation 6,588 feet (2008 metres).

ELK MOUNTAIN, north of the Chilliwack River and next to Mount Thurston and Ryder Lake, makes for a moderately easy hike. A favourite mountain of the local hiking community, it has superb views of the Fraser Valley and surrounding peaks. Elevation 4,698 feet (1432 metres).

Chapter Three

Mount Cheam, Lhilhequey, Mrs Cooper And The Crash

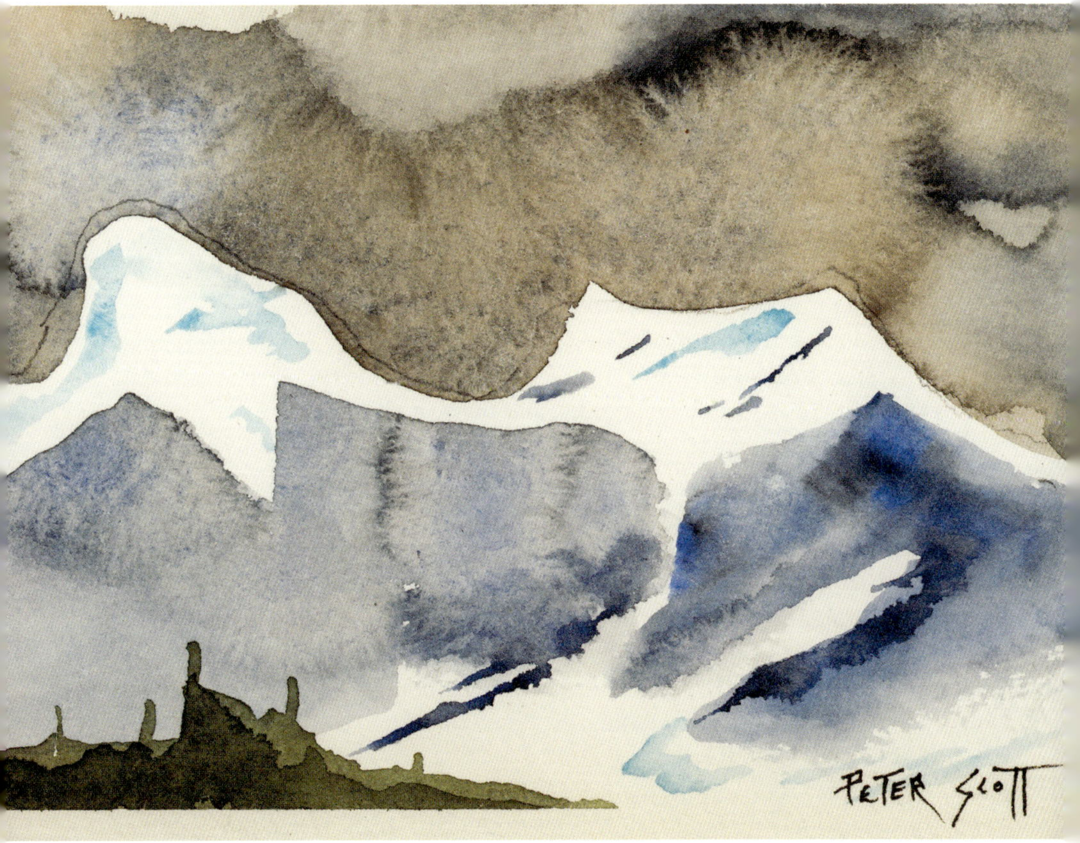

"Rain Over Mount Cheam and Lady Peak"

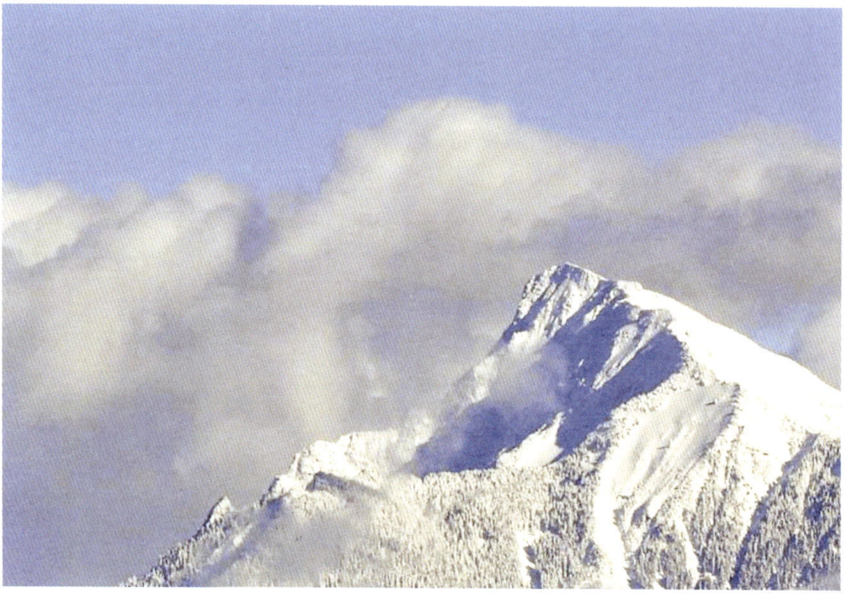

Mount Cheam. Photo by Skipper Fisher.

In September 1974 I began working as a grocery boy at IGA Foods in Vedder Crossing. That summer and fall, employees at the Rogers Sugar refinery went on strike and sugar was in short supply. The IGA had a stockpile of sugar in the basement, at the bottom of the stairs and next to the conveyor belt. On the morning of my first day at work I was unloading the milk delivery and moving stacks of milk cases on a trolley. As I passed the top of the basement stairs, I lost control of the milk cases, and they careened down the stairs and crashed into the sugar stockpile. The milk cartons exploded and soaked all the sugar!

My boss was standing in the storeroom talking to the milkman and witnessed the whole scene. To make the incident even more embarrassing, my dad was the milkman. I was in shock; my boss was in shock. My dad was laughing. Strike one, I thought. I was sure I'd be fired. Instead I was given the position of delivery boy, and every day at 4 p.m. I loaded the grocery orders into my boss's Mazda truck and delivered groceries all over Vedder Crossing, the army camp, the Soowallie reserve and several houses on Chilliwack Lake Road.

The last stop on my route on Thursday afternoons was at Mrs. Amy Cooper's little house, down near the Chilliwack River. She and her husband, Albert, were a very friendly elderly couple and would invite me in for supper every Thursday. I was unaware that Mrs. Cooper was a prominent elder in the Stó:lō community. During the 1960s she helped revive the Stó:lō culture in Chilliwack and was an important historian. During our supper sessions in their kitchen, she would tell me stories and Stó:lō legends of the local area. My favourite was that of Mount Cheam, an iconic mountain considered the mother and guardian of the Stó:lō, the "People of the River."

She stands proud, high above the Fraser River. Nowadays, flocks of people from the Lower Mainland hike to her summit to take in the superb views of the Fraser Valley. The mountain's Stó:lō name is Lhilhequey, pronounced "Theeth-ul-kay," meaning to rehydrate. One evening, Mrs. Cooper explained that Lhilhequey was a very spiritual place to the Stó:lō; she provided them with bear, deer, berries, various plants, and mountain goats. They gathered wool from the mountain goats and depended on the other animals for food. They would rehydrate their dried meat, fish and berries in the small lakes on and around Mount Cheam during hunting expeditions. Wild strawberries grew in the meadows below the peak.

Lhilhequey was the original home of the Goat People. Thousands of years ago, the powerful Transformer Xá:ls met a man from Pā'ku'm (Popkum) and transformed him into a mountain goat. This, she explained, is why there were so many mountain goats on Mount Cheam. One day, many mountain goats came down from Cheam and transformed into people. Many of their descendants live in the Chilliwack area today.

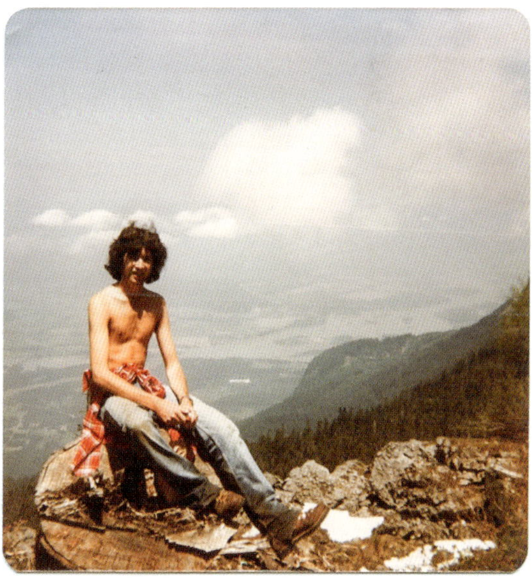

author on Mount Cheam

Mrs. Cooper told me that Mount Cheam is an area of religious importance. Spirit doctors trained there and spent long periods of time isolated in the Cheam highlands. Many of the various peaks of the Cheam Range as well as the mountain lakes, two caves, and the creeks that flow from these lakes all have special Indigenous names, she said, though she couldn't remember them all.

Eons ago, Kwelxá:lxw (Mount Baker), chief of the Nooksack people of Washington State, came to Te'ileque'uk, Chilliwack, looking for a wife. He met Lhilhequey, married her and took her home to Washington. They had three sons: Mount Rainier and Mount Hood however Mrs. Cooper couldn't remember the third son. They also had three young daughters.

One day, Lhilhequey decided to take her daughters and return to Te'ilque'uk, the land of her people. She told Kwelxá:lxw she was going home. Xá:ls, the powerful Transformer, changed Lhilequey, her daughters and her dog to stone so she could stand guard forever over the Stó:lō and the Staw-lo (Fraser) River, to protect them. The three small mountains below Mount Cheam are her daughters Séywot, the eldest, Oyewot, the second, and Xomó:thiya, the youngest.

Xomó:th'iya had an argument with her sisters as to who would stand in front. When she saw the Stó:lō people start to drown with the flooding of the lands below, she began to weep. Ever since, Xomó:thi'ya has stood in front. On a clear day, when mist covers her face, it is said she is crying. Her tears come down as Bridal Falls. Her mother and older sisters and her dog Squema:y (Lady Peak) stand as sentinels along the Cheam Ridge.

Much of this area has now been logged, and today plans are being made to build a gondola to the top of Mount Cheam. One night, after listening to one of Mrs. Cooper's stories, I returned in the delivery truck to Vedder Crossing. I had one more delivery to make. It was a dark, rainy, stormy October night. As I drove slowly along the side of Vedder Road, straining my eyes to find the address of my last delivery, I crashed into a telephone pole. That was not good. I returned to the store, went up to my boss and informed him I had bad news. He replied, "I know, you forgot the Coopers' potatoes." I told him the news was worse than that and led him out in the rain to the parking lot to show him his damaged truck. He was not amused. Again, I thought I would be fired, but again I was given another chance. After the truck was repaired, I returned to my delivery route and my weekly routine of having supper with the Coopers.

I thoroughly enjoyed those visits and the knowledge of the Chilliwack area Mrs. Cooper shared with me.

Cheam

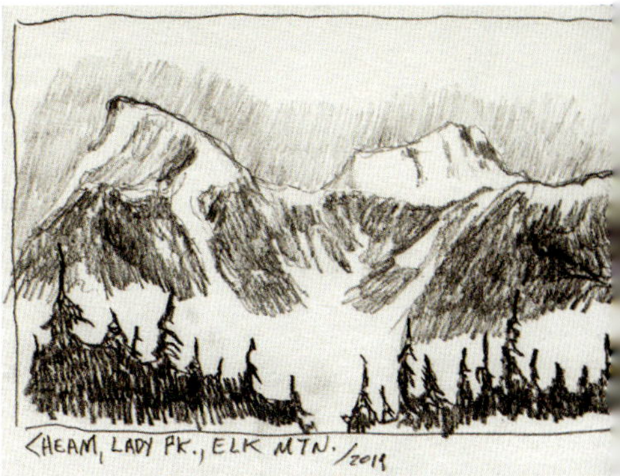

Queen Mother calls you Cheam,
The Creator named you Lhilheqey
Majestic in your stature,
high above the valley.

Kwelxá:lxw tried to own you;
You cannot own a Princess
Your people look upon you,
your beauty and your riches.

Forever and for always,
you will lead the Stó:lō
people. Prominent and regal,
you are nature's
steeple.

Time cannot destroy
you,
man will never own you.
Calm and solid Cheam,
river of time flows on around you.

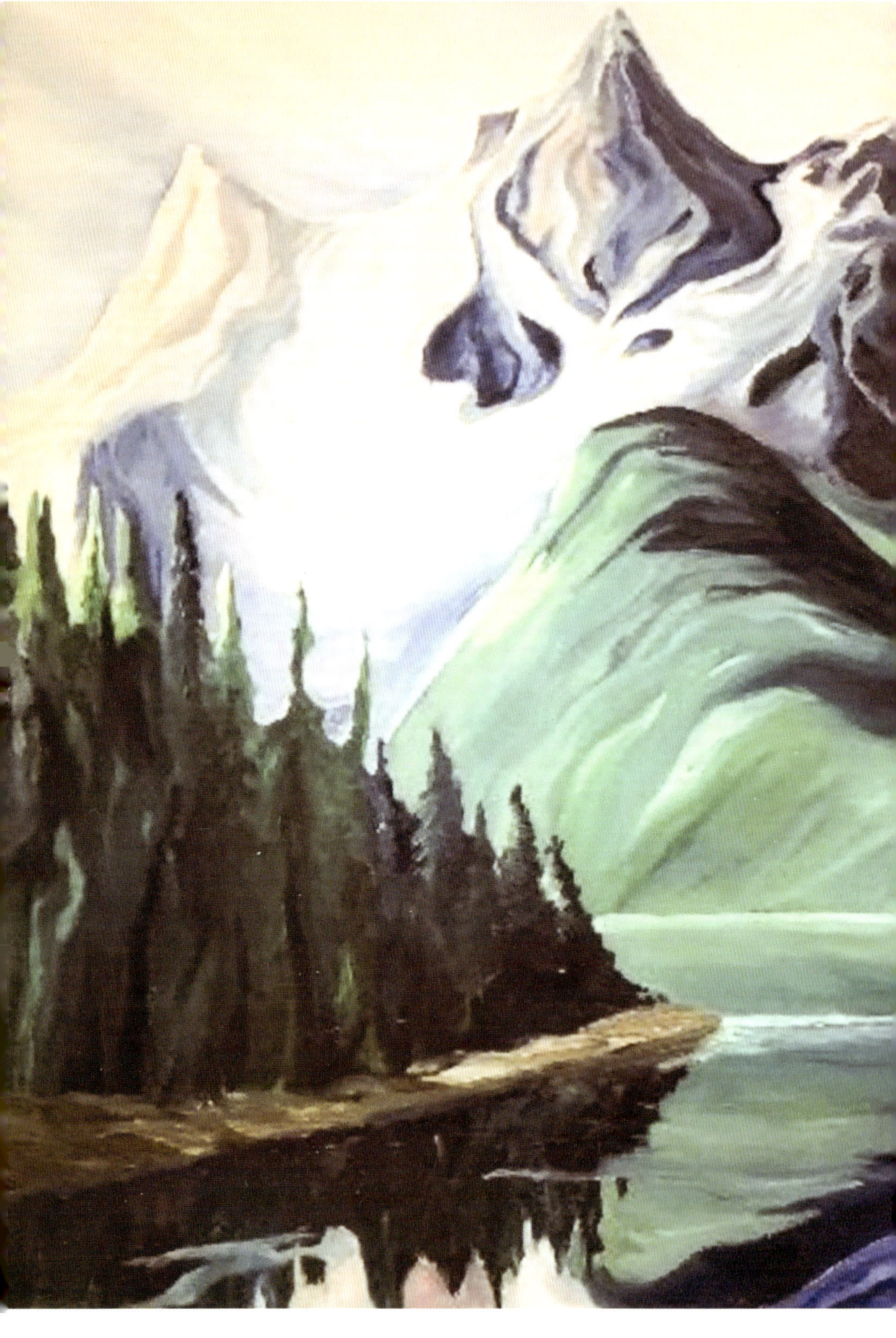

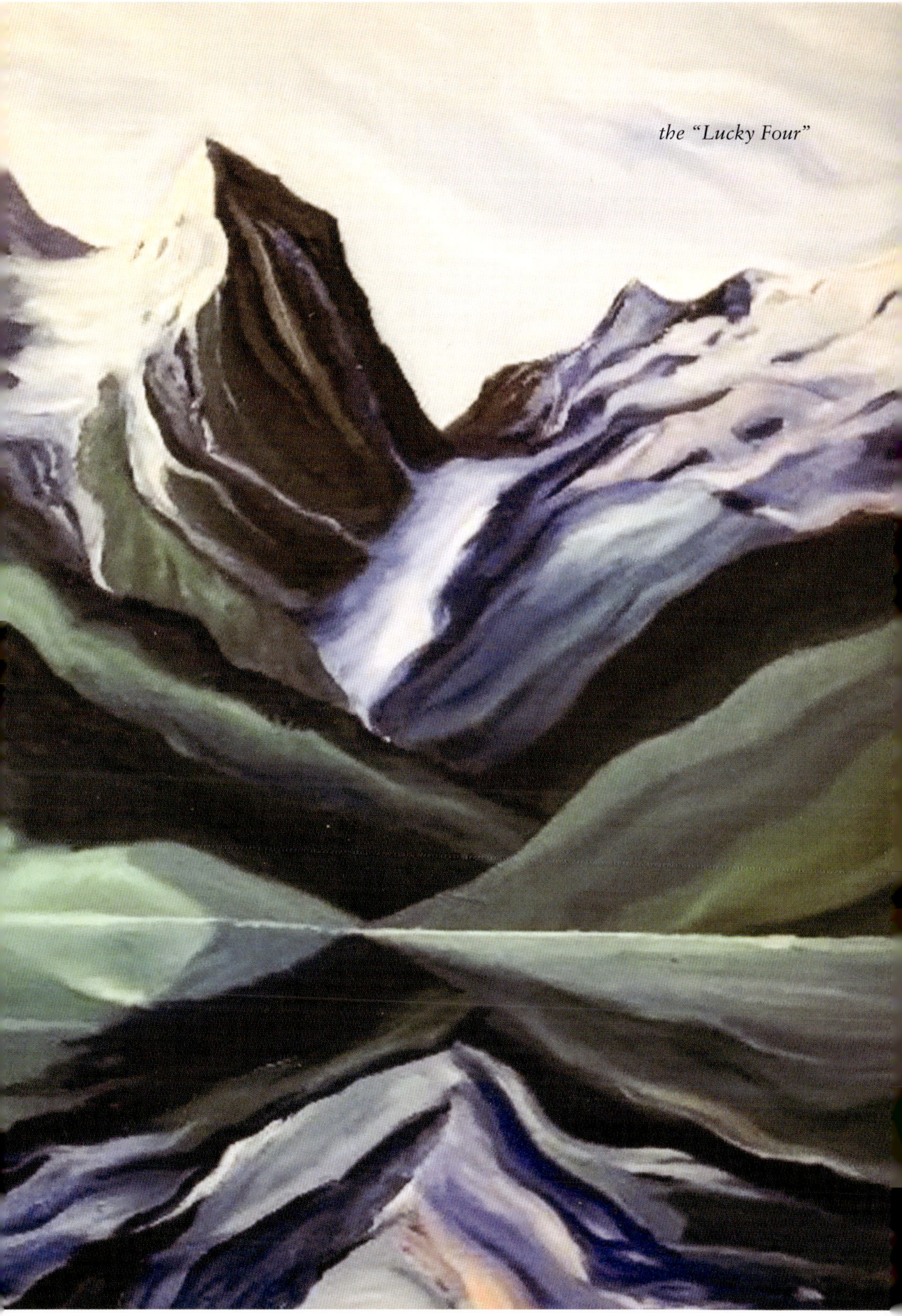

the "Lucky Four"

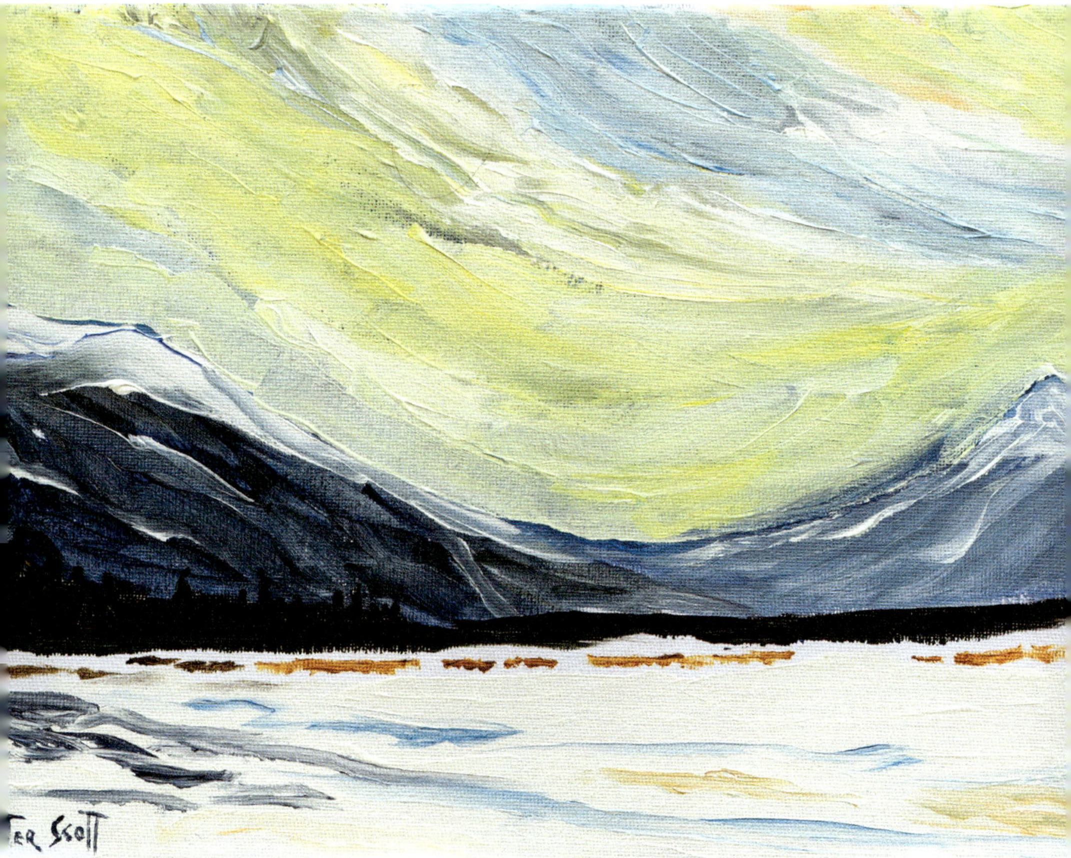

Chilliwack Lake Winter

Chapter Four

Who Are The Ts'elxwéyeqw?

The Ts'elxwéyeqw (Ch.ihl.kway-uhk) people are the First People of the Chilliwack River watershed, one of the tribes of the Stó:lō (STAH-lo), "River People." Archeological studies date the presence of Indigenous people in the area today known as Chilliwack and the Fraser Valley to about 10,000 years ago. It's thought that at the time of first contact, there may have been as many as 40,000 to 60,000 people living within Stó:lō territory.

Stó:lō tradition says that the land, resources, and geographical features were created by Xexaá:ls, the Transformers, the three sons and a daughter of Red-headed Woodpecker and Black Bear. In the mystic past, the four children journeyed down the Harrison River to the Fraser River, then upriver to the sunrise before travelling downriver again to the sunset. During their travels, they set out to make the world right, performing many transformations. People who acted wrongly were turned to stone. Others were transformed into valuable resources, such as cedar, sturgeon, and beaver. Xexá:ls fixed those people and animals that were not transformed into permanent forms, along with the mountains and rivers and other landforms. In this way, the world was made right. The land was transformed so long ago that it was "time immemorial." Ever since, the land has provided for the needs of the Stó:lō, the "People of the River."

The Ts'elxwéyeqw originally lived at Chilliwack, or Sxótsaqel, Lake for hundreds of generations, thousands of years. They built large, semi-permanent pit houses, pelát'tlq, dug partly into the ground and roofed over. To build these typically circular homes, they started by digging a deep pit, with posts to support the roof. The depth helped provide a cool and stable temperature in the summer and a warm and safe temperature in the winter. A pit house was large enough to house extended families. Pit houses existed in the Chilliwack River Valley long before the Pyramids of Egypt.

The Ts'elxwéyeqw descended from the four original Bear brothers: Siyámches, Th'eláchiyatel, Yexwé'ylem and Wilíléq. Wilíléq and his brothers moved the tribal headquarters from the outlet of Sxótsaqel Lake to a site in the Center Creek Valley called Stehiyoq, "place of the fish trap."

In 1782, a massive landslide buried an entire village, killing all the inhabitants. It also affected the local ecology by disrupting the salmon runs to Chilliwack Lake and coincided with a devastating smallpox epidemic introduced by European colonists.

Late in the 18th century, the Ts'elxwéyeqw people established a village named Thathemials, half a kilometer upriver from the bridge at Vedder Crossing. The area now known as Vedder Crossing was originally called Soowahlie, which means to dissolve, or make disappear.

At this time, the fifth man to bear the name Wilíléq was born. When he was older, he facilitated the final stages of the Chilliwack tribe's transformation from a Nooksack-speaking, high-elevation people to full- fledged members of the Fraser River–oriented Stó:lō community. Under Wilíléq the Fifth's leadership,

the Ts'elxwéyeqw people built a gigantic structure with an inverted gable roof at Soowahlie. Running down the center of the gable was a hollowed log capable of holding seven or eight days' worth of rainwater. This magnificent longhouse was named Qóqoláxel and was situated at what is now the south end of the Vedder Bridge. Using gates and levers, the water could be released during ritual events, adding drama to ceremonies. The "Watery Eaves House" became the focal point for Central Fraser Valley ceremonial life.

Wilíléq the Fifth established marriage alliances with prominent Fraser Valley Stó:lō families, as polygamy was still being practiced. He first married a woman from Swi:lhcha (Swee-ehl-cha)—Cultus Lake's original name—and a Katzie wife. Marriage alliances meant gaining access to the resources located along the Fraser River and the new wealth brought by the fur traders. When the tribe moved out into the lower valley of the Chilliwack River, there were times when it was difficult to get their canoes over the shallow waters where the stream spread out into several channels as it left Stito:s (Stee-taws), "the place of crossing."

The word Chilliwack, (Ch.ihl-KWAY-ulk), or Ts'elxwéyeqw, means "going back upstream" to as far as you can go in the shallow channels. When the canoe has reached the point where it can be paddled no further, you change to using a pole. According to Stó:lō elder Albert Louie, at that point the boat has reached what he terms ch'elxwiqw (chihl-AHL-qw), "as far as you can go with a canoe—you can't go no further."

One of the best authorities on Chilliwack history is the late Stó:lō elder Dan Milo, who worked with my grandfather at the B.C. Hop Yard. He told him the meaning of the word is "going back upstream," and explained that in Halq'eméylem, the prefix s, ts, or ch changes a noun to a verbal noun.

Hence the word Ch.il-KWAY is a name descriptive of action—"going back upstream." The action of "going upstream" described the people of the tribe in a canoe going to the head of the stream.

Sxótsaqel (S-HAW_Chyhk_uhl), the name for what is known today as Chilliwack Lake, literally means "head (-qel) of the lake."

Contact with Europeans, beginning in 1782, introduced unfamiliar diseases that decimated the Stó:lō population by 90 to 95 percent. When gold seekers first arrived in British Columbia in 1858, there were few aboriginal people left to meet the challenge of the intruders.

What Is Chilliwack?

The City of Chilliwack lies at the east end of the Fraser Valley, in the shadow of the beautiful Cascade Mountains. It is situated 75 miles east of the coastal port city of Vancouver, British Columbia.

Europeans first explored the valley in December 1828, when fur traders from the Hudson's Bay Company at Fort Langley sent out a party led by Francois Noel Annance to scout out the area. Prospectors followed the fur traders. Soon gold was discovered in the Fraser River at Yale, and the famous Cariboo gold rush was born.

Returning prospectors discovered new wealth in the Fraser Valley. By building dams and diverting streams, they created fertile farmland. To raise beef cattle, early settlers such as Isaac Kipp and Jonathan Reece claimed land in 1859. Reece built a butcher shop at Hope, and Kipp and a crew of men hacked a trail to Yale so they could drive their cattle to the first gold-rush community.

Soon after, the farms in Chilliwack were also producing oats at a yield of three tons per acre, at a value of one hundred dollars a ton delivered to the Cariboo. Later, to provide for their Oregon dairy cattle, James and Chester Chadsey pre-empted hay on Sumas Prairie. They soon produced a 2,500-pound supply of butter, sealed it, canned it and delivered it by ox wagon to the Cariboo at the price of one dollar per pound.

Michael Sweetman acquired a large piece of land between LUXUXUT (Luckakuk) Creek and Keatsey's Sly Slough. This fertile farmland now lies under gas stations, subdivisions, and the Chilliwack Mall. Previously it had been the site of the B.C. Hop Yard Company, the large hops-growing farm where my grandfather worked for 30 years. A brewery now sits where my childhood home used to be.

In 1867, A.C. Wells established the Edenbank Farm next to Luckakuk Creek, where he built the valley's

first creamery. His farm supplied butter and cheese to the Interior and coastal markets for years.

Postal service began in 1870; mail was delivered by riverboat twice a week, and Stó:lō men carried mail to the settlers by backpack and canoe.

The municipality of Chilliwack was incorporated on April 26, 1873, and held its first council meeting in the valley's pioneer Sumas School.

In 1897, prospectors discovered gold on Slesse Creek in the Chilliwack River Valley. Hundreds of gold-seekers flooded the area, filling hotels, buying supplies from local merchants and boosting Chilliwack's economy.

Chilliwack grew quickly, and today's population is over 102,000. The town's proximity to the largest centre in the province has opened Chilliwack to vast development. The area has also become the recreational playground for citizens of the Lower Mainland. Thousands flock to Chilliwack and the nearby mountains, lakes, creeks, and river to camp, hike, kayak, and fish.

People from across the country have discovered the beauty and mild climate of the Chilliwack area and now call this place home.

Chapter Five

The Chilliwack Search And Rescue And My Muse

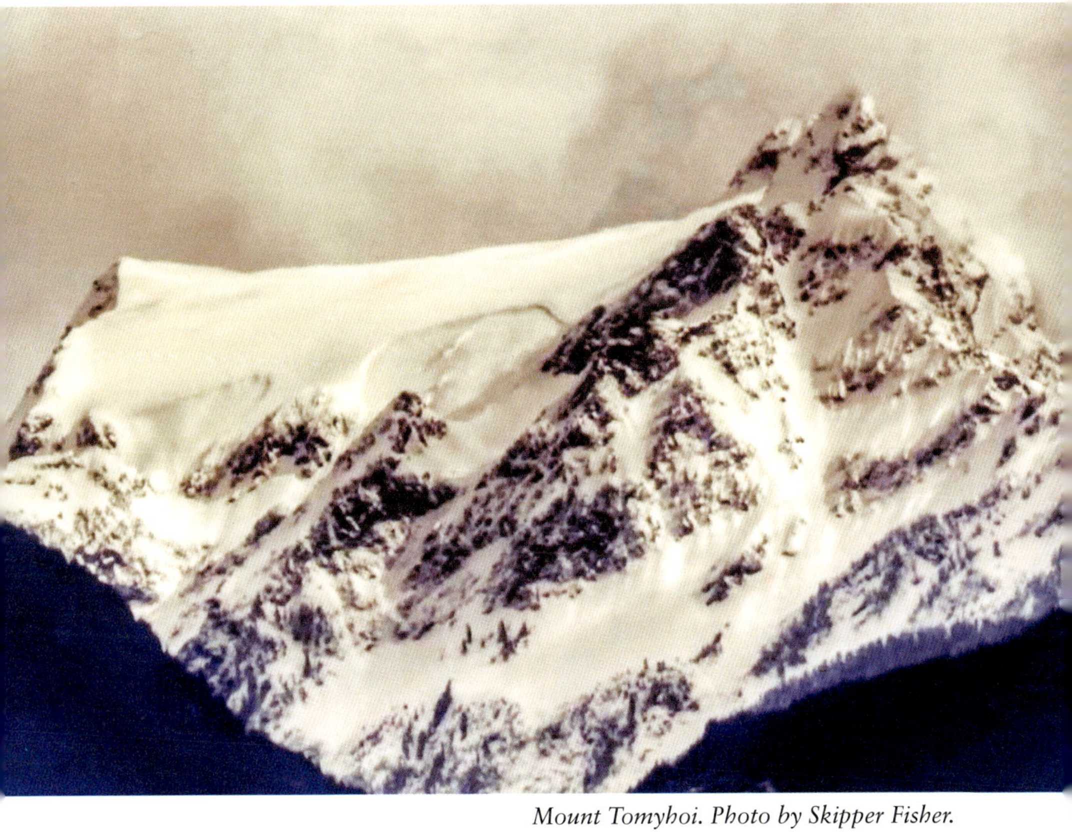

Mount Tomyhoi. Photo by Skipper Fisher.

In 1978, the Chilliwack Search and Rescue and local RCMP created a project to upgrade the forestry maps of the Chilliwack River watershed. They wanted to locate and record all the hiking trails within that area to improve their knowledge of the quickest route to a rescue. I was hired as project manager with a massive assignment to survey, map, upgrade, and build trails within the Chilliwack River Valley. I had a minor in geography and was studying cartography (map-making) as well as art at the University of British Columbia in Vancouver. This, along with my knowledge of the mountains, got me the job.

The Chilliwack SAR hired a crew of 14 other geography students to work on the project for the next two summers—eight months in all. I had two crew leaders, ten crew members, and two cartographers who worked on our maps at the SAR's building. We were an eclectic collection of characters. My team consisted of one crew leader, who also served as our first-aid attendant, one crew leader who specialized in eating granola and observing all things flora and fauna, one scholar who was also a backyard astronomer, one musician, one artist, two myopic mappers, one camp cook, one fly fisherman and five incredibly fit mountaineers, whom we dubbed the Alpine Tour Guides. Snow White had Seven Dwarfs. I had 14. Together we whistled our way through the woods.

We were happy campers and explored, mapped, surveyed, and built trails. We had many, many adventures in the Cascades, some of the best times of our lives. We began the project by obtaining large topographical maps from the local forestry branch and then highlighted all of the major valleys and tributaries of the area. My two crew chiefs and I began scouting out the territory, valley by valley, in an old but rebuilt, one-ton white Chevy truck the SAR had provided us. It had a high metal box to transport our crew, with two long, wooden benches in the back for them to ride on. It was a four-speed standard with dualies that gave it better traction than a 4x4. She wasn't pretty, but she was a powerful machine full of character and took us over mountains, through snowdrifts, mud bogs, game trails, and skidder tracks. We named her "the Elephant."

We identified as many existing trails as we could and had the two cartography students the SAR hired to create a record of those trails and forest service roads. They built a filing system that enabled the SAR to determine the quickest routes to a rescue. Once my team and I had outlined the major arteries of the area, we planned where to first send our crews to begin surveying and marking the trails. Many of these trails were in poor condition and needed repair. Several trails had to be slashed out and built.

At the end of each week, I would give the survey books to the cartographers, and they would transfer the coordinates and information onto the topographical maps and into their index files. This was before the computer age, GPS and Google maps. All the information had to be inputted manually. Those two young women were cartography wizards, and we soon had an efficient working system.

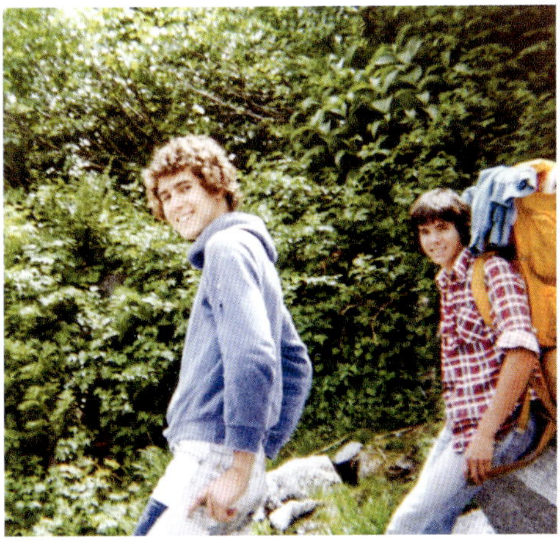

The Alpine Tour Guides

My crew were taught some basic rock-climbing techniques, and then we spent the weeks in the bush in some challenging conditions. We camped in our tents or slept under the stars among the mountain peaks. Three of my crew were in incredible physical condition and could climb like mountain goats. In the evenings, after our day's work, they would sometimes scramble to the tops of the mountains we were working on. On the weekends, they would bag local peaks for recreation. I depended heavily on those young bucks. During our eight months in the bush, none of my crew got lost, and not one of my crew quit the job. We loved what we were doing.

We started our project on the south side of the Chilliwack River at Tamahi Creek, placed between the Canadian Border Peak and and Mount Tomyhoi. The SAR would instruct us on the areas they wanted us to explore, and then we would struggle up the mountainsides with our axes, chainsaws, machetes, sandviks and backpacks. Two of my crew were young women, and they could out-hike most of the guys on our teams. Most areas were overgrown with slide alder and thick with blackflies. We went though many cans of repellent over the weeks. We would calculate our route, slash it out, survey it, mark it with red metal tags, and then have the coordinates and elevations transferred by the cartographers onto our maps.

We spent the next eight months working each valley—Tamahi Creek, Liumchen Creek, Slesse Creek, Nesakwatch Creek, Center Creek, Radium Creek, then the north side of the Chilliwack River among the Four Sisters, the Lucky Four Mountains, Ford Mountain, and the ridge to Williams Peak, and wrapped up the project by slashing a route from the south end of Chilliwack Lake up to Hanging Lake on the American border. I always carried a sketchbook and camera in my pack and used rolls and rolls of film to take an enormous number of photographs of the impressive peaks.

During the winter months, in the art studio at UBC, I painted large canvases of these mountains. Fortunately, people liked these paintings and purchased them. I became a professional painter, and so it was that I embarked on a 46-year career as an artist. The Chilliwack Cascades had gotten into my blood and poured out of my hands as paint, their images interpreted by my creative vision. These mountains will always be my muse.

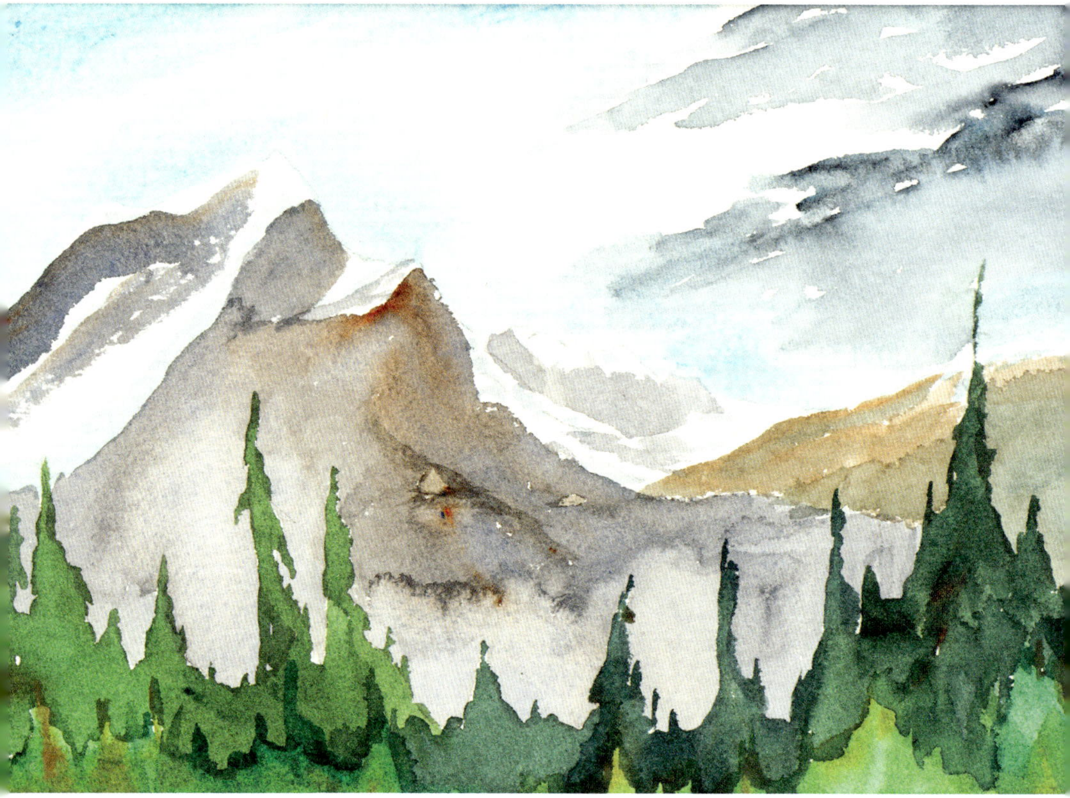

Canadian Border Peak

Chapter Six

The Elephant Takes Flight

In early May of 1978, my crew chief, Neil, and I took the Elephant for a drive up Mount Thurston Road so we could scout out the ridge and Chipmunk Creek area. I had just met Neil, and on the drive I regaled him with stories of my life's exploits. I got the impression he didn't believe me and took my stories to be tall tales.

We drove the Elephant as far up the road as we could, then parked her on the side of the road, blocked the wheels with rocks, donned our packs and hiked up to the ridge. We spent the afternoon scouting the area for trails. The weather was beautiful, the sky clear blue, and the view of the valley incredible.

At 4 p.m. we made our way back to the truck. As I tried to turn it around on the steep road, the tall metal box on the back of the Elephant made the truck begin to tip. I slid it into the ditch alongside the road and we crawled out of the cab. "Nice park," Neil said. The Elephant was grounded, on its side in the ditch. We couldn't get her out. We would need to have her towed.

We began our long walk back down the road to Foley Creek and then headed to Chilliwack Lake Road.

We got back to the bridge at 7 p.m. and decided to take a shortcut through the forest next to the Ford Mountain Prison Camp, with the thought of coming out onto Chilliwack Lake Road and hopefully hitching a ride into town. As we emerged from the trees and arrived at the road, a police vehicle from the prison camp came to greet us. The guards deduced that we were escaping prisoners, cuffed us, loaded us into the back of their vehicle and took us to the prison camp. They sat us down in the office and ran our ID through the computer. The information they received informed them that I was wanted on a Canada-wide warrant. This was news to me. I couldn't remember ever being arrested for anything, but there it was—someone with my same three names and birthdate and general description was a wanted criminal!

I told the guards I was innocent. They gave each other serious looks, said they had never heard that before, then broke out into laughter and locked me in a cell. Neil wet himself. As the evening turned into night, more information came in over the computer. Fortunately for me, the other Peter Douglas Scott, aged 20, was born in Ontario, and I was born in Chilliwack. This discrepancy made them release me, and as they drove us back to Sardis, they informed me they would let me go this time, but if I was the wanted guy, the authorities would eventually get me. Comforting to know. By the time we arrived back at town it was midnight, and I could tell Neil was beginning to believe that my tall tales were real and not exactly tall. He also had to change his pants.

Long day.

The next morning, one of the SAR members drove Neil, me, and two of our crew up to our truck in his 4x4, with the mission of towing the Elephant out of the ditch. We chained up the Elephant and, with much effort, extracted her from the ditch so that the truck was now facing downhill on the steep logging road.

While my crew were loading their saws and equipment into the back, I put the gearshift into reverse, engaged the emergency brake and was in the process of blocking the front wheels when suddenly the Elephant broke free and began a rapid descent down the steep logging road. I chased it, jumped in, and desperately tried to jam it into gear, but it was rapidly accelerating and was heading to a sharp switchback. I jumped, and as I was sliding down the bank in a cloud of dust, I watched the Elephant take flight. She left the mountain and dropped a hundred feet down into a grove of alpine fir and immediately started a fire.

My crew thought I had died. I thought I'd died. The SAR member was quick to call his superiors on the satellite phone and in a very excited voice told them what I had done. He was livid; he couldn't believe what he'd just witnessed. Neither could we. We climbed down to our truck and extinguished the fire. On the way back to town, sitting in the 4x4, Neil looked at me with saucer eyes and asked me, "Who are you?'

I replied, "One of a kind, man. Welcome to my life.

Next day, the SAR sent up a tow truck. While trying to haul up the Elephant, the weight of our truck immediately ripped out the rear end of the tow truck. The SAR then sent up a large diesel truck that finally was successful in hauling up our truck. On the way down, the tow truck driver chain-smoked all the way, as the tow truck was wider than the logging road. He asked me how I got the Elephant up there. I replied, "Getting it up there wasn't the problem; getting it down was the hard part."

We repaired the Elephant, and she carried us through the mountains for many more months and adventures. I loved that old truck, and the guys and girls on my crews. They were the best.

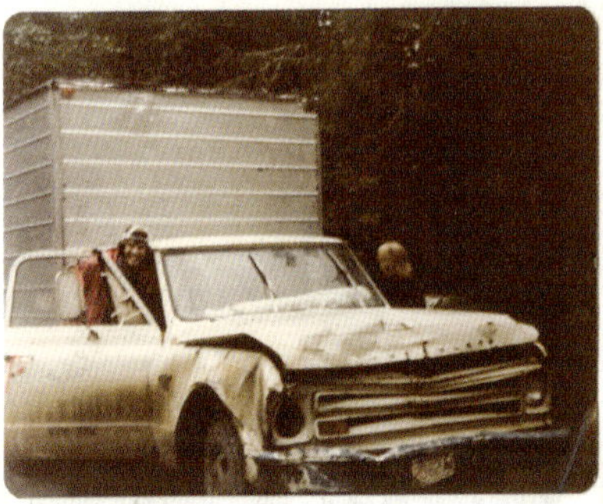

"The Elephant"

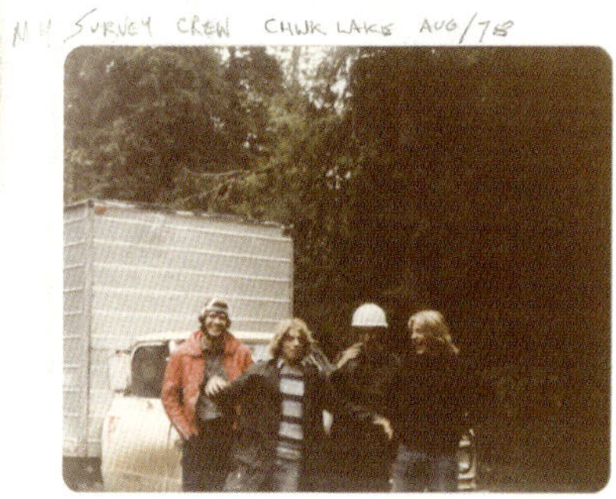

The Crew in front of The Elephant

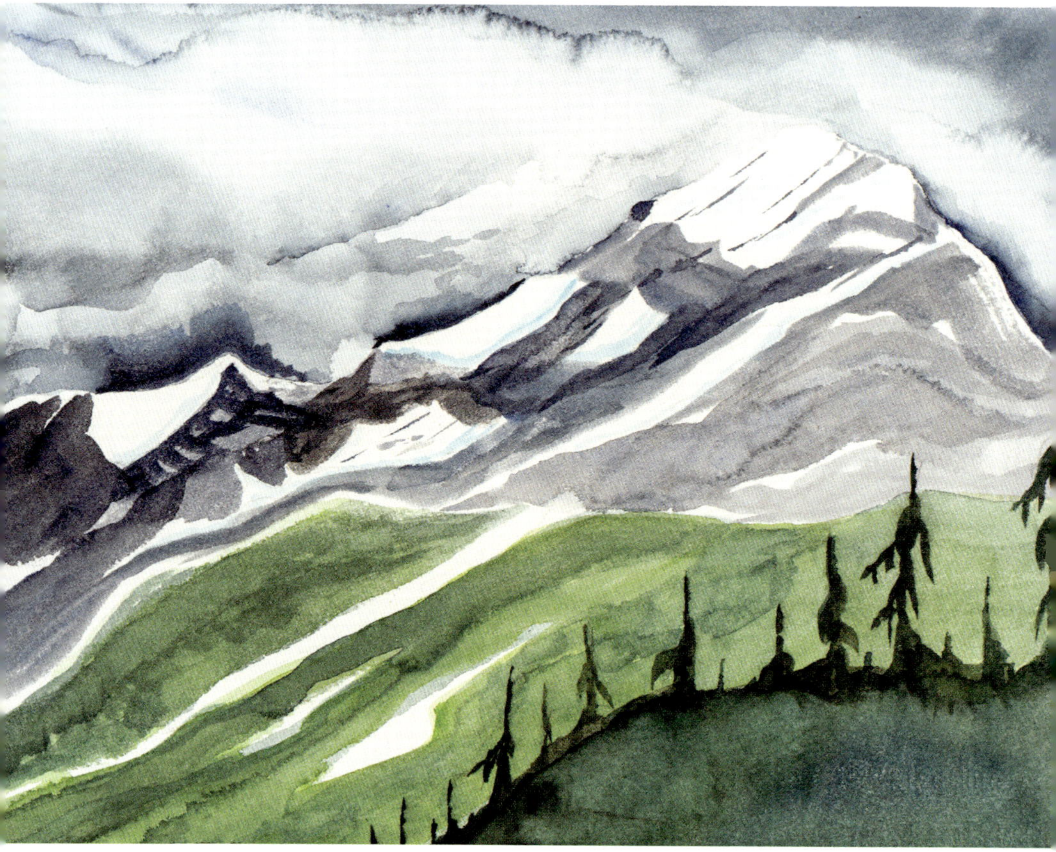

Mount McGuire

Chapter Seven

Mount McGuire

Mount McGuire is a prominent mountain in the Chilliwack Cascades, clearly visible from anywhere in the Fraser Valley. It stands at 6,620 feet (2018 metres) and is two miles north of the Canada-United States border, twelve miles southeast of Chilliwack. The steep western side drops into Tamahi Creek. The mountain was originally named Tamahi, Tamiye ho:y, by the Stó:lō. This Halq'eméylem word means deformed. Mount Tamahi was the place of the deformed.

According to Mrs. Cooper, deformed babies were once left on this mountain to die of exposure. The mountain attained the name McGuire In 1917. During the first week of August 1978, my crew and I hiked up the old Borden Creek Forest Service Road on McGuire. The road was reached from the mouth of Slesse Creek and branched off to the west and through the old logging camp. That was as far as we could go in the Elephant. The road was overgrown and not driveable. We had a long slog to get to the top. We followed Borden Creek to a washed-out bridge that was difficult to crawl across. The day was hot, the blackflies insufferable, and our packs heavy.

Bugs are a curse to most hikers in the bush: blackflies, deer flies, mosquitoes, and the most hated, no-see-ums.

These flies want to suck our blood. Female blackflies, mosquitoes, horse flies and biting midges all require a feast of blood to maximize their egg production. The males do not need blood and leave humans alone. The females seek to inhale carbon dioxide and are then attracted to heat. If you happen to be warm-blooded, you become her target. After a female has tripled her weight in blood, she retires to a sheltered place to let her eggs develop. After she has laid her eggs, she searches for more blood and the cycle continues. Mosquitoes prefer standing water and blackflies prefer running

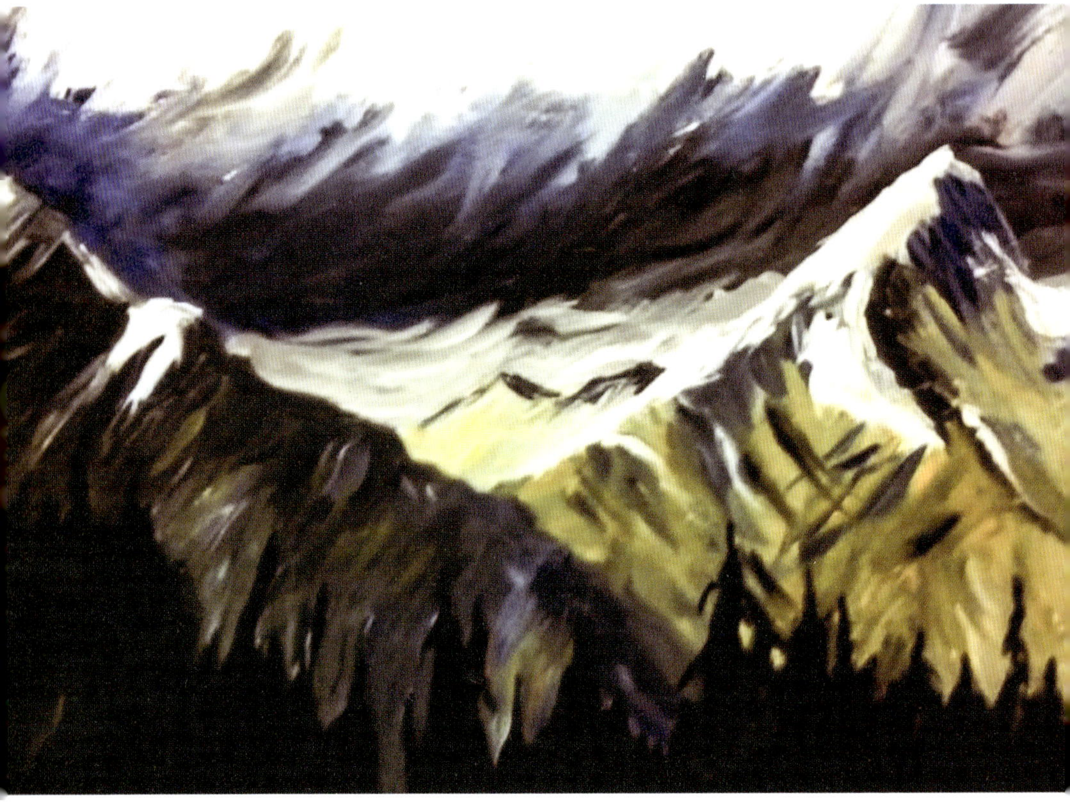

Border Peaks Morning

water, as their larvae develop in creeks and streams. Mosquitoes prefer the warm, humid early hours and evening hours, while horse flies and deer flies thrive in the hot afternoons. I used to laugh at my crew as clouds of adult female blackflies would descend on them as they took their breaks near a stream. I always sat a few yards away from water while eating my lunch. A good woodsman knows these things. My crew used hundreds of cans of bug repellent over the course of our project.

My mother told me of an Avon deodorant product that she found discouraged annoying insects. The product was called Skin So Soft. She used it while picking berries. I tried it and it worked! From then on, my crew could not figure out why the bugs left me alone.

My Stó:lō aunt once told me the story of an old cannibal woman who lived in a cave above Yale. She would lure children into her cave, poke out their eyes and roast the children on a spit over a fire and eat them. One day, two boys surprised her and pushed her into the fire. The flames danced high as she roasted to death. The embers from the fire became mosquitoes. Like the cannibal woman who drank children's blood, now the mosquitoes drink yours.

A good woodsman also knows not to eat bananas in the bush. The sweet oils and sugar in the fruit attract the mosquitoes.

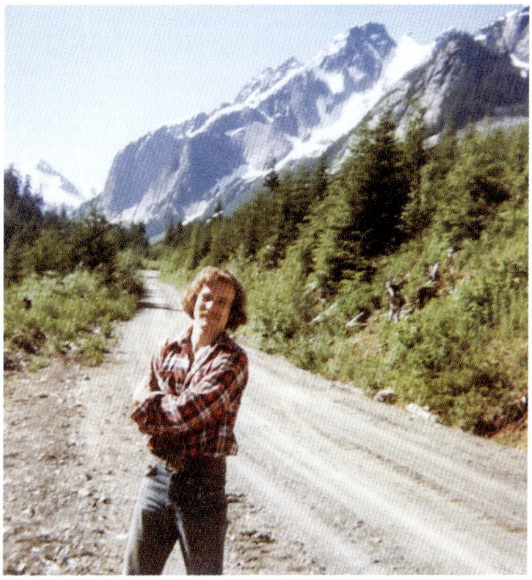

One of my crew leaders was a guy named Leon. He was a happy, amiable, granola-eating kind of guy, a fun guy to have on our crew. He sometimes wore a pair of bright yellow shorts that earned him the nickname "Neon Leon." While we were filling our survey books with valuable data, Leon would be filling his survey book with notes on the local flora and fauna, location of wild mountain blueberries and good areas to cross-country ski in the winter. Because he was so easily distracted by his surroundings, he was always getting into mishaps that added humour to our days. He was fun to prank. We would fill his hiking boots with cold water, put ants in his sleeping bag, and fill his underwear with shaving cream. We also told him bananas repel mosquitoes; he would eat bunches of them. We told him it would be more effective if he rubbed the peels on his arms and neck. Leon thought he was cursed by the mosquito gods.

That day on McGuire, we finally arrived at the bowl and decided to make camp. We slept under the stars that night and philosophized on the origin of the universe. Our resident scholar and backyard astronomer pointed out the wonders of the heavens to us. It was the beginning of the Perseid Meteor Shower, and the sky over us rained with shooting stars. We were mesmerized.

The next day we discovered the trailhead, but it didn't seem to go anywhere. We finally found a rough trail, and it led us to a boulder field. It was slow to cross, but once we did, we discovered a deposit of fossils that resembled sea stars. At one point in history, this area was covered in seawater.

The top of McGuire consists of limestone and always looks like there is snow on top of the mountain. As we marvelled at this feature and made our way along the ridge, Leon suddenly had an attack of indigestion. It might have been the water he guzzled out of Borden Creek the day before or his overindulgence on high-mountain blueberries. He developed debilitating cramps, then erupted like Mount Vesuvius. Leon had the runs. Leon's neon shorts were no longer bright yellow. We left him to deal with his predicament and finally reached the summit of Mount McGuire.

We had scrambled to the top on loose rock. The views from there were stunning. The entire Fraser Valley and surrounding mountains—Mount Slesse, Border Peaks, Mount Tomyhoi and the Cheam Range to the north—lay before us. The descent was tricky, but we eventually made it back to the overgrown road. We found that Leon had survived his ordeal. We did a rough survey of our route to the top and had the information transferred onto our main map when we returned. It had been a difficult trip, but it was worth it.

Chapter Eight

Lightning On Ford Mountain

Once upon a time, that is in 1978, the Chilliwack Search and Rescue sent my crew and me to the top of Ford Mountain to repair, survey, mark, map, and try to slash a route along the ridge to Williams Peak. Ford Mountain is at the south end of the ridge and is 4,672 feet (1424 metres) in elevation. This was going to be a tough job, as there was no clear route along the ridge. We drove the Elephant as far up the road as she would go, then unloaded our gear, saws, and axes and made the climb up the road to the trailhead. The trail was steep at first but slowly levelled out. Once we were on the trail, it was approximately a 45-minute hike to the top, mostly in the shade of trees but then opening up to a clearing on the top of the mountain.

The old BC Forestry tower there was to be our base camp. The tower was many years old; the paint was white and faded and she looked tired, however she would be our home for the next two weeks. The tower had two old metal cots, a table and chairs, a potbellied stove, and cupboards where we stashed our supplies. At the bottom of the tower was a large cistern full of cold rainwater. Being extremely thirsty on this hot July day, we dropped our packs and filled our stomachs with cold mountain rainwater.

Then we saw the dead rat floating in the cistern.

After emptying our stomachs of cold mountain rainwater, we set up camp and removed the plywood that covered the tower's glass windows. The view was spectacular, a 360-degree view of the surrounding mountains, Mount Slesse, Rexford, the Border Peaks and the Cheam Range to the north. Our crew of six spent the first night sitting out on the balcony, taking in the

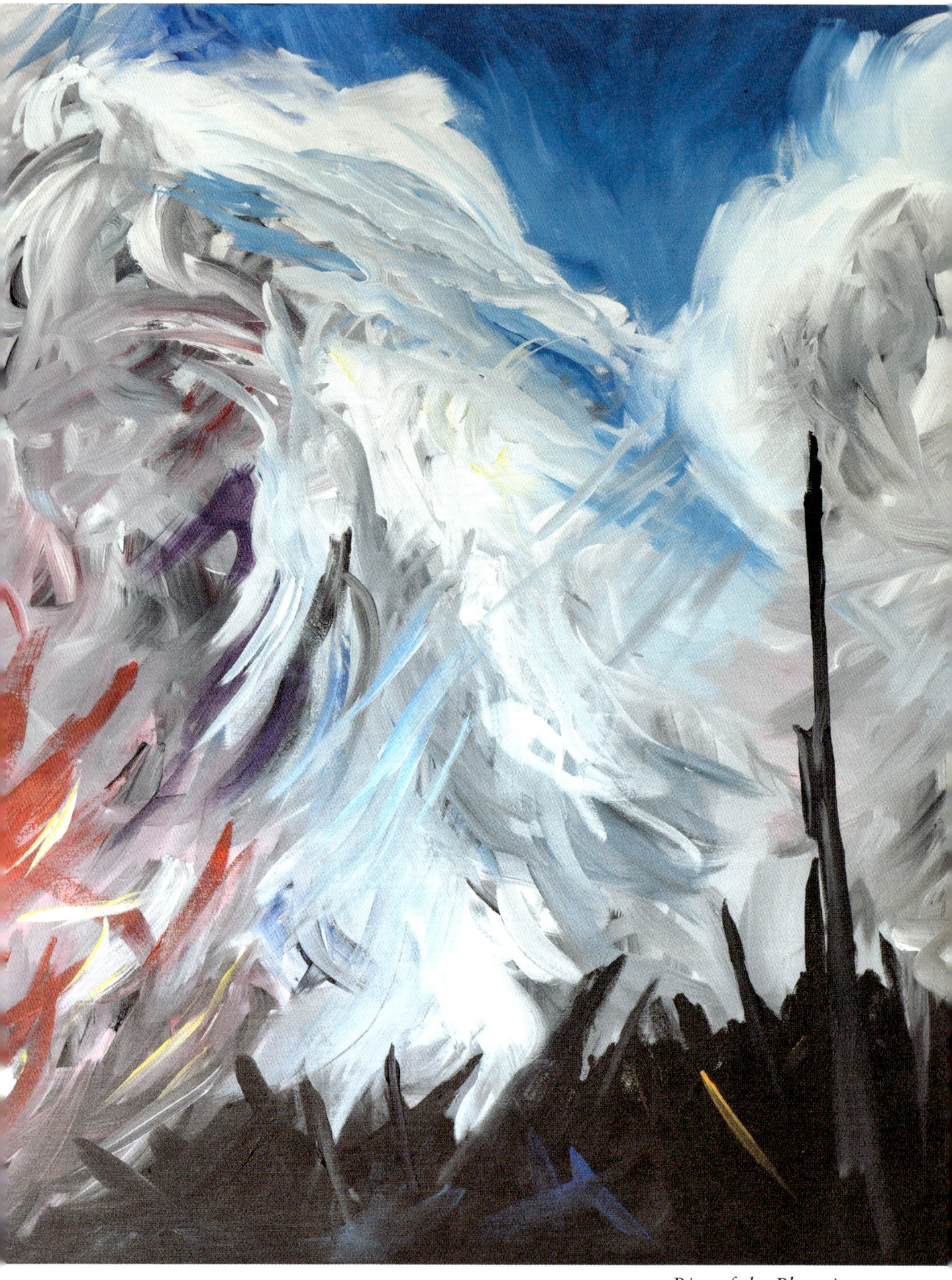

Rise of the Phoenix

view, and then watched a star show in the sky above. Two of the crew camped in a tent alongside the tower.

Hernaldo, our camp cook, made us a spectacular breakfast in the morning that attracted some wildlife. We had to scare them away by banging pots and pans and yelling. Hernaldo kept us well fed during our stay.

We spent the first day hiking along the ridge, hacking out a rough route and having chainsaw wars. The next day we flagged a route along the ridge to where we met up with the trail that comes up from Foley Road.

The next two weeks were spent falling trees, bucking up logs and slowly making our way along the ridge. One afternoon, a mountain storm blew in and enveloped the ridge. The claps of thunder were deafening, and the rain came driving down. With lightning flashing around us, we raced, soaking wet, across the clearing to the tower, hoping not to get electrocuted—and Leon wearing a metal hard hat! We knew the tower was grounded with a lightning rod and we would be safe there. We rushed into the shelter and briefly locked Leon outside. Then, as we were laughing and drying off in the tower, lightning struck the forest below us and plumes of smoke began to rise above the trees.

This got our attention. We realized we would need to race down

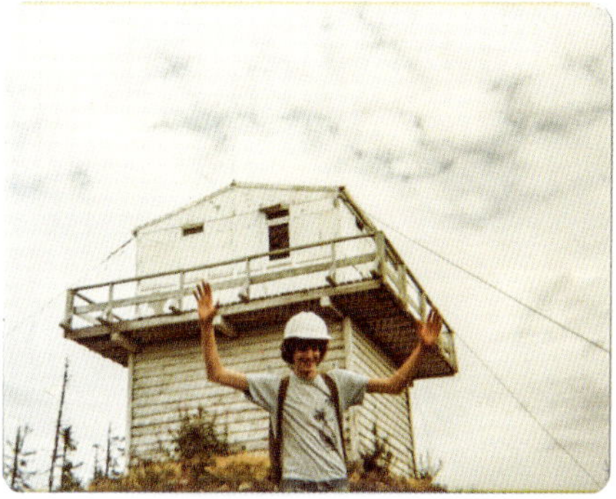

Ford Mountain Look-Out Tower

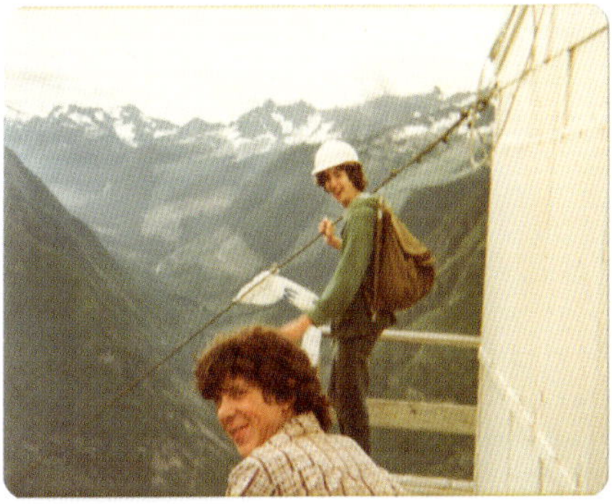

Crew members on the deck of the Ford Mountain Look-out

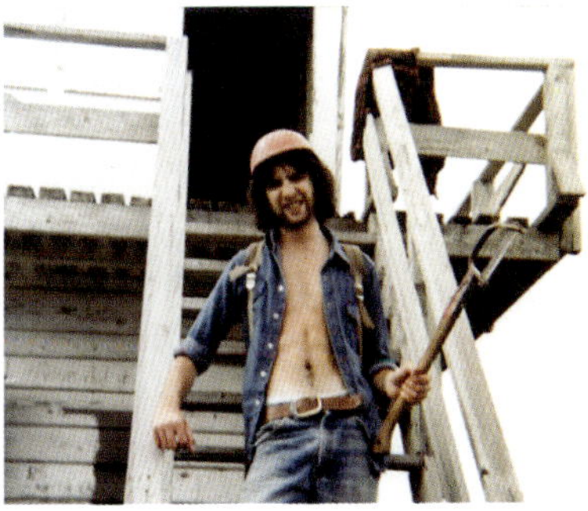

Crew chief on the steps of Ford Mountain Look-out

to the Elephant and make a quick trip around the fire. We quickly donned our packs, grabbed our tools and ran down the trail. We loaded everything into the truck, turned the key—and nothing happened. Elephants aren't supposed to forget, but our Elephant had forgotten how to start. The battery was dead, and we feared we would we be too if we didn't get past the blaze.

Fortunately, the pouring rain suppressed the fire and we made it down the mountain through intense smoke. Even the Elephant lived.

Once again, we'd survived another adventure in the beautiful Chilliwack Mountains.

Chapter Nine

The Mountain Project

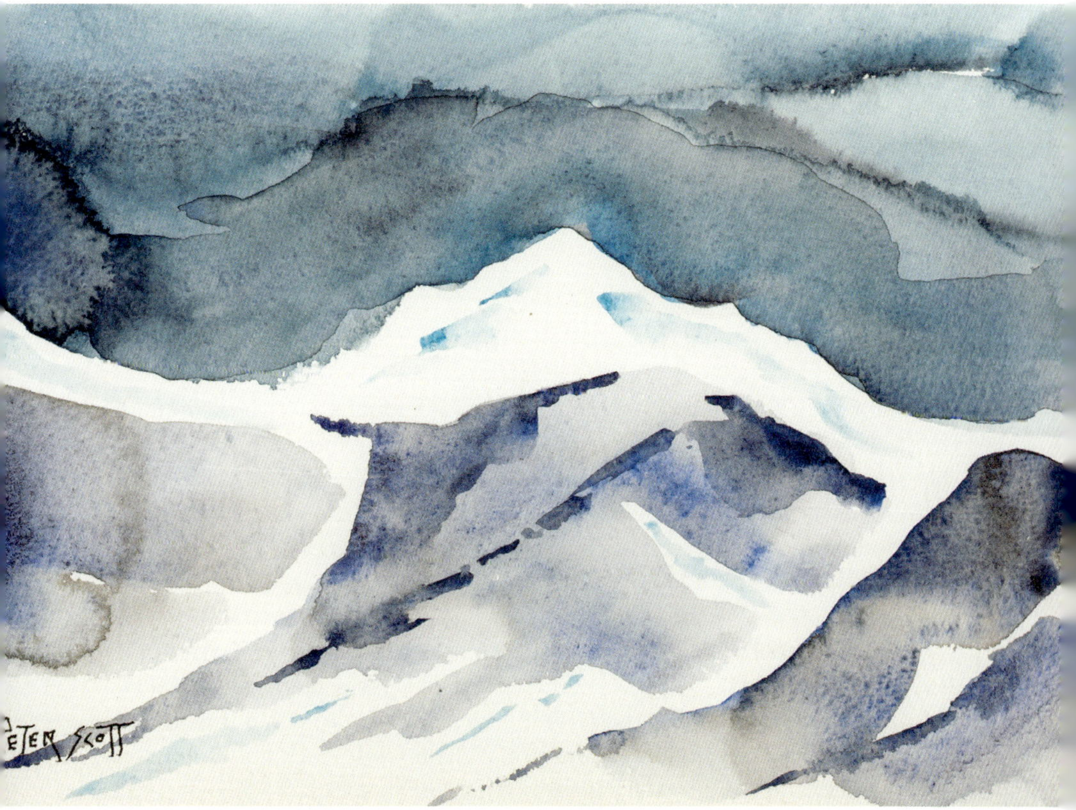

Isolation Peak

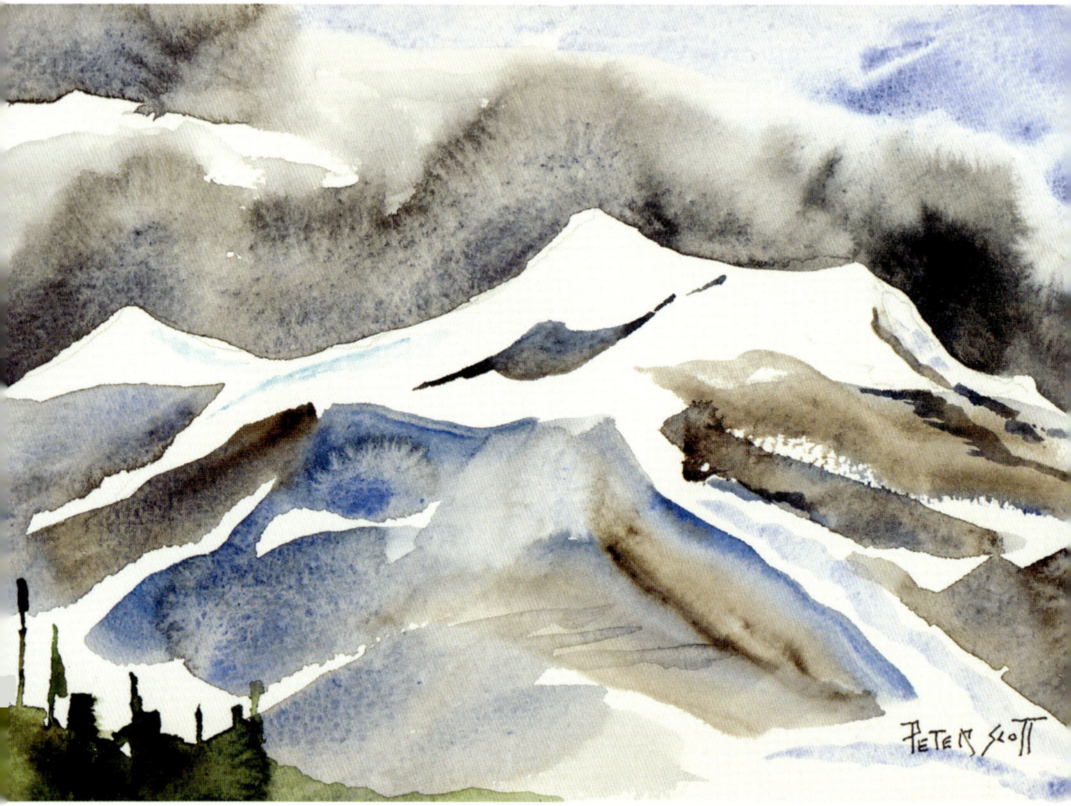

Mount MacFarlane

The Mountain Project was created by Chilliwack mountaineer Neil Grainger in the 1980s to honour local servicemen by dedicating mountains after these heroes. Climbers of the Chilliwack Search and Rescue participated in the Mountain Project by scaling these peaks and placing crosses on the tops of the mountains.

Mount Macfarlane

Mount MacFarlane was the first local mountain to be honoured after a deceased veteran. Mount MacFarlane rises to 6,778 feet (2066 metres) and is southeast of Chilliwack in the same range as Mount Slesse, just south of Pierce Lake. It is named for Ronald E. MacFarlane, who was born Dec. 26, 1921, in Chilliwack and graduated from Chilliwack High School in 1939. He joined the RCAF in February 1941 and went overseas that October. Ronald was attached to an RAF bomber squadron and captained a Lancaster bomber. In January 1943, his plane was attacked by three German Junkers on his way home from a bombing mission. The plane was badly damaged over Germany; several of his crew were wounded and his upper gunner was killed after their Lancaster was raked with bullets. MacFarlane was able to shake off the attacking fighters and with much difficulty and heroism was able to return to his base in England. He was awarded the Distinguished Flying Award Medal by King George VI. However, that Dec. 16, Flight Lieutenant MacFarlane was shot down by German night fighters over Holland. None of the crew survived.

Grainger Peak

Grainger Peak is named after local airman Frank Grainger. He joined the RCAF in 1941. He became part of an aircrew flying on Atlantic Patrol from northern Scotland. On Oct. 16, 1943, he was killed in Northern Ireland. He was 20 years old. Grainger Peak is north of Chehalis Lake on the north side of the Fraser River.

Mount Northgraves

Mount Northgraves is named for George Allan Northgraves. He was born in Youngstown, Alberta, on April 10, 1920, and moved to Chilliwack in 1938. He worked in the hop fields before joining the 16th Light Anti-Aircraft Battery in Vancouver, and was posted to England in 1941. George Allan Northgraves was officially reported missing in action during the Dieppe raid in 1942. Mount Northgraves is 6,791 feet (2070 metres) high and is near Welch Peak in the Cheam Range.

Mount Archibald

Mount Archibald stands 5,511 feet (1680 metres) west of and on the same ridge as Mount Cheam. Mount Archibald is named for Ronald Earl Archibald, who was born on Sept. 29, 1920, and attended Rosedale Elementary and Chilliwack High School. In November 1940, he graduated as a pilot of a Lancaster bomber. On a bombing raid over Germany on June 4, 1942, his plane was hit. Captain Archibald ordered his crew out and then went down with his plane. Mount Archibald overlooks his hometown of Rosedale.

Mount Rexford

Mount Rexford is the tallest and most impressive mountain in the Illusion-Nesakwatch-Rexford group near Chilliwack Lake. Mount Rexford's elevation is 7,641 feet (2329 metres) and

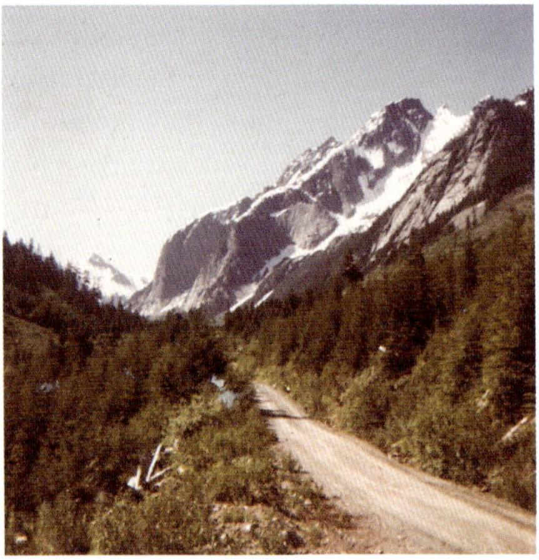

Mount Rexford

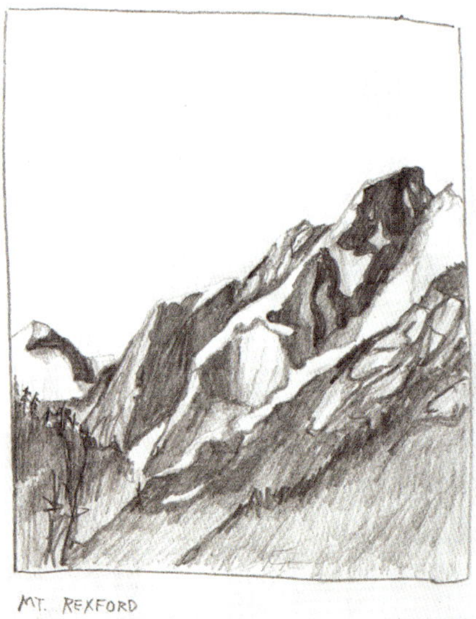

Sketch of Mount Rexford, 1978

is five miles south of the Chilliwack Lake Road, along Center Creek valley.

According to Neil Grainger in his book The Mountain Project, "Mount Rexford is known as a mountain climbers' mountain, as there are no easy ways up or down, only many interesting routes for qualified people. Mount Rexford is not for casual hikers."

Mount Rexford was named for a local soldier, Douglas Rexford, who attended school in Sardis and served in World War II. He was killed on Dec. 15, 1941, at the age of 18.

Conway Peak

North of the Chilliwack River. Named after Leading Seaman Archibald Henry W. Conway, Royal Canadian Navy, killed in action. He was originally from Chilliwack. Elevation 6,549 feet (1996 metres).

Mount Corriveau

West of Chilliwack Lake, south of Post Creek, this was named for F.O. Arthur J. Corriveau of the RCAF, killed in action during World War II. He was from Agassiz.

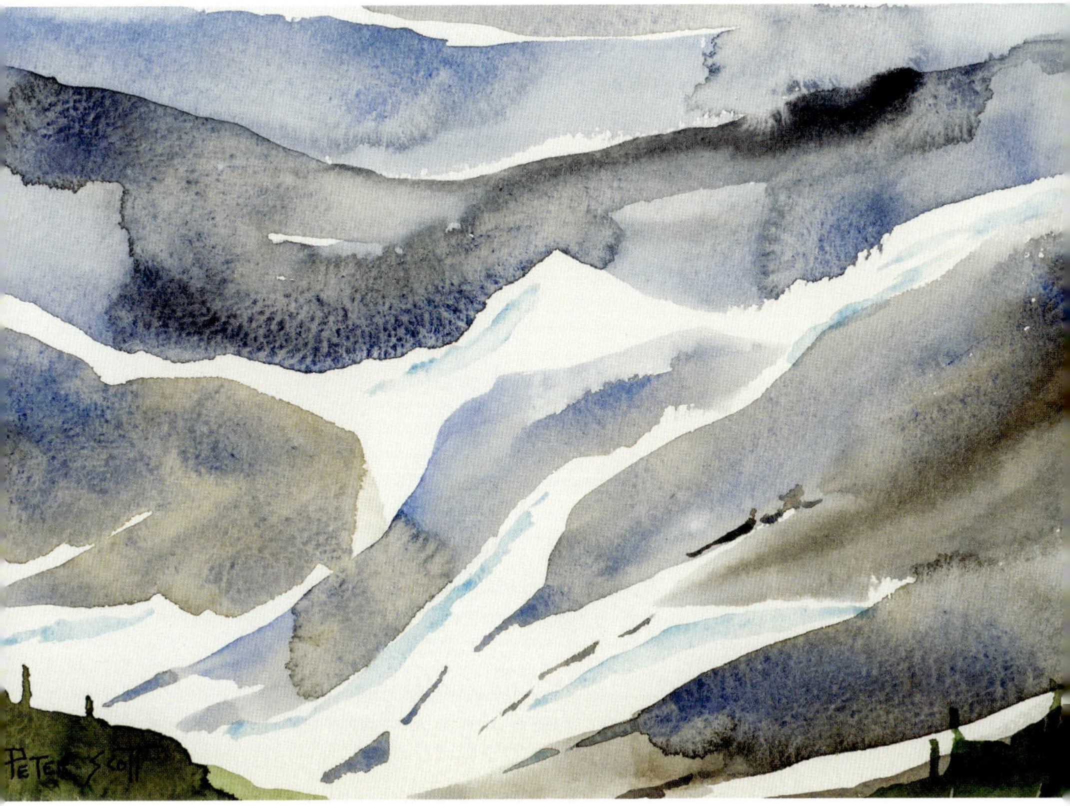

Williams Peak In Summer

Mount Edgar

East of Chilliwack Lake, it was named after F.L. John R. Edgar of the RCAF, killed in action. Originally from Chilliwack. Elevation 6,762 feet (2061 metres).

Ford Mountain

Located north of the Chilliwack River, west of Chilliwack Lake, this mountain was named for F/S Harry K. Ford of the RCAF, killed in action, from Chilliwack. A BC Forestry lookout tower stood on the summit of Ford Mountain and was in operation during the 1960s and 1970s. It was dismantled in 1980 due to vandalism. Elevation 4,659 feet (1420 metres).

Goetz Peak

Northwest of Chilliwack Lake, it was named after Private Rudolf Goetz, Canadian Army, killed in action during World War II. He was originally from Yarrow.

Mount Laughington

This peak, north of the Chilliwack River and Larson's Bench, was named after Private Harry Laughington of the Canadian Army, killed in action. He was from Agassiz.

Macdonald Peak

On the west bank of Chilliwack Lake, this mountain gets its name from Flying Officer Robert D. Macdonald of Atchelitz, also killed in action during World War II while serving with the RCAF. Elevation 7,372 feet (2246 metres).

Mount Mercer

Northwest of Chilliwack Lake, it was named in remembrance of Private Wesley R. Mercer of the Canadian Army, who died in action. He was from Rosedale. Elevation 5,571 feet (1698 metres).

Williams Peak

Williams Peak is named for John "Jack" William Williams, born on Feb. 2, 1922. He received his education in Chilliwack and joined the RAF in October 1940. He was posted to Malta in the Mediterranean Sea and flew as a Spitfire pilot. His nickname was "Willie the Kid." He was awarded the Distinguished Flying Cross in August 1942 for his devotion to flights over Sicily and Malta. Not long after, his Spitfire crashed into the sea during a dogfight with a German plane.

Williams Peak, elevation 6,853 feet (2089 metres), is visible from Chilliwack Lake Road, just north of Chilliwack Lake. The peak is shaped like a pyramid and is recognizable from any direction. A cross for John "Jack" Williams was placed on the summit of Williams Peak on July 21, 1984, by a member of the Chilliwack Search and Rescue, thus completing the Mountain Project.

Chapter Ten

The Elephant Rides Again

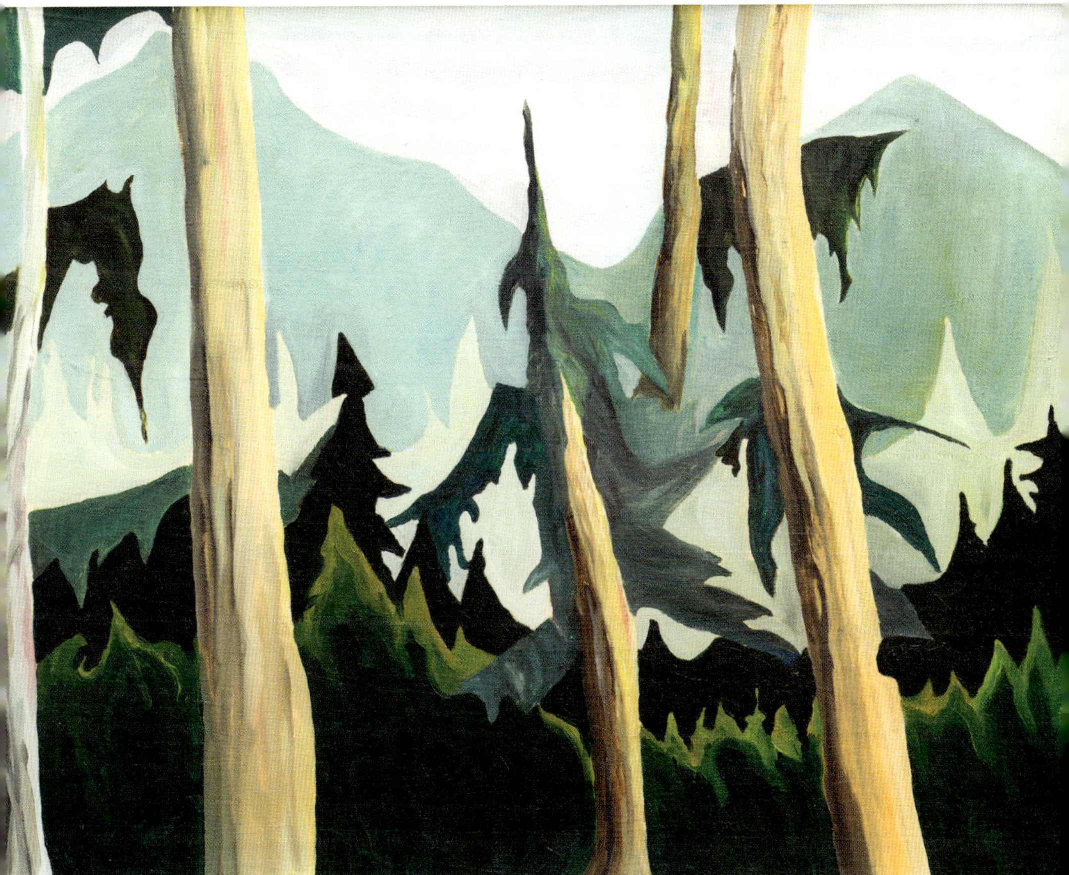

Mount Liumchen Through the Trees

Many, many, many years ago, the CHWK SAR sent my crew up to Liumchen Ridge to clear and mark the trail up to Liumchen Mountain, try to make repairs to the old trapper's cabin, and swim in Liumchen Lake.

We loaded our gear into our old Elephant and started our journey down Sleepy Hollow Road, through the Soowalie Reserve, across Liumchen Creek, first dubbed Loyumthel (which means, water swirling out in gushes), and up the long, long, old logging road up to the ridge. The road is steep, with a sheer drop off to one side and a steep slope on the other. To the left is Church Mountain.

It was a beautiful, sunny August morning as we made our slow drive up the mountain. Three-quarters of the way up, we suddenly came to a large washout that left a huge gap in the road. I began trying to coax the Elephant around the washout, but the screams from my crew in the back of the truck made me stop. There was no way around it. My crew quickly scrambled out of the truck, happy to be alive, gathered up their packs and chain saws and started the trek up to the ridge. My crew chief, Neil, and I were left to deal with the situation.

We couldn't drive past the washout, and the grade was far too steep to park the truck, so it was either try to "jump" the gaping hole or back the truck all the way down the mountain. I decided to try and jump.

Having seen the Elephant fall off a mountain earlier in the summer, I didn't have much faith in her ability to fly. However, what the heck, we would try again. Neil happily got out of the truck and crawled past the washout. He was going to "flag" me in for the landing. I backed up the Elephant, put her in gear, did ten quick Hail Marys, closed my eyes and hit the gas. Then I hit the mountain.

When I opened my eyes, I was staring at a long drop-off to the bottom of the valley, the Elephant was teetering on the edge of the road, and Neil was running away. I felt like Hannibal, although his elephants had actually crossed the mountains.

Having jumped out of her once this summer to save my life, I decided to stay in the truck and try to back her out of the hole and back down the mountain. Then my side mirrors fell off.

Neil came back to guide me. I put the Elephant in reverse and, with much praying, swearing and biting of nails, I got her out of the washout and back on the road. And then, driving blind, with Neil frantically yelling directions, I finally got our old truck back to the bottom of the mountain. Then all we had to do was hike all the way back up the long road to the ridge and rejoin our crew. The journey was made, and we spent the next week working on the trail and the cabin. We made camp on a bluff above Liumchen Lake. Near our camp was an overhanging rock. At night we made our campfire in this semi cave and the flames reflected off the steep rock sides, keeping us warm during the chilly nights.

At the end of the week, we celebrated by playing poker and dancing around the fire late into the night. Leon accidently danced in the fire, and his jeans ignited.

We quickly grabbed him and threw him in the lake. Then we remembered Leon couldn't swim. Two of the guys dived in and saved him. Other than emerging with two leeches stuck to his face, Leon was unscathed, and the flames on his jeans were extinguished.

The view from Liumchen Ridge is spectacular. At 5,500 feet on a clear day, you can see all the surrounding mountains. Kwelxáilxw, Mount Baker, dominates the skyline. During our time there, we basked in the splendor of Tammiax (Mount Tomyhoi), the Border Peaks, Slesse and the Cheam range to the north, and the alpine flowers were all in bloom along the ridge. We had a great week and then, packing our heavy saws and packs, made the long descent back to the Elephant, who was happily waiting for us in the shade down by the creek.

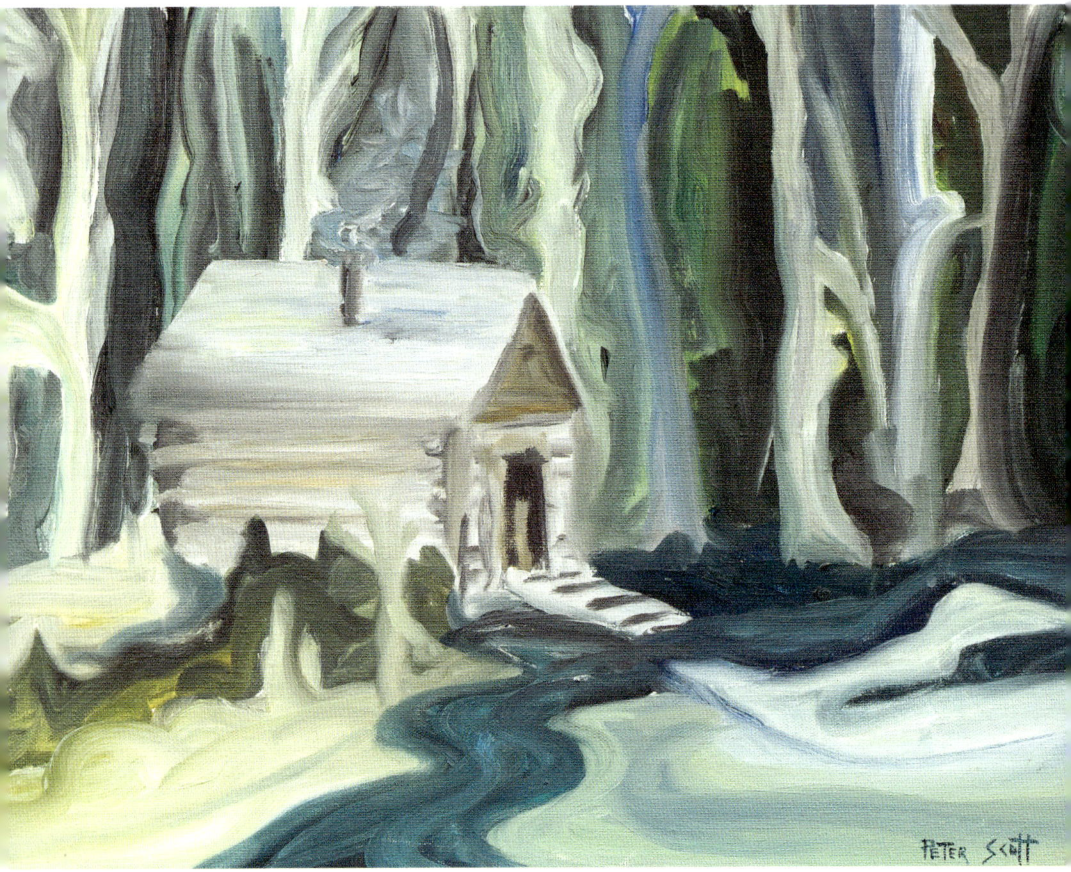

Cabin at Red Mountain Mine

Chapter Eleven

Gold Rush, Red Mountain Mine And The Bear Escapade

Back in August 1978, the Chilliwack Search and Rescue sent my crew out to survey, map and mark the route up to Red Mountain Mine. Red Mountain Mine is an abandoned gold mine in Whatcom County, Washington, one half mile south of the U.S. border at the south end of the Slesse Creek Forest Service road. The mine lies at 4,715 feet on the north slope of Mount Larrabee, formerly known as Red Mountain. Mount Larrabee is part of a group of 7,000-foot peaks known as the Pleiades.

In August 1897, three prospectors, Jack Post, Russ Lambert, and Lyman Van Valkenburg, discovered large grains of free gold in the waters of the south fork of Slesse Creek near the international boundary. A few days later, they found gold as large as peas in a stream up the southern slope of Bear Mountain, above the west fork of Slesse Creek. Over the next few days, the men staked five claims; each claim covered an area of 1,000 by 2,000 feet. They took their gold findings to Sumas to assay and register their claims. The assay revealed a value as high as $10,750 per ton. Their claims became known as the Lone Jack claims.

A gold rush to the area soon ensued. Overnight, news of the find had spread north and south of the international border. The easiest route to the area was along the bank of the Chilliwack River to its confluence with Slesse Creek, where it began a strenuous six-mile climb alongside the banks of the creek to the international boundary and from there another four miles to the Lone Jack claims.

Other prospectors staked a thousand claims, which encompassed Red Mountain, Tamahi Peak, and areas alongside Slesse Creek. The area was named the Mount Baker Mining District. By the early fall of 1899, the small town of Chilliwack was swarming with prospectors. All the hotels were filled, large quantities of mining supplies were being sold by local merchants, and pack horses were hired out. The original prospectors, Jack Post and his two partners, soon realized they lacked the funds to develop a gold mine and accepted an offer, selling their five claims for $50,000.

The new owners formed the Mount Baker Mining Company and soon began building their mining operation. They built a bunkhouse, an office, and a cook shack; purchased a large quantity of supplies from Chilliwack merchants; and hired a herd of packhorses.

Soon after, five gold quartz veins were discovered on Mount Larrabee by Americans C.W. Roth and Associates. They staked their claims, and the Boundary Red Mountain Mining Company was established. By this time the Mount Baker Mine had found a very rich four-foot-wide vein at a depth of a hundred feet. It milled between $3000 and $4000 per ton in free gold. The ore was much richer than that at the surface of the vein, where the gold rush had begun with Jack Post's discovery.

The Mount Baker Mining Company sold original shares at a mere 50 cents each. In 1901, miners removed 44,000 tons of ore from its site. By that point it was common to see pack trains of 50 to 75 mules loaded with supplies for the mine. In 1904, the company spent $6000, at $80 per ton, to pack more than 75 tons of supplies to its site. The mine had provided a continuous profit for its owners from the beginning of operations at the Lone Jack claim in 1899, eventually bringing a value of $1.25 million to the shareholders, but that came to an abrupt end in 1907, when a fire destroyed the mine's mill and the owners had to cease operating.

Mining at the Boundary Red Mountain Mine began in 1902. They struck a four-foot vein at the 4000-foot level, which carried gold of a higher value than what was initially found. During its highest production years, the mine consisted of a power plant on Slesse Creek, with thousands of feet of phone and power transmission lines, several bunkhouses, an office, ten stamp mills and an aerial tramway. In 1914, gold production reached about $150,000. The following year, the mine added five stamp mills and produced $148,578 worth of gold.

A packer from Chilliwack, Ed Allison, was the main transporter of supplies to the mine. He used up to 40 packhorses to take in supplies, food, and heavy machinery. The last three miles of the 25 to the Boundary Red Mountain Mine were the hardest, as the rough trail gained 1,700 feet in elevation over 32 switchbacks.

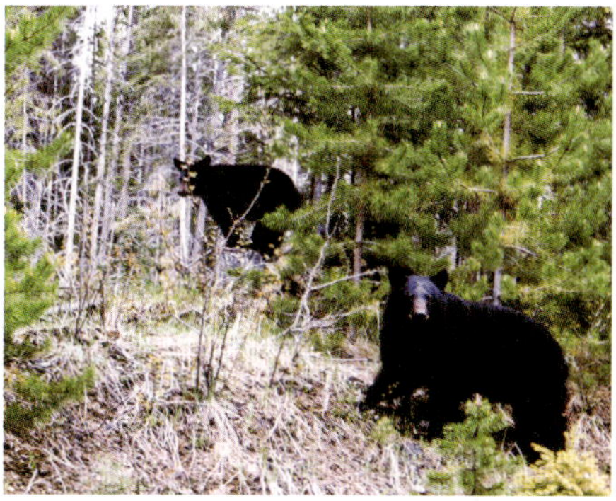

Mama Bear and her cubs

By 1921, the mine employed 80 miners and shipped out gold and bricks equivalent to $140,000. The miners worked in harsh conditions, thanks in part to a river of ice-cold water that flowed through the mine consistently from a glacier behind the mine. Labour turnover was constant; there were always three crews—one coming, one working, and one going. In just one month, September 1921, 96 percent of the workforce left and had to be replaced.

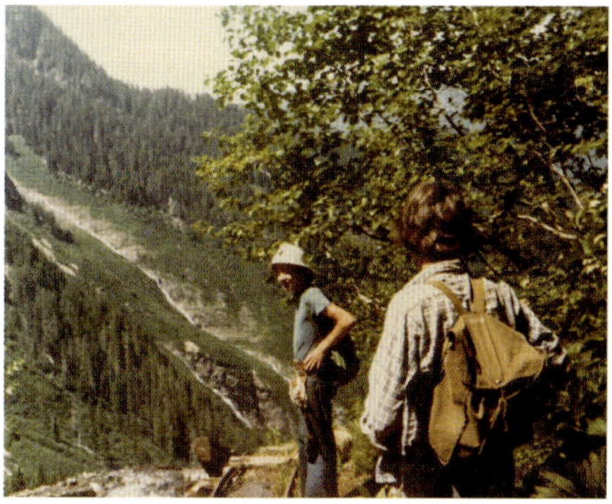

Crew at Red Mountain Mine

A snow slide during the winter of 1942 destroyed the Boundary Red Mountain's mill, bringing an end to 44 years of mining activity. The mine had produced gold and silver worth $950,000 in total, most of it gold.

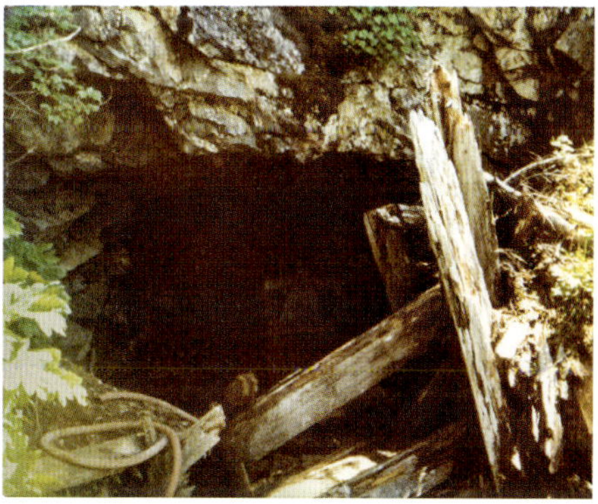

The Red Mountain Mine

Today, the international border is marked by an automated alarm system that is monitored by the US Border Patrol. The pack trail switchbacks over the border in many places and is heavily overgrown.

In 1978, there were no alarms or border patrols.

We loaded our gear into the back of our truck at the crack of dawn and drove the Elephant to the end of the Slesse Creek Forest Service road. To the east of us was Slesse Mountain; to the south was the route to the mine. The old pack trail was heavily overgrown with slide alder and rife with blackflies.

Halfway up the trail, we finally broke through the dense bush and came face to face with a mother bear and her three cubs, gorging on mountain blueberries. The cubs went up a nearby tree like three little rockets, and the mother bear came at us like a crazed linebacker.

The rule of the bush is that you're safe if you can outrun everyone else. We dropped our packs and scattered like dust in the wind. Out of the corner of my eye, I saw two members of my crew run into each other at full speed, and the rest of us scrambled up old alpine fir. Mother bear made a "bluff charge," then turned and, with her young cubs following her, raced up a steep slope faster than anything I'd ever seen move. We gathered our gear, changed our underwear, thanked our lucky stars, and carried on up to the mine.

The mine site was overgrown with bush, but we were still able to get to the opening. The rails still led into the mine, and an old ore car was still sitting there. A cave-in blocked the tunnel a few yards within the entrance, and cold mountain water gushed out of the mine. There were still pickaxes and shovels, water pipes and assorted old machinery scattered about the site. The buildings had all been destroyed over the years by fires and avalanches. Most of the mill equipment lay in ruins where it fell after the camp burned in 1942.

As we sat and ate our lunch, we marvelled at what had been accomplished over 40 years at this mine.

We couldn't imagine how difficult it must have been to keep it all in operation. It was difficult enough for us, and all we had to do was carry packs and chainsaws and dodge bears.

Another great day in the mountains.

Chapter Twelve

The Night Of The Storm And Crash Of Flight 810

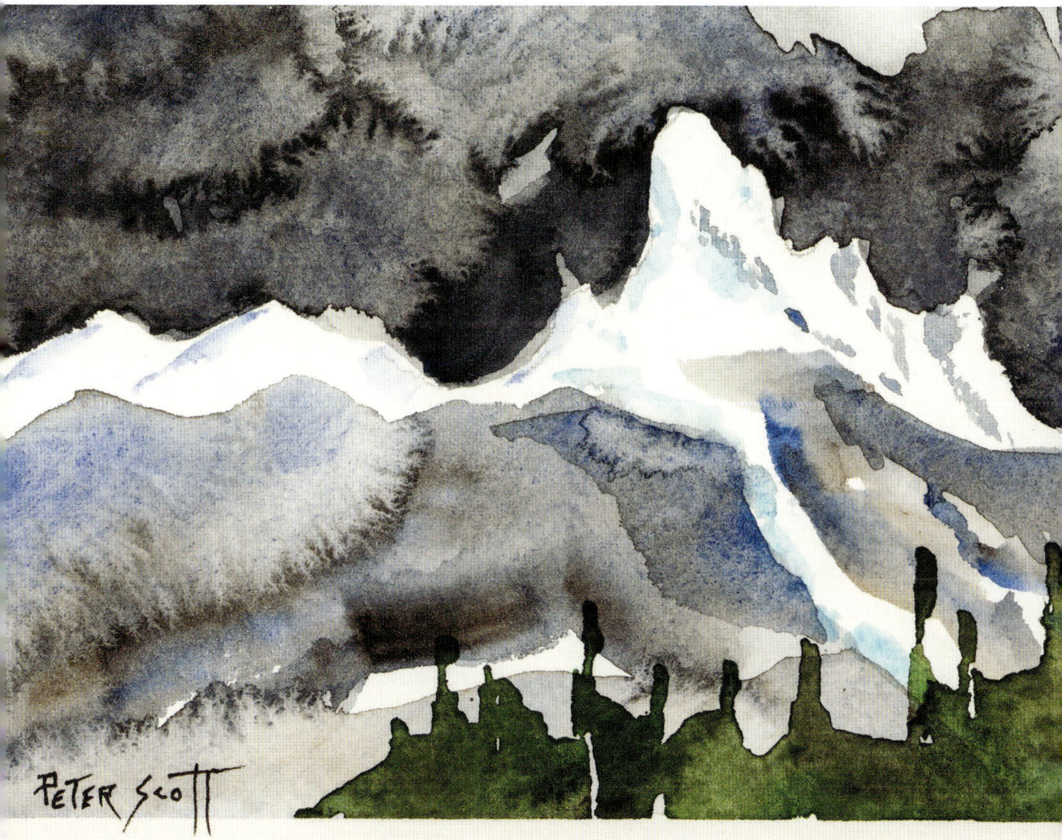

Night of the Storm, Mount Slesse

The worst Canadian air disaster occurred during a violent winter storm on the night of Dec. 9, 1956, near the small farming community of Chilliwack.

It began at the Vancouver International Airport at approximately 5:30 on a dark, rainy Sunday afternoon. Fifty-eight people were waiting at Gate 5 for a flight on Trans-Canada North Star Airliner Flight 810 en route to Calgary, Regina, Winnipeg, Toronto and Montreal. The plane they were waiting for was more than four hours behind schedule because of storms it had encountered over the mountains.

Among the 58 impatient and weary passengers were four members of the Saskatchewan Roughriders team of the Canadian Football League, returning home from the annual Shrine All- Star football game at Vancouver the previous day. Mel Demarco, formerly of Detroit, Mel Beckett of Indiana, Ray Shyrnk of Redwater, Alberta, and Gordon Sturtridge of Winnipeg had each purchased $100,000 in life insurance from the machine in the terminal. Racing into the terminal, late for the flight, was another CFL player, Calvin Jones of the Winnipeg Blue Bombers, who had also played in the All- Star game the day before. He had missed an earlier flight, and now TCA agents squeezed him onto Flight 810, taking one of the two seats reserved normally for the stewardesses. There were now 59 passengers waiting to board the plane.

Behind the football players were six Chinese passengers. One was Kwan Song, whose address was The Bowery, New York City, and who was returning from Hong Kong. He had apparently left the Crown colony under the watchful eye of British Intelligence, and his progress through Canada was under the surveillance of both the RCMP and the FBI. Kwan was believed to be bringing $80,000 in U.S. currency back to New York to pay the fees of Chinese students who had been studying at U.S. universities, and whom the Communist government hoped to persuade to return to China to help its technological program, including nuclear projects.

Other passengers boarding Flight 810 included football fans, World War II veterans, a Mountie, three women returning from a Hawaiian holiday, and women with young children.

The flight crew of Flight 810 consisted of pilot Captain Allen Clarke, 35, of Montreal, co-pilot First Officer John Boon, 26, of North Vancouver, and the lone stewardess, 24-year-old Dorothy Bjornson of Swan River, Manitoba. Clarke had been a bomber pilot in the RCAF Bomber Command in the Middle East during World War II and had survived 47 combat missions. Both he and Boon were more than capable pilots.

Clarke and Boon spent considerable time conferring with the weather forecaster, studying the weather charts and speaking with pilots from westbound flights. They decided to operate routinely to Calgary, 400 miles away, beyond the Rockies. After both men signed the flight plan, they ran out through the rain and boarded the North Star to prepare for the trip. They completed their cockpit check and eased the lumbering aircraft to the take-off position.

The plane carried 27 bags of mail, 1000 pounds of freight and express, 500 pounds of fresh flowers, the 59 passengers, three crew members, the passengers' baggage, jewels, and money, including Kwan Song's $80,000, and 13,394 pounds of high-octane aviation fuel, bringing the take-off weight of the plane to 76,850 pounds.

The North Star roared down the runway into the east wind and lifted off at 110 knots. The plane climbed at 500 feet per minute through light cloud. Heavier formations lay ahead, and tremendous thunderheads erupted with lightning. At 6:29 p.m., Flight 810 passed over the radio checkpoint at Cultus Lake and was now climbing at 15,000 feet, a mile above the jagged peaks below.

At 16,000 feet, the pilots reported they were encountering turbulence and that icing had begun to coat the plane's surfaces. A westbound flight 20 miles to the north of Flight 810 reported to Captain Clarke that there were clear skies at 21,000 feet and if he could attain that altitude he could escape the turbulence. This message may have influenced Clarke's decision to continue. At 6:48 p.m., Clarke's North Star was at 19,000 feet and battling extreme turbulence; clear skies were just four minutes away, and the plane continued to go on and up.

Then, at 6:52 p.m., a light flashed on the North Star's instrument panel, indicating an engine fire. Clarke shut off engine number two, on the left wing. The plane was now somewhere over Manning Provincial Park, five miles north of the U.S. border and 35 miles southeast of Hope. Clarke radioed Vancouver, reported what was happening, and then made the crucial decision to turn back to Vancouver. He flew through violent thunderstorms, ice and a headwind of 90 miles per hour. With an almost full load of fuel, a full passenger compartment, heavy freight and one inoperative engine, he continued to fly through treacherous updrafts in a storm growing more furious by the minute.

At 6:56 p.m., the plane was losing altitude, and a minute later it was down to an altitude of 14,000 feet. The radio controller wanted to know when the descending aircraft would cross the radio intersection at Hope. At 7:07 p.m., the plane had still not reached the radio intersection, indicating to the Vancouver controller that the aircraft was struggling against a terrific headwind. By now, the air traffic controllers determined that the plane was making a ground speed of only ninety miles per hour; the nose winds were blowing at 100 miles per hour.

The plane requested a descent to 10,000 feet. This was granted. The mountain peaks were now less than 2,000 feet below. The iced-up, crippled plane pushed onward and downward, frantically fighting the fierce thunderstorm. The ice was forcing it lower and lower. The minimum safe altitude in that area was only 9,600 feet, leaving Clarke and Boon little margin for error. The passengers by now must have been beyond terrified as lightning flashed around them while the plane violently dropped and rocked.

The NORAD station at Birch Bay in northern Washington had been watching Flight 810 on their radar and were the only ones to witness the next event: the blip of Flight 810 suddenly disappeared from their radar screen. One of the operators phoned the Vancouver tower and yelled, "Your Flight 810 has gone off our scope."

Flight 810 was dead, and so was its compliment of 59 passengers, a young stewardess and two fine pilots. It had exploded 7,950 feet up on Mount Slesse.

Chilliwack residents reported explosive thunderclaps from the mountains and said it was the worst winter storm they had ever experienced. The explosion on Mount Slesse rattled our windows and shook our house in Sardis, yet the air controllers could not pinpoint the site of the crash. They believed it had crashed on Silvertip Mountain, near Hope. The residents of the Chilliwack River Valley knew better; however, search officials refused to heed their advice.

It took authorities almost two and a half hours to decide the flight really was missing. All-weather RCAF CF-100 jet fighters were sent to search the Cascades. Pilots reported the air turbulence was so violent that their safety straps were breaking and equipment was flying all over the place. The jets were recalled, and the search was called off until the next day. Hope that there might be survivors diminished with each passing hour.

The RCAF spent weeks flying over the Silvertip Mountain and Mount Cheam area, to no avail. For one afternoon there were 24 official planes over the region, as well as 26 civilian planes. Several amateur mountain climbers rushed into the wilderness, and many of them had to be rescued, some by helicopter.

After five months, there was still no trace of TCA Flight 810. Finally on Sunday, May 12, 1957, three mountain climbers from Vancouver stumbled upon a fragment of the downed aircraft when they were lost in a snowstorm while climbing Mount Slesse in the Chilliwack River Valley. The trio of Efreda Pigou, an alpinist from Vancouver, Geoffry Walker, 28, and David Cathart, 23, discovered a piece of a paper map and a fragment of metal at

7,500 feet on the slopes of the mountain. They made it down and next day took the evidence to the RCMP. The piece of aluminum had the numbers CA 37-3-2000-63B on it. Trans-Canada officials identified the evidence as part of the wing of the missing North Star.

Immediately, helicopters and expert climbers were sent to search the northeast face of Mount Slesse. After two days of searching, experienced alpinist Walter Broda found a a four-metre section of fuselage, a child's shoe, a tiny human hand, fragments of luggage, and a pair of men's pants. None of these were marked by fire, indicating that the plane had been blown apart in a violent explosion. The mountaineers found that the North Star had crashed into the peak only fifty feet from the top. At the point of impact was a blackened spot of granite. Embedded in the spot were the wires of the pilot's headphones, the outline of his head and hat clearly visible. The plane's steel control cables trailed down the sheer sides of rock. A hundred feet below was a twisted propeller; a hundred feet below that, another chunk of fuselage. The bodies of the victims and the principal wreckage were found half a mile below this. Because of the dangerous, steep terrain, officials decided it was best to leave the bodies of the victims where they had perished.

In 1994, the province of British Columbia declared the east-face slope of Mount Slesse as the Mount Slesse Commemorative Site, protecting it from commercial exploitation and development. A cairn with a plaque and propeller were placed on the slope.

Slesse

High above the forests
of the valley far below.
Above the clouds and echoes
of the river,
far above the snows,
    Stands a mountain
    Stands a Lady
    Stands a killer
No one knows,
the beauty that's Slesse.
Eight thousand feet
or taller,
watching on forever
over forests, lakes and rivers,
    Slesse with her beauty
    Slesse with her wisdom
    Slesse with her stature
Daughter of the Cascades,
Queen of all around her.
No one knows the beauty
    Of the Lady
    Of the killer
    Of the mountain
No one knows the secret,
in her heart and in her soul.
The essence of the mountain,
    Slesse stands majestic
    Slesse stands forever
    Slesse stands so proud
She stands so tall and lonely
high above the clouds.

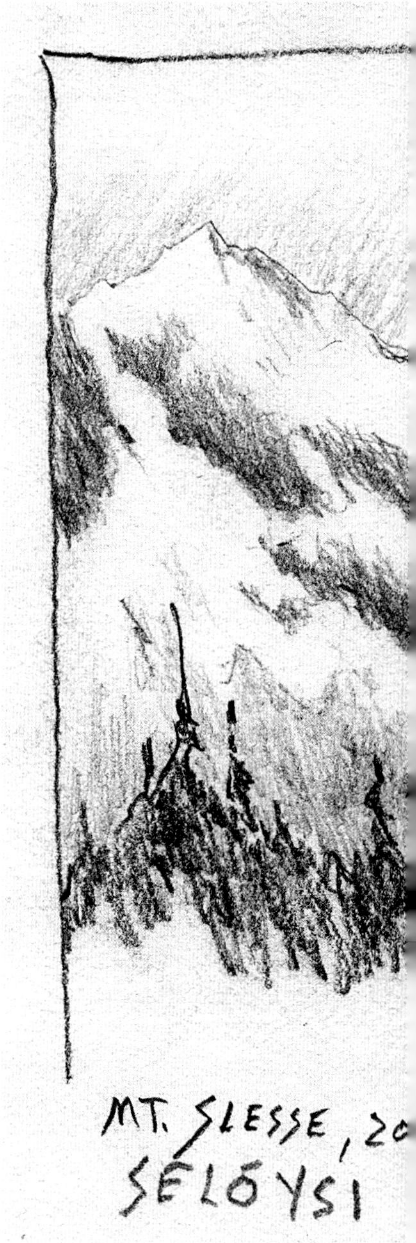

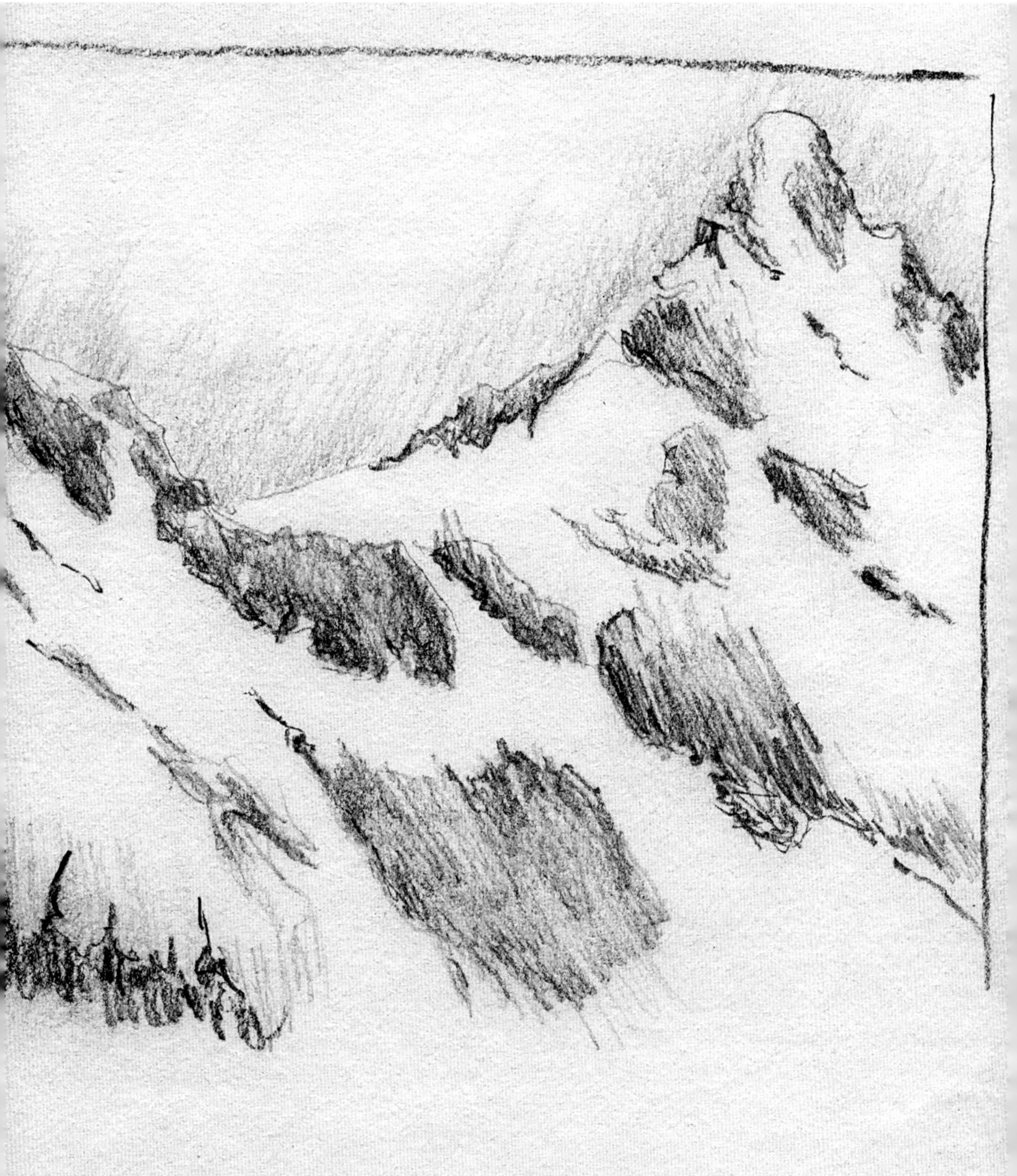

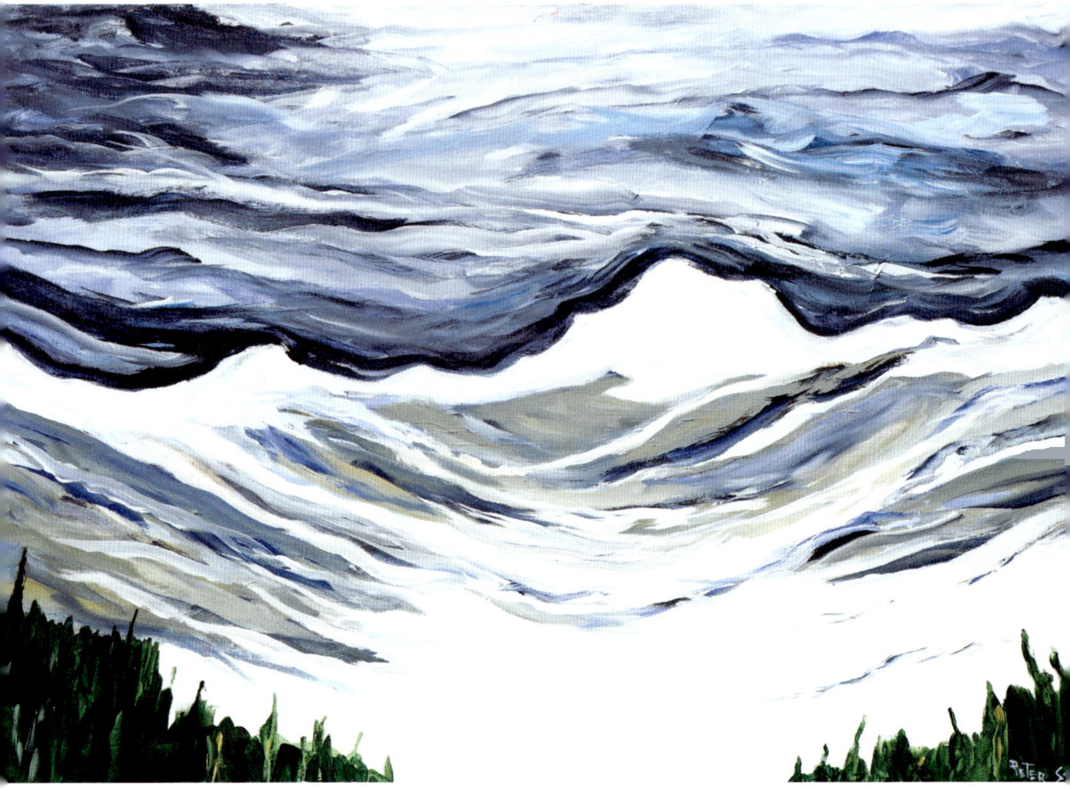

The Sky is Crying

Chapter Thirteen

Air Disasters In The Chilliwack Cascades And The Curse Of Mount Slesse

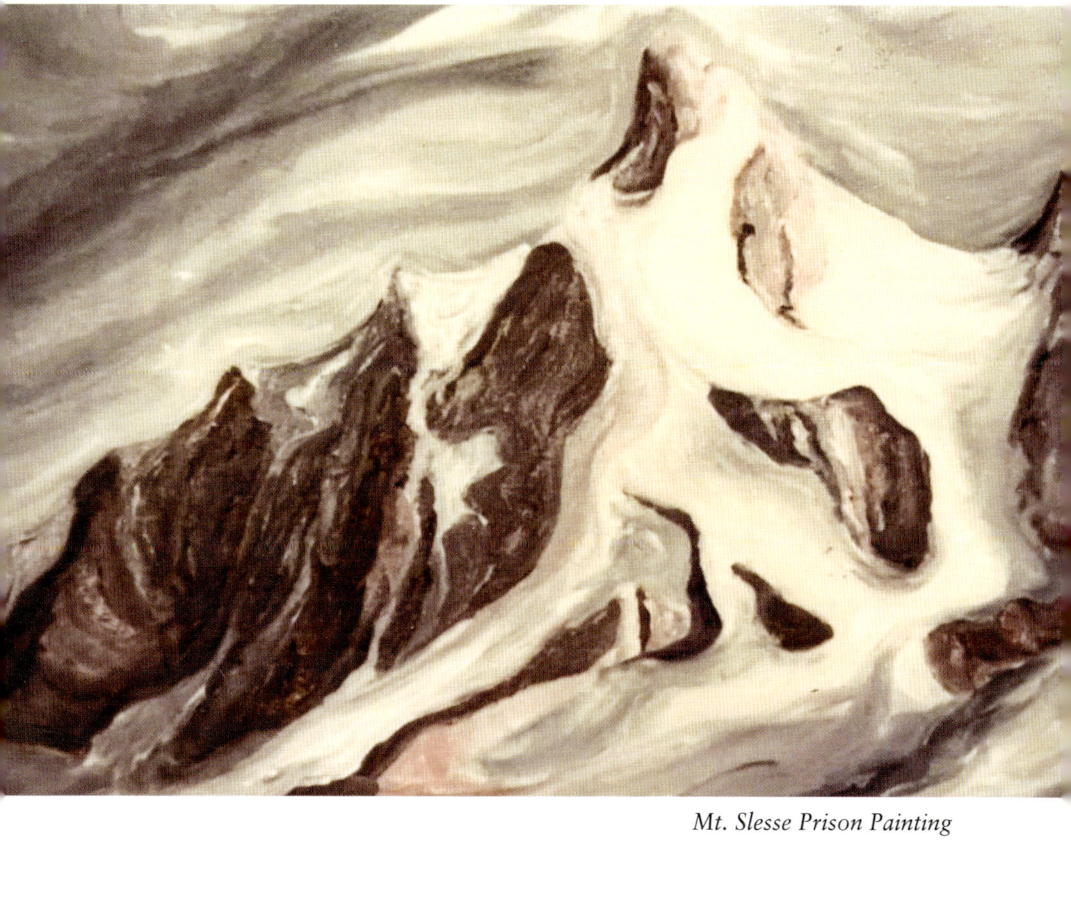

Mt. Slesse Prison Painting

In addition to the crash of Trans-Canada Air Lines Flight 810 on Mount Slesse in 1956, the towering mountains above Chilliwack have been the scene of two other airplane disasters. The first occurred five days before Christmas, in the winter of 1942.

A Canadian Pacific Airways Lockheed Super Electra left Prince George on a routine flight to Vancouver. Aboard were three crew members and ten passengers. The two veteran pilots, Captain Ernest Kubek and co-pilot William Holland, had 6,500 and 8,500 hours of flying time respectively.

Reports of a low-flying airplane were made by residents of Chilliwack in the early evening of Dec. 20, 1942. The plane was flying low during foul winter weather and was overdue at Vancouver International Airport. When it didn't arrive at its destination that night, authorities initiated an extensive air and ground search for the aircraft.

The search focused on three areas within the Chilliwack River Valley: Liumchen Mountain, the west side of the Elk Mountain ridge, and the eastern end of the valley. After ten days, the air search was suspended and a ground search began alongside the Chilliwack River and eastward to Chilliwack Lake, but to no avail.

Eight months later, on Aug. 9, 1943, a pilot spotted glistening aluminum wreckage on the upper slope of Mount William Knight.

A crash inspection team made the difficult climb to within a few hundred feet of the crash site until the steep terrain halted their ascent. From where they were, they could see aircraft propellers hanging from rocky cliffs. A few days later, on Aug. 18, a team of experienced climbers reached the site and found wreckage scattered over a large area on two sides of the mountain peak.

The team deduced the plane had been flying in fog and clouds, searching for its lost radio beam. One of the propellers had caught the ridge, ripped loose and embedded itself in the rock face. The plane hurtled over the ridge, dropping onto the opposite side of the peak, smashing into millions of pieces. The pilot had come close to clearing the ridge. The other propeller rested on the southwest face of the mountain.

There were no survivors.

* * *

On June 1, 1945, a Royal Air Force crew left the RCAF base at Abbotsford on a navigational flight exercise to the Penticton area and back to Abbotsford.

The crew was flying a B-24 Liberator. It had a maximum speed of 247 miles per hour at 28,000 feet and a range of 1,540 miles.

Summer thunderstorms were over the mountainous route, but posed no reason to abort the flight. The crew consisted of Flying Officer Hill, second pilot Officer Gilbert Long and navigator Sergeant Graham Murray, plus two radio operators, Sergeants William Swatton and David Lansans. The crew also included bomber Sergeant James Hammond and air gunners Sergeants William Drummond, Stanley Aloripso, John Dale, Isaac Gibsons, and Albert Broadbent.

The B-24 Liberator left Abbotsford at 9:06 a.m. heading east on the three-hour flight. Their last radio transmission occurred 35 minutes later, at 9:40 a.m.

An air search was initiated, but there was no sighting of the aircraft. For the next two weeks, heavy rainfall and low clouds hampered the search. A ground search focused on the mountains of the Chilliwack River Valley, Mount McGuire, Lady Peak and Elk Mountain. After fifteen days of intensive ground and air searching, an RCAF plane located the B-24 Liberator wreckage a hundred feet below the summit of Mount Foley in the Cheam Range, at an elevation of 7,730 feet.

Poor weather delayed climbers from reaching the crash site. Five days later, on June 20, a climbing party reached the wreckage. They removed the bodies from the downed plane and buried them in a common grave at 6,600 feet on Mount Foley. A wooden cross bearing the names of the airmen was erected.

The Department of Transport could not determine why Flying Officer Hill, who had been exactly on course, had been flying 2,000 feet lower than the stipulated altitude of 9,600 feet when the crash occurred. The cause of the crash remains unknown.

* * *

I have always been fascinated with Mount Slesse, suh-LEE-see, "Fang" in the Halq'eméylem language, situated in the Chilliwack River Valley. I grew up in the shadow of this awe-inspiring mountain. She was framed by our living room window. At 8,002 feet (2439 metres), she dominated the skyline. To me, she was beautiful. She didn't look like a fang; to me, she appeared a peaceful and majestic Madonna. Over the years I hiked on her, camped on her, and sketched and painted her many, many times.

After my graduation from art school at the University of British Columbia, I entered a painting I had done of Mount Slesse at an art exhibition in Chilliwack that also involved several other artists. A man kept coming over, admiring my painting. He seemed captivated by its mysterious allure and told me he wished he could own it. I told him the price and suggested he could buy it. He informed me he wasn't allowed any money. Intrigued, I asked why. He explained he was an inmate from Kent Prison who, along with other inmates, was there to exhibit his wood carvings. Finally, I made him an offer. I traded my painting of Mount Slesse to him in exchange for two of his woodcarvings. The transaction was made, much to his pleasure, and Mount Slesse went to prison.

I always record the names of people who own my paintings. Twenty years later, while I was watching the BCTV News Hour, a story was broadcast about an ex-convict who had recently been released from prison, moved in with a local woman and her two daughters in Chilliwack, and then committed a triple murder. I recognized his name, checked my records, and was stunned to find he was the con who owned my Slesse.

Where is my painting now?

Another layer of intrigue added to the legend of Mount Slesse.

Chapter Fourteen

The Magic And Mysteries Of Cultus Lake

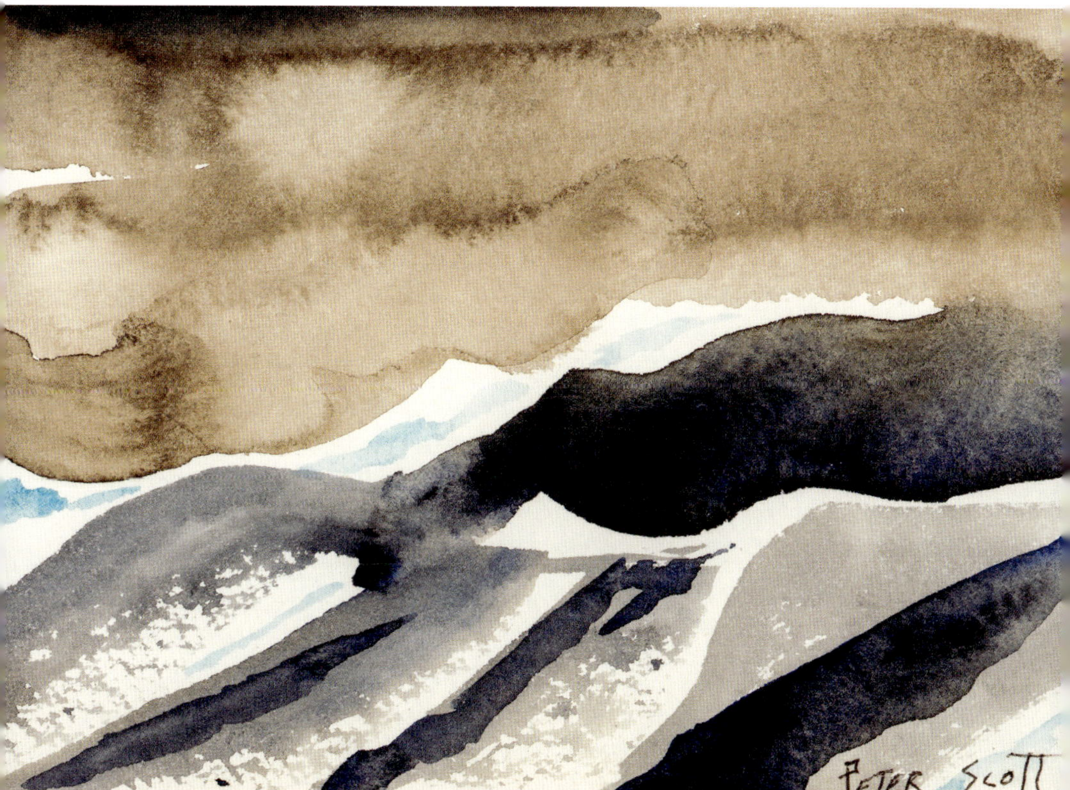

International Ridge

Cultus Lake is a jewel in the Chilliwack area. Situated below the International Ridge at the western end of the Cascades, it has been a playground for Chilliwack residents for many decades. In the 1940s, 1950s and 1960s, there was a roller rink, pavilion, and store at Main Beach. During the long, hot summer months we would ride our bikes from Sardis to Cultus Lake and spend the day swimming at Main Beach. There used to be a tall diving tower and slide there. People would frequently get injured doing unintentional belly flops off the diving tower, so eventually it was dismantled. The roller rink and dances at the pavilion were major attractions. Locals had summer cabins nearby, mostly rustic buildings with screened-in porches looking out at the lake.

Other popular beaches were Entrance Bay, Maple Bay, and Lindell Beach. I had years of summer fun taking swimming lessons at Main Beach, sliding headfirst down the tall metal slide, and daring friends to jump off the diving tower. Unfortunately, every summer there would be drownings at Cultus Lake, and if you didn't dry off thoroughly after swimming you would develop the dreaded cedar itch, a painful rash caused by the cedar logs in the lake.

According to Sto:lo legend, Cultus Lake was originally an empty basin. Water in the basin flowed into an underground river, leaving the basin dry. A community settled there. A young man from this community named Koothlak used to go swimming in a small lake he built on the side of a mountain. He dammed the lake, so it would fill with more water. Boys in his community used to tease him about going to swim there every morning, until one day he released the waters of the lake. When Koolak released the water, the branches of the dam went into the underground river, stopping it up, and the lake we called Cultus Lake was formed, drowning everyone in the community.

The lake became a source of both power and danger. Men desiring the power of Indigenous healers often ventured to the bottom of the lake. Once, a powerful doctor dug a small hole from a small lake and ended up in Cultus Lake. People believed there were tunnels below the bottom of the lake. Several people who swam in the lake went under and did not resurface; their bodies were found some time later, after they were transported through the underground river to Mud Bay, Washington, at the southernmost reach of Puget Sound. The tunnel, so the story went, was able to transport and kill those who were unworthy of the powers granted by forces living under the lake.

One time, some youth wanted to see if they could conquer the lake, believing that if they could, they would become medicine men. One young man didn't take anyone with him on his quest to conquer the lake, and when he came to, he found himself on a beach on the other side, in Bellingham,

Washington. He was said to be the only person who had ever survived the tunnel travel from Cultus to another location.

The tunnel remains a part of the spiritual geography beneath Cultus Lake. The exact location of the tunnel entrance has been lost, although some believe it is at Entrance Bay, thus the name of the present-day bay.

Stó:lō healers continued to go to the lake to obtain powers, but eventually, after thousands of years, the spiritual power was all used up. The "magic" was gone. The Stó:lō named the lake Swiltcha, (Suh-WEELT- zuh), meaning useless, worth nothing. In the Chinook language, it was called K'ehl or Kul, meaning bad.

Stó:lō legends also have it that man-eating serpents live in the reed beds of Cultus Lake. They suck the flesh off people and leave the bones. In Oliver Well's 1970 compilation book Myths and Legends of the STAW-Loh Indians of South Western B.C., locals Bob Joe and John Wallace tell a story of a youth who was seeking to undergo his SUH-Lee-ah (puberty rites) at Cultus Lake, home of the Slollicum (SHLAH-lah-kuhm), underwater serpents. He dived in and landed on the roof of the Slollicum's dwelling at the bottom of the lake. The Slollicum creatures swam out of their dwellings to investigate. They carried him into their house, where he discovered they were sick. Using his powers, he healed them. In return for this, they gave him the tluh-KEHL, which resembles a stout icicle. He stayed a while and then rose back to the surface of the lake with his tluh-KEHL.

He returned to his people and became a great healer, qweh-LAM, and cured the sick with his tluh-KEHL.

One day, a man from the lek'-EH-mel tribe and a friend set out on Cultus Lake without the knowledge of the Chihl-KWAY-Uhk people. They took a rope, STAY-quihm, and went out into the middle of the lake in a canoe. One man tied one end of a rope around his waist and descended into the lake to visit the Slollicum. After he had been down there a long time, his friend pulled up the rope. All that was left was the fleshless skeleton of his friend. He had been devoured by a serpent of the lake. The survivor gathered up the bones of his friend and went quickly home. After that, no one sought to look for the Slollicum of Cultus Lake.

Men continued, however, to try to obtain powers by going down into the lake. Always there were just bones left. Or men would disappear when they went into the area around Cultus Lake. This area became known as SOO-WA-lay territory—a word that means to disappear or dissolve.

On the May 24 long weekend in 1974, a group of my friends, my brother's friends and I went camping at Entrance Bay. On the Saturday morning, I got up early, left my tent, and drove into Vedder Crossing, as I had to work that day at the IGA store. When I arrived back at our campsite that night, everyone was

sitting in the camp, quiet and sad. The girls were crying. During the afternoon, one of my brother's friends had drowned. He had left the wharf at Entrance Bay and swam out past the log barriers, suddenly disappeared and never resurfaced. It was a hot day, and they had decided to go swimming, even though the water was quite cold.

The RCMP divers recovered his body in the reed beds 30 feet below the surface; his left arm had been injured and was missing a large part of flesh from his radius.

The coroner speculated that he had suffered cramps from the cold water and had sunk to the depths.

He couldn't account for the wounded arm.

Today, Cultus Lake is a tourist mecca. It is very developed, with beautiful multimillion-dollar homes. In summer the beaches are packed with people, and tourists swim and frolic in the water. The magic has returned to Cultus Lake.

One day during the summer of 1979, my crew and I were sent to scout out the route to International Ridge, high above the lake. The old logging road heading out from Edmuston Road led to an old, overgrown site that had been logged many decades before. Now all that was left was a variety of large stumps with springboard cuts, an old rail bed, and some scattered equipment. At one time the logs had been sent out by rail. I found an old railway lantern and sledgehammer there.

Once we found the trail, we discovered it was heavily overgrown with slide alder and stinging nettles. The trail was extremely steep. We had to slash our way through with machetes and sandviks. It was a long, long afternoon. We made it to the ridge and marked it with flagging tape. The trail follows the Canada/U.S. border.

As I stood on the ridge and looked out over the lake and the beautiful Fraser Valley, I could see a large cloud of yellow-brown pollution approaching the valley from the west. I became aware that soon our valley and the whole Chilliwack region would change. Progress and unimaginable development were headed our way. Cultus Lake and the Chilliwack Valley would never be the same. Change was coming; however the mysteries and stories of Cultus Lake remained.

Cultus (Sw ltcha) Lake

Swíltcha, lake of mysteries,
stories that are told.
Legends from millennia,
handed down from old.

Slollicum in reed beds,
magic tunnels far below.
Spirit powers in the water,
where they come from no-one knows.

The magic, gone forever,
suddenly is bad.
The people say it's useless,
only knowing what they had.

Now the lake is strong again,
its beauty people see.
Hundreds live around it,
Cultus for eternity.

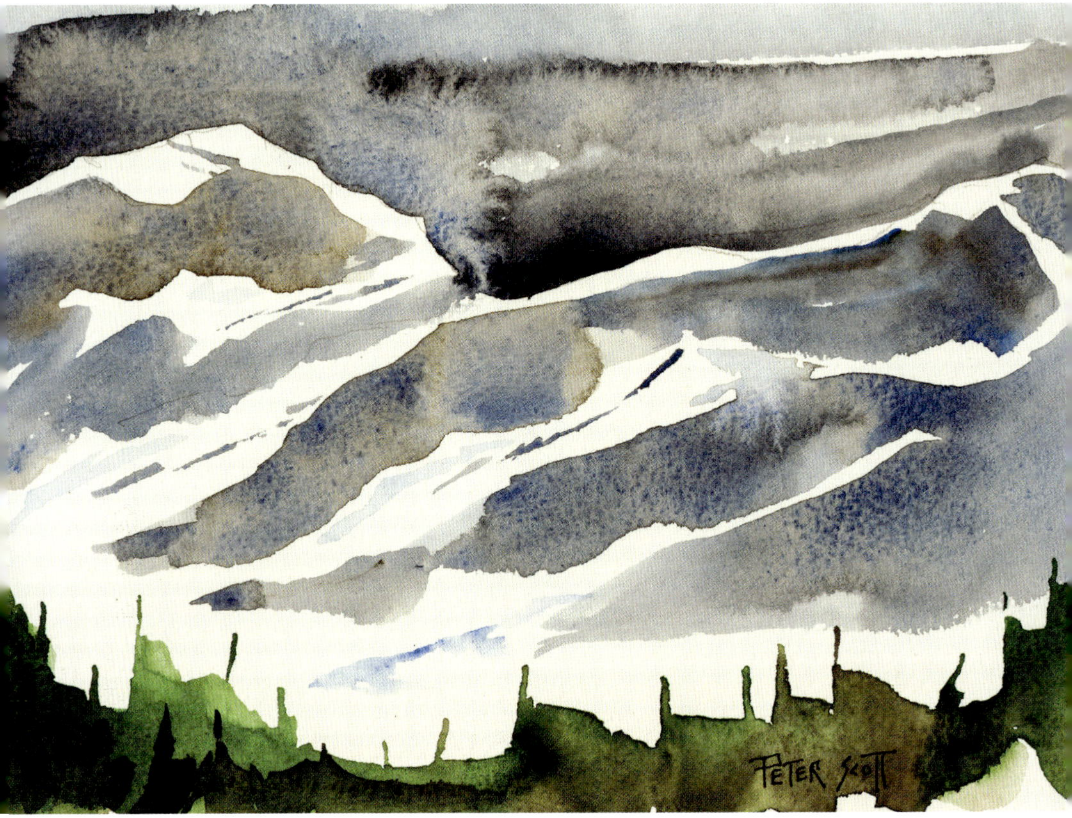

Mount Webb

Chapter Fifteen

The Chilliwack Lake Wild Goose Chase

One rainy afternoon during the summer of 1978, my crew and I were hiking back to our campsite at the south end of Chilliwack Lake after a long day of working in the bush. As we were walking along the sandy beach, tired and exhausted, Leon tripped over something sticking out of the sand. It was a large wing. We dug it up and found it was attached to a very large Canada goose. This was strange. Canada geese usually fly south; they don't bury themselves in the sand. Perplexed, we decided to rebury it in the beach.

After a swim in the lake, we made supper and then sat around the campfire until late in the night. I kept hearing strange sounds, but I thought it was my crew, as we'd had beans for supper. The next morning, when we emerged from our tents, we discovered extremely large bear tracks that went through and around our campsite.

These tracks were enormous. We re-examined the prints and the size of the claws. This was no black bear. These were the prints of Ursus Arctos horribilis—a grizzly!

Grizzlies aren't known to dwell in the Chilliwack River Valley, but someone forgot to tell this bear. Over the years, there have been rare reports of a stray grizzly who has wandered through the high country and down to the valley. Old man Lindeman, a local trapper, had a large pelt stretched out on the side wall of his cabin at the north end of Chilliwack Lake. I had seen it there when I was a kid. Our bear must have come over old man Lindeman's mountain.

If a grizzly encounters a human, the bear usually makes the human disappear, especially if the human(s) has unearthed his food cache. Why were we still alive?

Grizzlies are not only extremely large animals, but they are also HUGE, powerful, and mean. Their skulls are massive, their incisors enormous, and their claws long and razor sharp. We were lucky to still be breathing.

The monster had recovered his goose from the beach and explored our camp during the night. According to grizzly protocol, he should have torn our packs, tents, and us to shreds. Instead, he chose to eat and run.

Years later, when I had relocated to the Cariboo district, the wilderness was populated with grizzlies. A person was not wise to roam the wilds of the Cariboo Mountains without a rifle. A very large rifle. One afternoon, though, I took my son and his friends on a hike along the shores of Bowron Lake. We were camping near the Bowron Lake Lodge. Guns are not allowed in the park, so we were hiking armed with nothing but jackknives and water bottles. As we were hiking along, I suddenly noticed a large patch of bark missing from the trunk of an old jack pine. The swatch was eight feet from the ground and bore large claw marks. A grizzly had been marking his territory, and we were in it. We made a hasty U-turn and headed back to camp to pack up our tents and get out of there. While we were packing, my friend arrived in his pickup truck and began excitingly telling us he had just passed a thousand-pound grizzly up the road. The boys and I had unknowingly flushed the bruin out from the shoreline, and he headed through the bush to the road.

Tom loaded us into his crew cab, and we headed back up the road to find our bear. We rounded a bend in the road, and there he was. He let out a snort and headed into the trees. We drove to the spot, shut off the engine and rolled down our windows and listened for him. He didn't make a sound. It's amazing how animals that size can be so quiet when they are being stalked. Tom had a rifle in his truck, and we were outside the park boundaries. We knew he was staring at us from somewhere in the bush. Then the trees started to shake and we heard crashing through the bush. We decided to quickly leave before he had a chance to rush out and attack our truck. That was one large bear, and we were one very lucky group of campers.

Forty miles southwest of Bowron Lodge lies the small, former gold-mining town of Wells. The population in the 1960s and 1970s comprised approximately a hundred hippies, draft dodgers and old gold miners. The hippies and draft dodgers had revitalized the ghost town, and the place was alive again. The lone RCMP officer who was posted to Wells had a routine where he would extract a drunken, rowdy local from the Friday night dances at the Wells Community Center, or from the Jack O' Clubs Hotel, and then drive the drunken individual several miles out on the Bowron Lake road, drop the drunk off and let him walk back to town in the dark to sober up.

This was known as the dreaded "grizzly walk." I only made that walk once, and once was enough.

In the spring of 2002, an old prospector was returning to Wells from his diggings on Antler Creek when his truck broke down. All the swearing in the world couldn't restart the truck. Begrudgingly, the old-timer decided to walk the rest of the way to town in the dark. Bad decision. Along the way, he surprised a sow grizzly and her cubs. That was the last thing he did on this earth.

The next day, a local found the remains of the old gold miner. He had been brutally mauled and was lying in the middle of the road. His head was missing. He must have left his rifle in the truck.

There is a rule in the Cariboo. If you encounter a grizzly bear in the wilderness and you have forgotten your rifle, or if all you brought with you was a bag of granola, don't run. Instead, bend over and kiss your ass goodbye. The old gold miner never recovered from his mistake.

Another victim of Ursus arctos horribilis was a young German tourist who was enjoying his wilderness canoe trip on what is known to canoeing enthusiasts around the world as the Bowron Lake Chain. In the summer of 1993, he and his girlfriend had embarked on their trip of a lifetime, or for him a forgettable trip of the end of a lifetime.

Europeans and Americans love making the trip to this famous canoeing chain of lakes. It takes approximately ten days to round the chain in the beautiful Cariboo Mountains of central British Columbia. Along the route are a few old trapper's cabins and remote campsites.

Our German tourist friend and his girlfriend had decided to stay in one of the old cabins. They cooked their dinner and sat on the front porch and gazed at the stars. Suddenly, out of the dark, emerged Mr. Horribilis. The girl ran to the canoe and set off across the lake for help. Her brave boyfriend ran into the cabin and slammed shut the door. The bear knocked down the door. The girl escaped. The boyfriend didn't. The bear dragged the boyfriend onto the beach.

The next morning, park rangers found the body of the boyfriend on the beach in front of the cabin. He had been mortally mauled. A large chunk of his gluteus maximus was missing. The moral of the story: follow your girlfriend.

Knowing these legendary stories, my crew and I were extremely happy to pack up our gear and leave our camp on the shores of Chilliwack Lake.

Moral of story #1: if you trip over a goose wing buried in the sand on the beach, go back to your truck and get your bear spray.

Another wonderful day in the beautiful Chilliwack Mountains.

Lindeman (Suxwi:ts) Lake

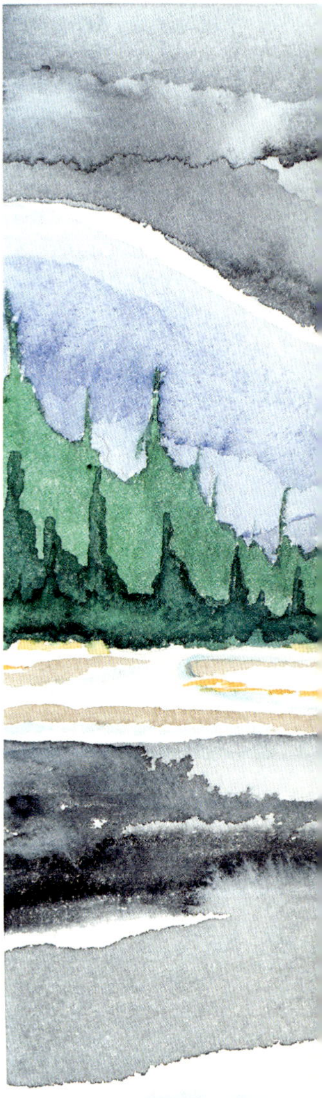

Lake of turquoise waters,
a quiet calm of bliss.
Shimmers in the sunlight,
through the morning's mist.

Echoes of the mountains
and their cascading falls.
Ripple o'er the waters,
and the lonely coyote's calls.

Suxwi:ts through the ages,
thousands of years old.
Mountain glacier waters,

turquoise, green and cold.

Forever holds a magic
to anyone who goes.
Spring, or summer, autumn,
or through the winter's snows.

A place of calm tranquility,
a place where spirits live.
Hiding in the shadows,
with their gifts to give ...

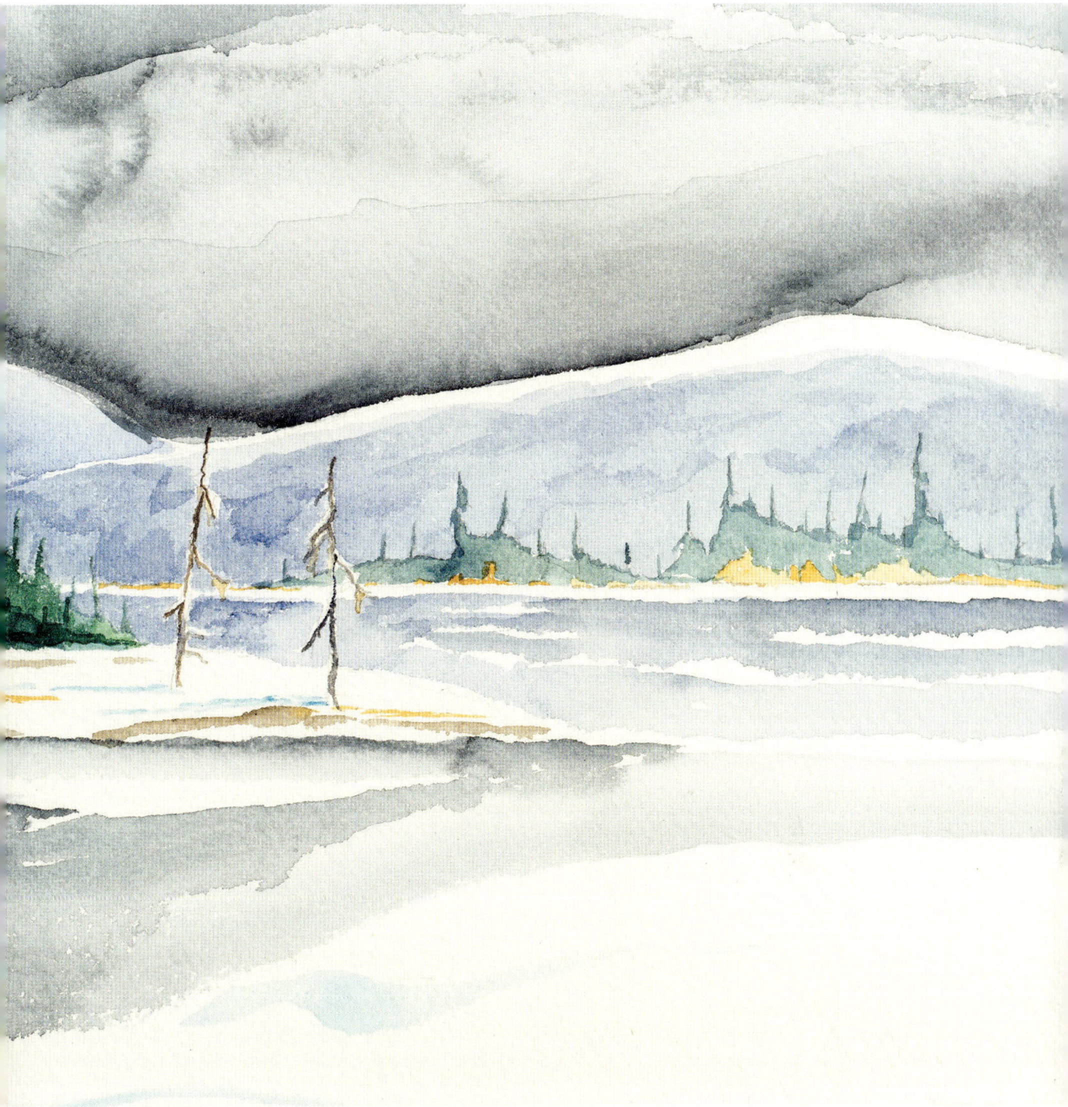

Lindeman Lake Below the Ice

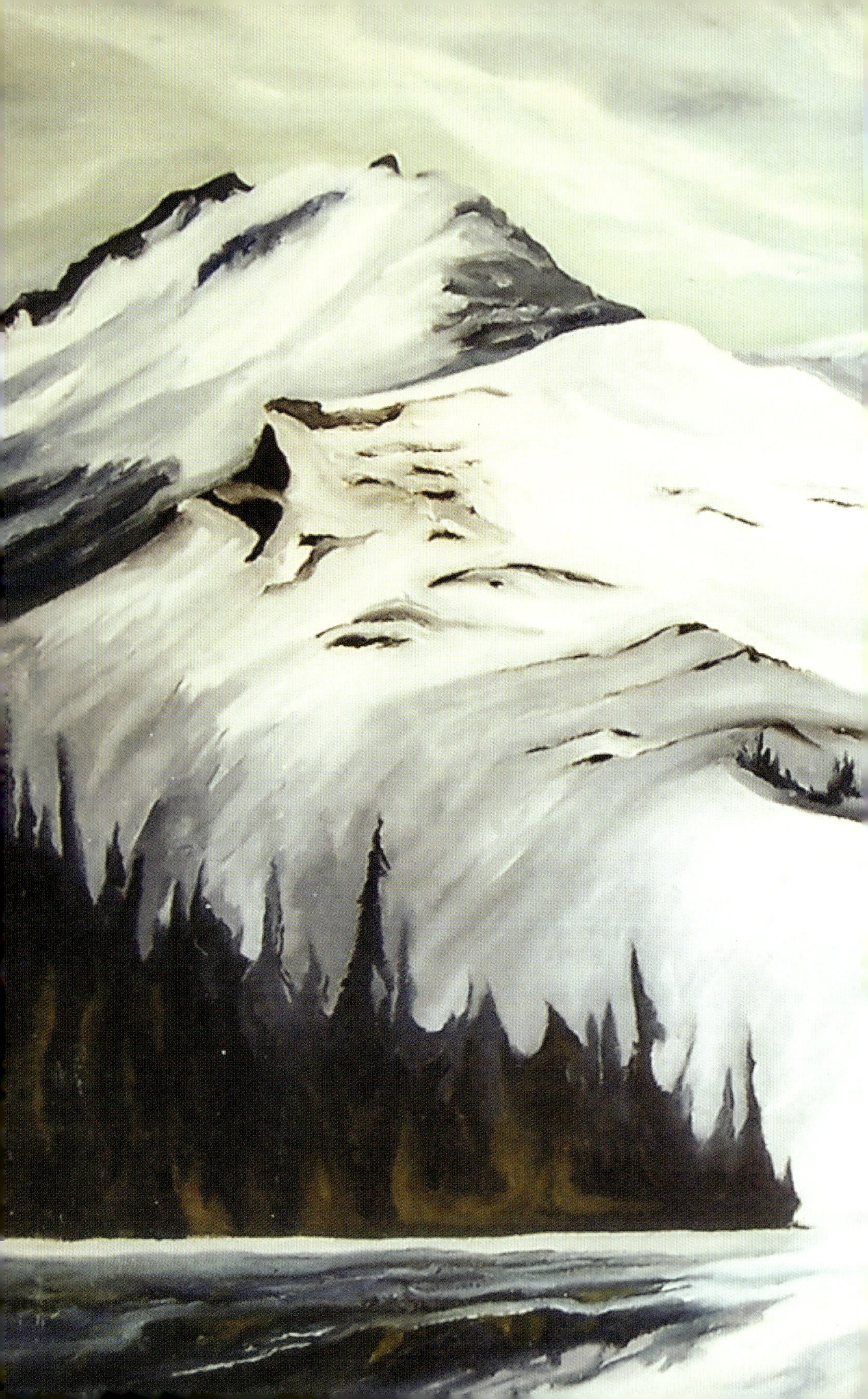

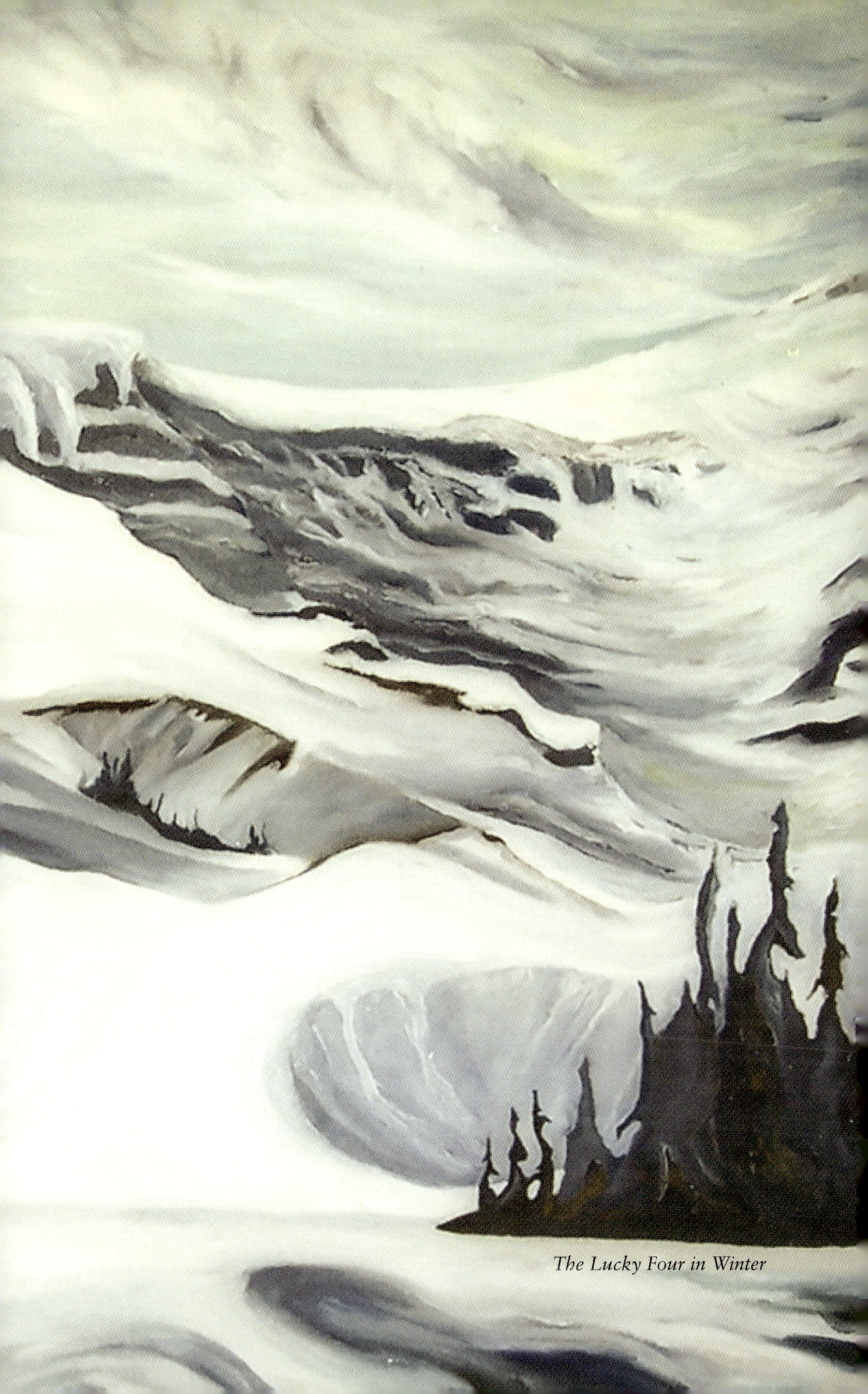

The Lucky Four in Winter

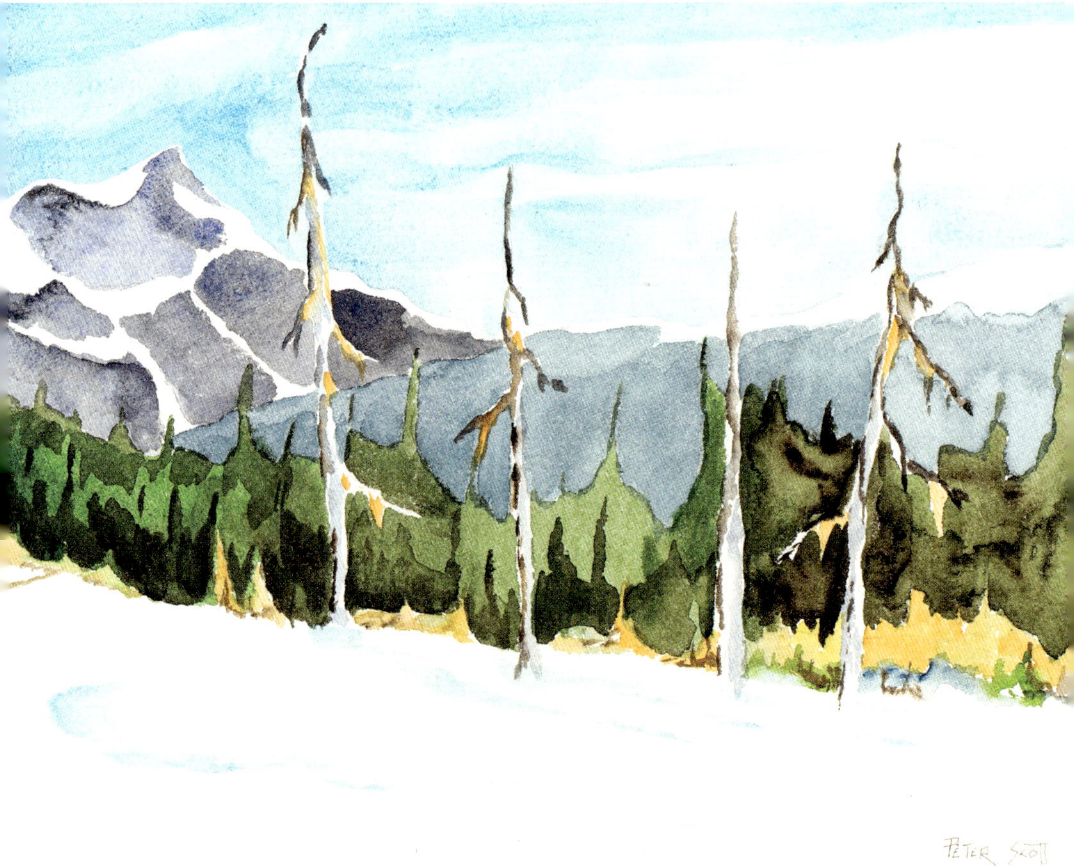

Red Mountain

Chapter Sixteen

Goodbye Stranger, The Lucky Four Mine And Night On The Ledge

In August 1979 the Chilliwack SAR sent my crew and me to Waleach (Jones Lake) to hike up and check out the route to the old Lucky Four Mine. The Lucky Four mountain group consists of Mount Foley, Welch Peak, Knight Peak and Stewart Peak. The mountains are located at the south end of the lake, and the view of them is spectacular. The lake itself in late summer is not scenic. The north end is full of stumps.

Welch Peak, Mount Foley and Stewart Peak are named after the three partners of the Lucky Four Mine, which is on the face of Mount Foley below the ridge, near the cirque formed by Conway Peak and Mount Foley. The glacier in the cirque is Lucky Four Glacier. The highest point in the group is Welch Peak at 7,976 feet. Prospectors from Hope discovered the showings of silver, copper and some gold in the fall of 1915. They staked a group of claims on the Lucky Four.

In 1916, the claims were optioned to A.S. Williams, of North Vancouver. In 1917, the engineering firm of Welch, Stewart and Foley acquired the property. This was an early American-Canadian railroad construction firm, owned and operated by Patrick Welch and J.W. Stewart, of Spokane, Washington, and T. Foley of St. Paul, Minnesota. It was the largest railroad construction company in North America at the time. They built miles of track for railways that included the Great Northern Railroad, North Pacific Railway, Grand Trunk Pacific, and the Pacific Great Eastern Railway.

Diamond drilling began soon after acquisition of the mine. Six holes were drilled from the snowfield above, collecting 0.06 ounces of gold, 8.33 ounces of silver and 12.05 percent copper. The mine later consisted of two main lateral shafts coming in from the face of Mount Foley at elevations of 5,400 feet and 6,300 feet.

1919 saw the demise of the firm's ownership of the mine, and over the next few years various companies worked the operation. The mine continued to produce modest amounts of copper and silver. In 1957, Chillicopper Corporation Limited acquired a controlling interest in the mining operation and continued to produce returns. The lower shaft was drilled into a 45-degree slope. The entrance was high above a glacier, which made for dangerous access to the shaft. Working the operation was extremely hazardous because of the extreme angle of the shafts, avalanches, and the height of the mine.

We drove the Elephant to Waleach Lake on an overcast morning and then proceeded to travel along the east side of the lake until we came to a fork in the road. In the words of famous New York Yankee Yogi Berra, "When you come to a fork in the road, take it." We took the left branch and followed this until we came to a large washout. We decided not to try to make the Elephant jump this obstacle, so we parked her there, donned our packs and headed up the road until we came to the trail. This new trail had been built in 1971 and was in good shape. It led up through the forest, eventually meeting with another old road that had a corduroy section.

At this point, thick clouds and a summer storm rolled in. The clouds obscured our visibility. We finally got out of the trees, and then we were really travelling blind. There was no such thing as GPS back then. We only had our compasses, dead reckoning, and our noses to follow. All we could do was keep going up. We blindly stumbled our way through meadows. The rain started and soon was driving in sheets, and we had no idea where we were. We thought we might be at Mile High Camp, so we set up our tents and camped for the night.

One member of our crew was the younger brother of one of my guys and had been hired by the SAR mainly because he needed a job. Why, I don't know. He had no experience in the bush and was now panicking in the thick fog and cloud. He stayed in my tent, and I tried to calm him down. It was a long night. Finally, at daybreak he rolled up his sleeping bag and said he was going down. As he was packing, he started singing the lyrics to a Supertramp song, "It's early morning yesterday, I was up before the dawn, I really have enjoyed my stay, but I must be moving on. Goodbye stranger, it's been nice, hope you find your paradise." Then he disappeared into the clouds. I was

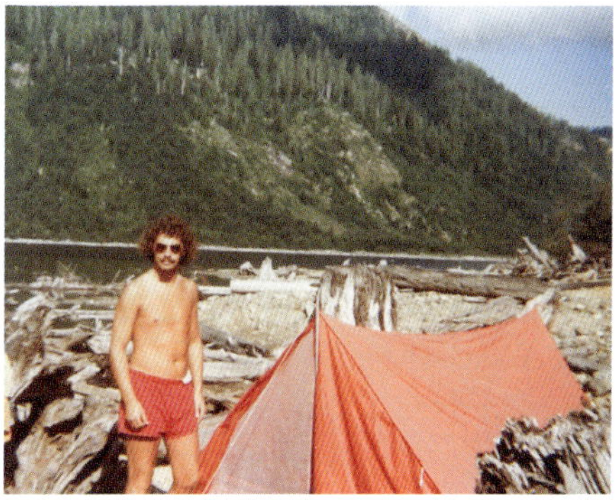

Rookie on the Beach

laughing so hard, I didn't try to stop him. An inexperienced hiker, zero visibility, the edge of a cliff—and away he went. I should have gone after him, but my crew was already packing up, determined to find the mine. Finally, there was a break in the clouds, so we made our way across the ridge and headed south to Foley Mountain. We found the mine. It was below us, on a steep slope high above a glacier. We decided not to venture down to it. Old planks were hanging out of the mouth of the shaft, and we couldn't believe people would work at such a dangerous place.

The clouds cleared as we made our way back down to the Elephant. As we arrived at the lake, there was our deserter, sun-tanning on the beach. He had miraculously found his way. We loaded him into the truck and said goodbye to the Lucky Four, which were now clear of clouds and stood impressive and beautiful against the blue sky. I drew a few quick sketches and took some pictures, and when I returned to the studio at UBC the next month, I stretched a 4-by-6-foot canvas and painted The Lucky Four.

In 2012, the Quesnel Art Gallery acquired the painting from me. I wish I still owned it. I consider it my masterpiece. Whenever I visit Quesnel, I head back to the gallery and look at the painting. As I stand there, looking at it, I hear in my mind the lyrics to that old song. "I really have enjoyed myself, but I must be moving on." I laugh and remember the good old days … high in the mountains, lost in the clouds above the Lucky Four Mine.

The Lucky Four

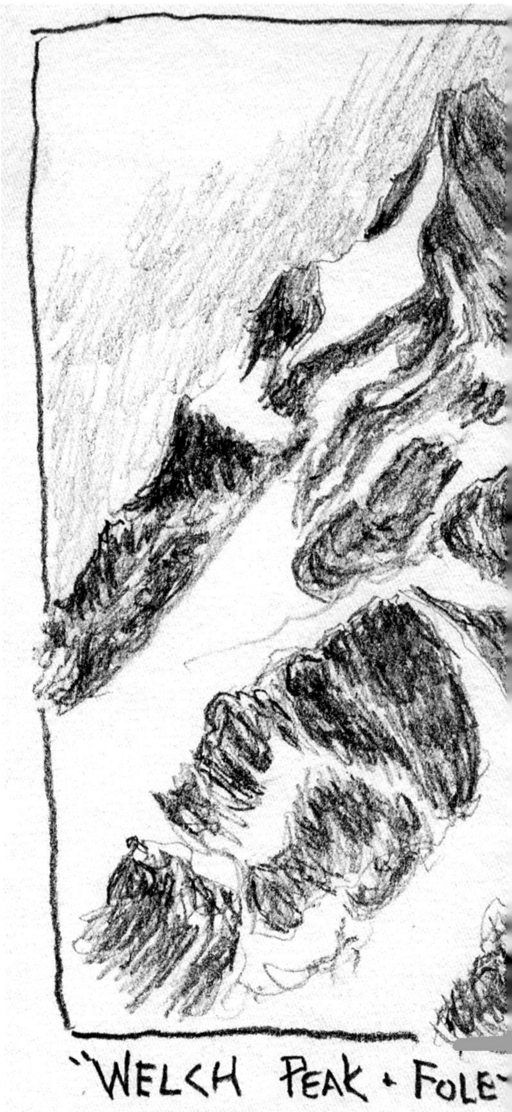

Mountain peaks and glaciers
reach up through the clouds.
Cries of ghostly miners
Echo clear and loud.

Cascading falls and avalanche
pour into the streams.
Abandoned mines and memories

fade to ancient dreams.

Below the lake is shimmering,
mountains out of reach.
Remnants of man's folly,
The gold was out of reach.

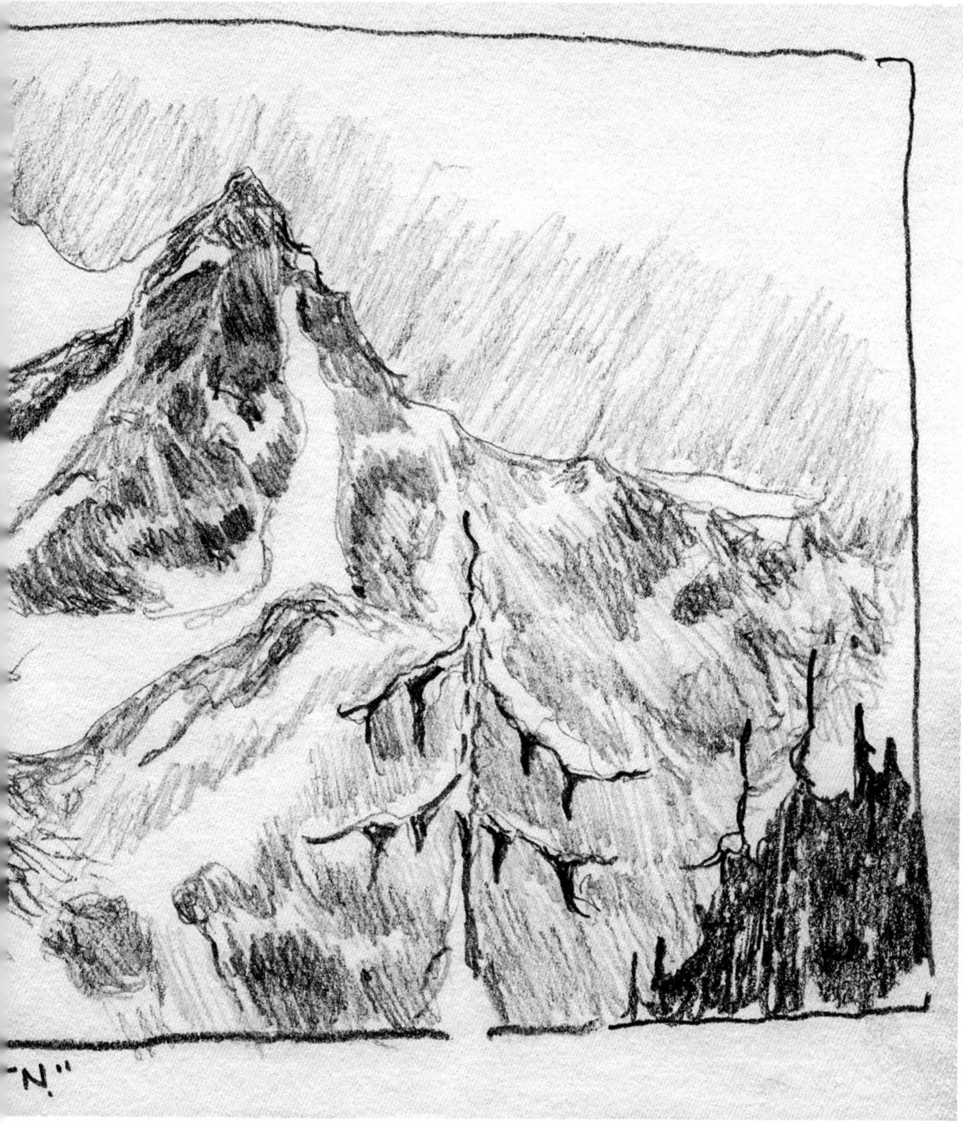

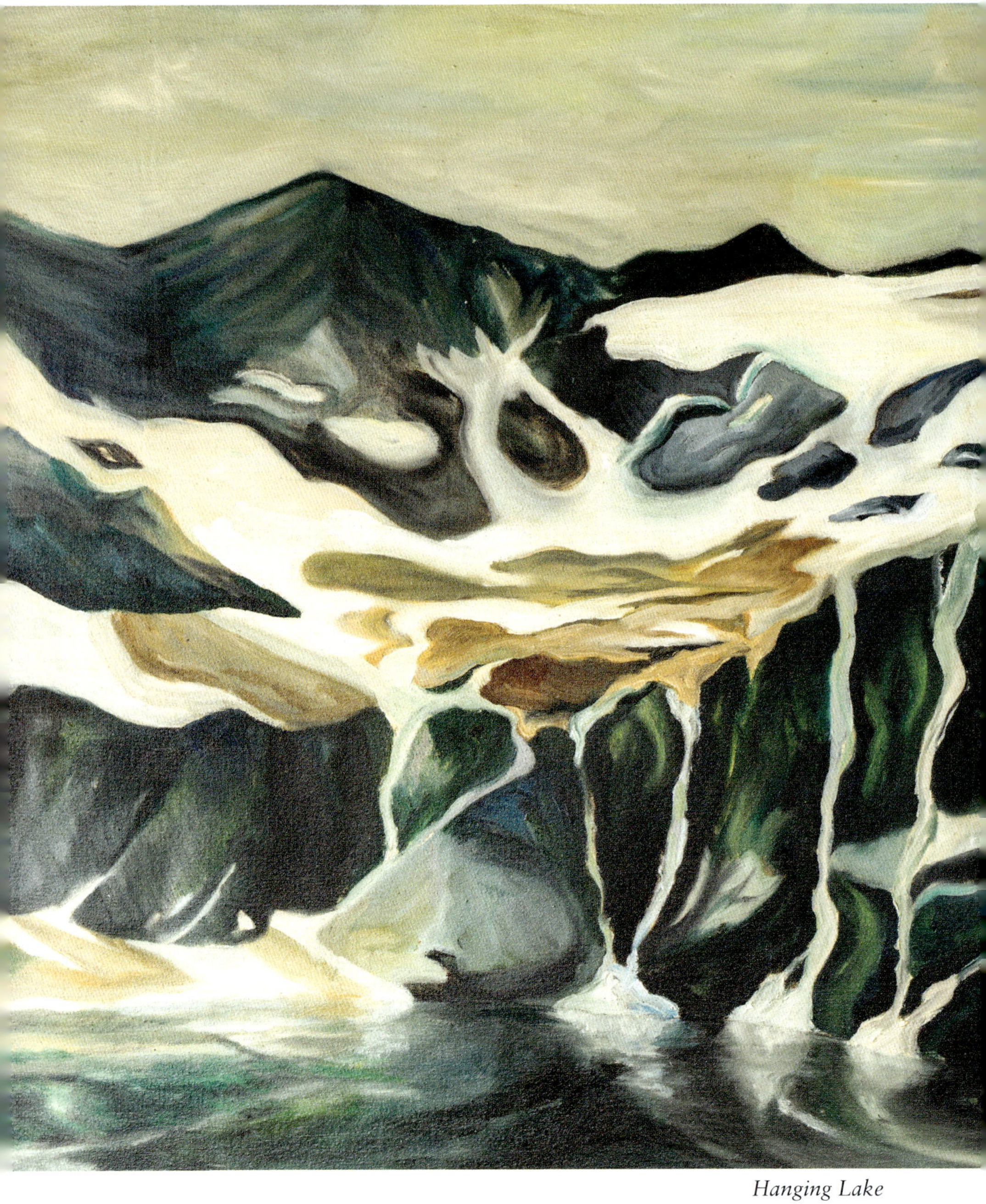

Hanging Lake

Chapter Seventeen

Hanging Lake, A Broken Leg, And A Bear

My favourite site in the Chilliwack River watershed is Hanging Lake. I used to go there for inspiration and solace. It is difficult to get to; the perfect location for a painter seeking solitude. Hanging Lake is a spiritual place. It is so quiet you can hear the spirits of the Ts'elxwéyeqw, those who have called these mountains and lakes home for thousands of years. To me, this place has a natural inner power that comes from somewhere else, a mystical place where the ghosts exist.

During the last half of August 1979, my crew and I set out on our last assignment in the SAR project, to slash, survey, map and mark a route up to Hanging Lake. Hanging Lake is on the U.S.-Canada border, high above the south end of Chilliwack (Sxótsaqel) Lake.

We drove the Elephant to the far end of Sxótsaqel one early, sunny morning. On the drive from Sardis, something was wrong with the Elephant. She was struggling. Her age and adventures in the mountains these last two summers had worn her out. She was covered in dents and scratches from bouncing off trees along the narrow roads and skidder tracks we drove her on, as well as the damage she acquired from her famous jump off Thurston Mountain the summer before. Now, she was constantly stalling, overheating and limping along the gravel road to the far end of Chilliwack Lake. We knew the end of the Elephant was near, and so was the end of our magical eight months exploring these mountains. However, one more adventure remained: Hanging Lake.

We donned our packs, picked up our chain saws, axes, machetes, and shovels, and headed up the trail through giant, old-growth cedar forest. The trail was in good shape and the hike along the Little Chilliwack River was pleasant. Along the way, we would stop and marvel at the size of these enormous old cedars. Several of us could stand around the trunk of these trees holding hands, their trunks were that large.

Once we made our way through the cedar grove, we had to cross a fast-flowing stream on a narrow, slippery log and then use our machetes to slash our way through thick bush. The old trail went straight up into a massive boulder field. We spent several days working on the lower end of the trail and camped at Sapper Park at the end of Chilliwack Lake.

After a few days, we had a route cleaned out that led to the boulder field. In the center of the boulder field, which was covered in chest-high wild mountain blueberry bushes, stood a grove of trees. We set up camp in there for a few days while we slashed our way across the boulder field. It was a great place to break a leg; there were large holes between the boulders, obscured by the bushes. Leon was busy sampling the berries and making notes of the flora and fauna in his survey book and always seemed to be the last guy in our column as we hiked up the trails. I often hiked behind him in an effort to speed him up. One day, as we were crossing the boulder field, Leon was studying a hawk through his binoculars. He proceeded to stumble and fall forward into a hole between some boulders. He fell awkwardly, and we heard a cracking sound. The screams that followed would wake the dead. He had fractured his leg. Not a great situation. I had left the satellite phone in the Elephant. As I was the leader of the group, it was my responsibility to hike down to the truck and notify the SAR. The crew, meanwhile, got Leon back to our camp in the trees and tried to ease his pain with rum. It wasn't a bad break; we thought it was a spiral fracture, as the bone wasn't protruding through the skin.

I left the crew in the late afternoon and was headed through the chest-high berry bushes, trying to follow our slashed-out route, when I saw him. A large black bear. It looked to be a male, as I saw no cubs. He was busy munching on berries. Bears have poor eyesight but rely on their keen scent of smell. The breeze was blowing my way, so I could smell him, but as yet, he hadn't smelled me.

I was stuck. I needed to get past him; time was of the essence, and dusk was setting in. However, he was in no hurry to go anywhere. Finally, I took out my whistle and blew it loudly while waving my arms around. Startled, he stood up on his hind legs and sniffed the air. I was on the verge of having a heart attack when suddenly he turned and ran. I also turned and ran. Who was more scared—the bear or me?

When I was sure Yogi had left, my breathing was restored and my pulse settled, I continued down the trail and eventually reached the Elephant. I made the call to the SAR, and they were sending a team up to extract Leon. I returned up the trail with my head on a swivel and all my defence mechanisms on high alert, as by now it was dark and I wasn't sure if Yogi was still in the area. I made a lot of noise as I pushed my way through the berry bushes over the boulders and made it to camp. Leon had been well medicated by now and was feeling no pain. Leon was drunk.

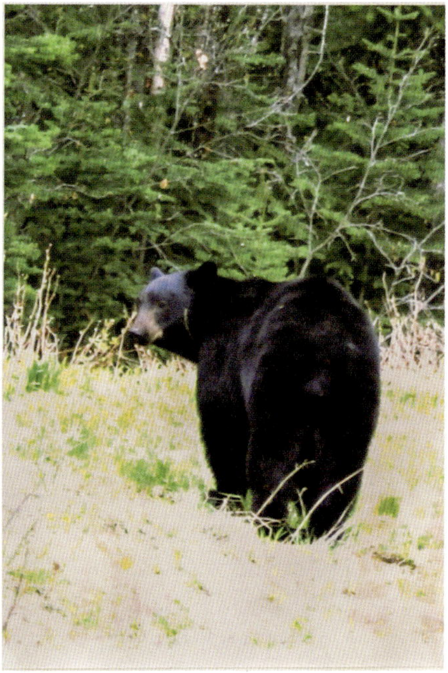

Yogi

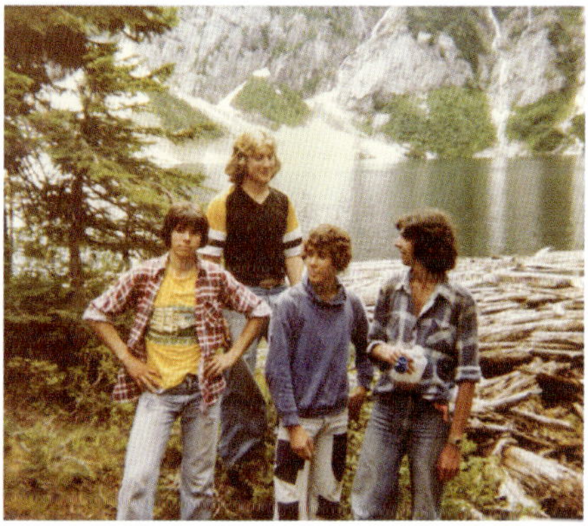

The Alpine Tour Guides at Hanging Lake

After that fiasco, once Leon had been successfully rescued, the crew and I got back to work. It took two more days to slash a route across the boulder field. Our crew was now reduced to seven, and the work was intense. Finally, we broke through the bush and found ourselves at the bottom of an extremely tall waterfall. Great. Now we had to cut a trail straight up through the trees with our chain saws and axes.

It took us five days to push a passable trail to the top of the waterfall. From there, we built a trail along the fast-flowing stream to Hanging Lake. It was impressive: 12 waterfalls cascading down from the glacier above the lake. We dropped our packs, guzzled ice-cold mountain stream water, and set up camp. We stayed at the lake for three more days, dropping trees and bucking up logs to make the trail more passable. We spent our last day swimming and relaxing in the waters of the lake. I did several sketches and shot two rolls of film of the scenery. Hanging Lake was going to turn into a painting when I returned to the studio the next month.

That night, we celebrated. It was a bittersweet end to the SAR project, but we danced around the campfire and howled at the moon! The next day we hiked down to the Elephant, marking the tree trunks with red metal tags as we passed. Once we were down to Chilliwack Lake, we fired up the Elephant. She sputtered and coughed but finally came to life. On the way down Chilliwack Lake Road, the wire holding the Elephant's hood snapped; the hood flew open, broke off its hinges and flew up and over the tall tin box on the back of the truck. The hood became a large white kite, and we were hoodless! No one was hurt, but it's not every day your hood flies off. The end of the Elephant was near.

We arrived back at the SAR headquarters, parked the Elephant and paid our respects to our old friend.

I met with the directors of the SAR the next night. The project was over. We had built miles of trails over the past eight months, explored the vast area of the Chilliwack River Valley, and climbed to the tops of many peaks. We had also been on two rescues, one successful and one that ended tragically for a young hiker, who had fallen into a ravine and drowned in the stream below. I was with the young girl's uncles when the call came in that the divers had found her lifeless body. Two SAR members brought her up the steep sides of the ravine with ropes and a stretcher. Then one of my crew and I had to carry the stretcher to the awaiting ambulance. A horde of reporters and cameramen strained against the yellow tape as we loaded the poor girl into the ambulance, and as we fought off the reporters, we could hear the wails of the distraught mother. That was a rough day. Fortunately, my crew and I only had to experience something like that once.

Overall, the mapping project was a huge success. Our maps were used for many years. For me, it had been an experience of a lifetime, working in the beautiful Cascade Mountains. We held a wake for the Elephant and said goodbye. I kept her last remaining hubcap.

Hanging Lake

Serene waters flowing from the glaciers up on high.
Hanging Lake lies peacefully, below the dancing sky.
Whispers of the Ts'elxwéyeqws, floating on the breeze.
Misty, ghostly figures, ancient faces in the trees.
Soaring hawks and eagles, mountain air that speaks. Hidden gold and memories, high up on the peaks.
Among the alpine spirits
that are poised along the shore. Frozen for eternity,
for now, and evermore.

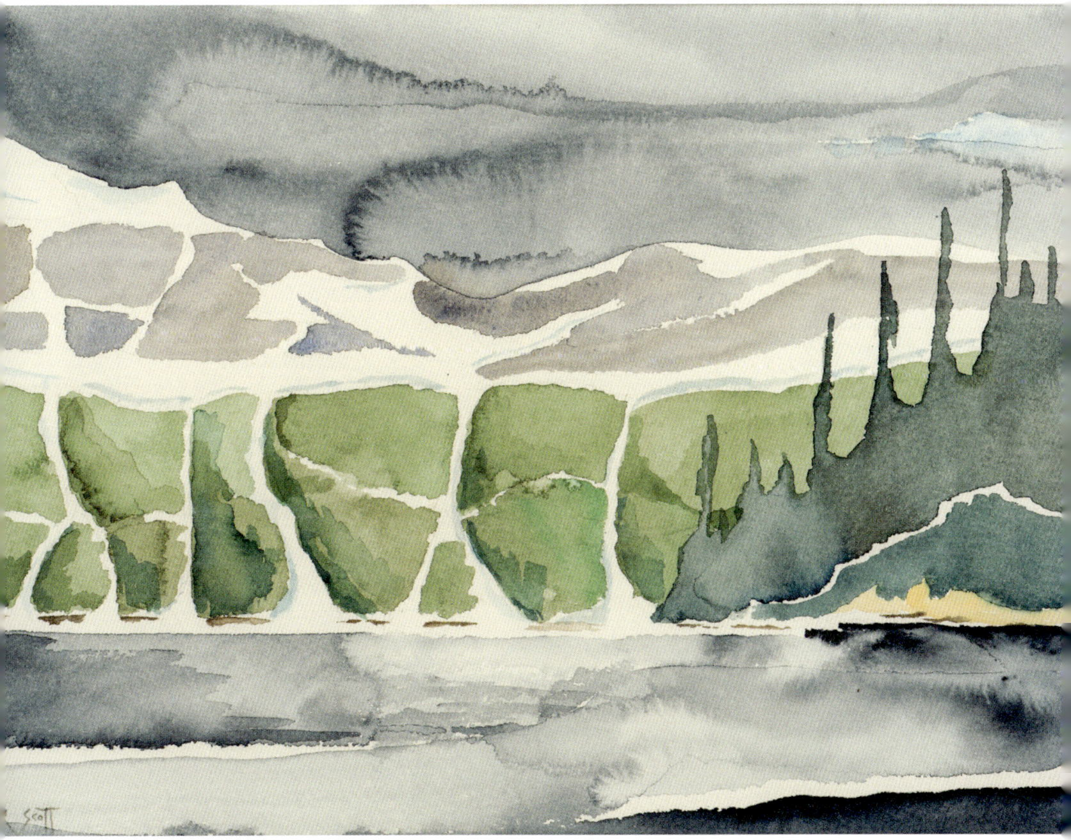

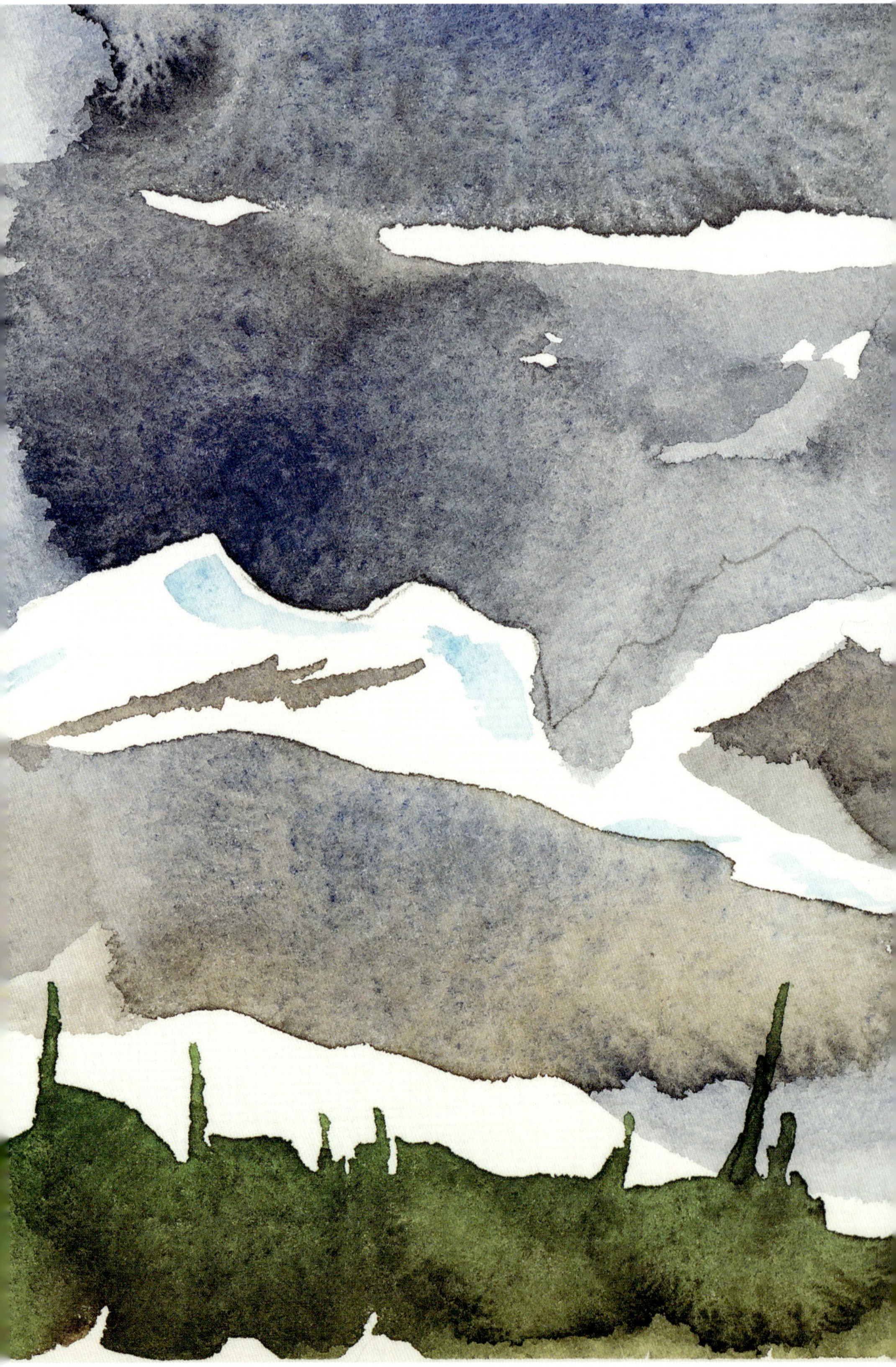

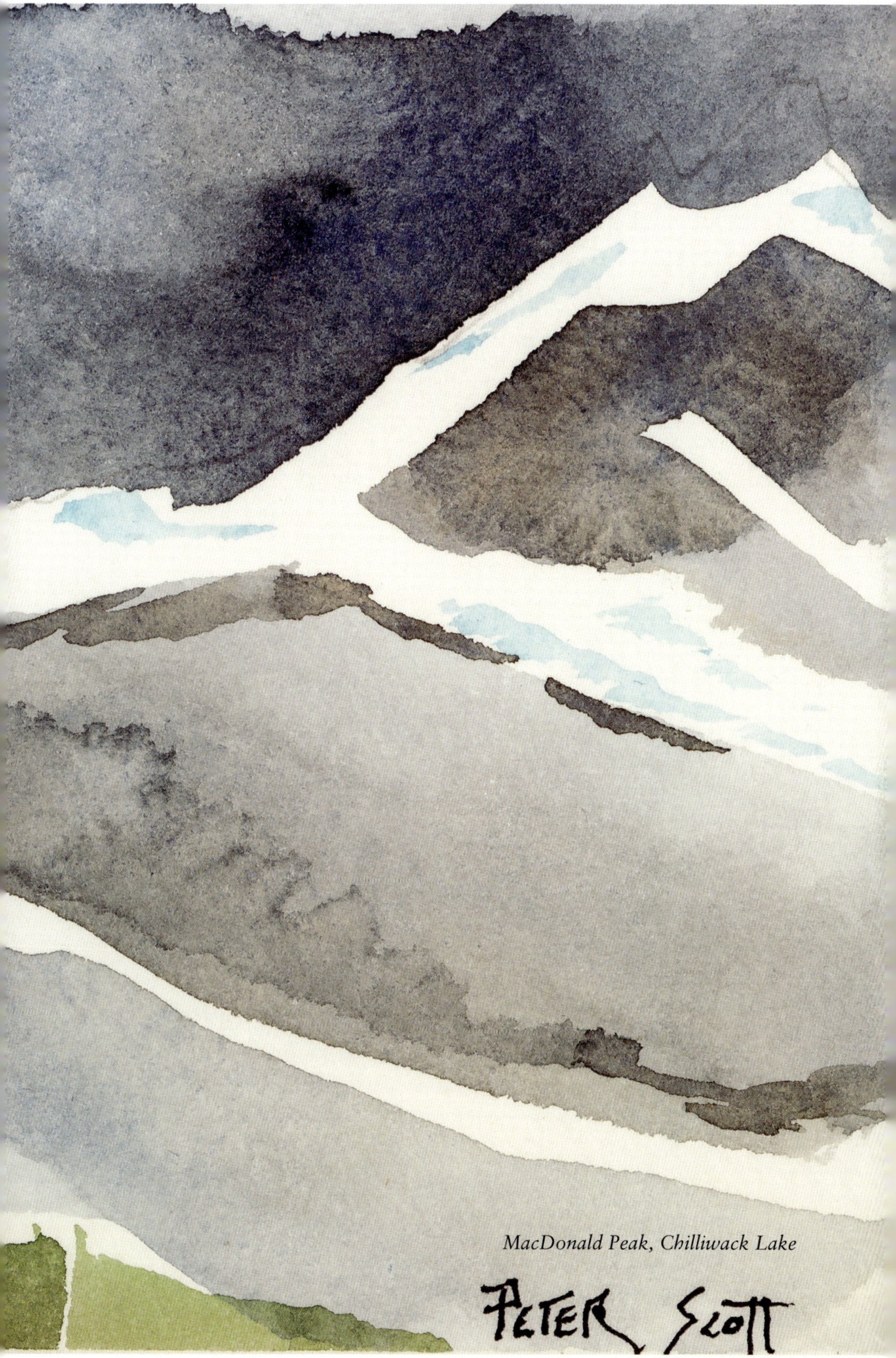

MacDonald Peak, Chilliwack Lake

Chilliwack Lake Sx tsaqel

Lake of grey, green waters,
she lies beneath the mountains,
of forest clad dark cedars.
Tall and noble fir
stand along the shoreline.

Ice pack glacier snow line,
melts into your waters
and shimmers in the daylight,

cool and calm in darkness.

Holds the life within you,
Kokanee and Rainbow swim
far below your surface, rising,
to feed upon the bounty
that glides upon your face,
and lie in cool dark corners.

In the heat of summer,
the creeks flow violently into you.
Ripples from the raindrops
refill you in the winter.

Streams from mountain heights,
life abounds around you.
Mountain purity and strength,
fill your mountain waters.
Sxótsaqel lives on forever, and forever
in the mountains.

Chapter Eighteen

The Mysteries Of Chilliwack Lake

Chilliwack Lake is a mystical place, sacred to the Stó:lō people. Its traditional name is Sxótsaqel, and it is said to be home of spiritual beings, water babies: Só:lmexw (S-all-mux-w). They are believed to live at the south end of the lake, under the rocks. The rocks have been worn smooth by their feet. Water babies are said to look like little mermaids, about two feet long, that play in and out of the water. If someone catches a water baby, a heavy mist comes out of their mouth and the water level of the lake rises until the water baby is released.

It is said by locals that water babies are there; they are real. You just have to believe in them. According to legends, these creatures make a sound like a baby crying, an ominous, eerie cry that means someone is going to drown.

The waters of Sxótsaqel Lake are cold all year round, and drownings are frequent.

An American soldier, Michael Brown, working on the U.S. Boundary Commission's survey crew drowned at the southeast end of the lake on Oct. 10, 1885. His body was found, and he was buried at the mouth of Depot Creek in a coffin made from a cedar log, 150 yards from the lake. Today a marble headstone marks the site and bears his epitaph.

Depot Creek is close to the south end of the lake. Near it is a large, smooth rock outcropping that slopes into the lake. When wet, it is very slippery. In the fall of 1979, I took my young brother-in-law camping at Depot Creek, which has a beautiful sandy beach at its mouth that makes it a good place to camp. We had canoed down the lake to this spot, and the next day we went fishing on the large, sloping rock. It was an overcast, cool day, a good

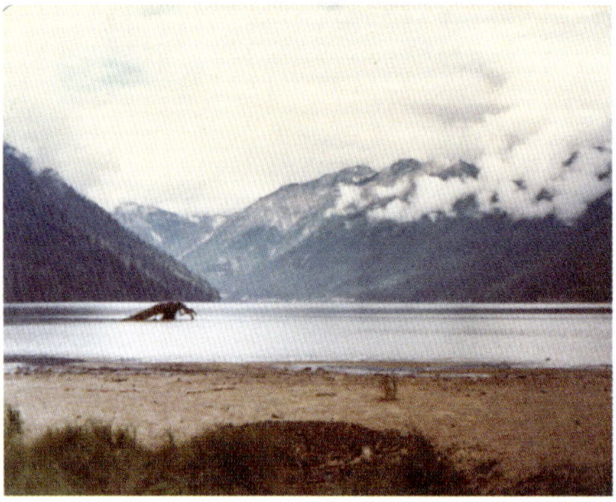

Creature in Chilliwack Lake

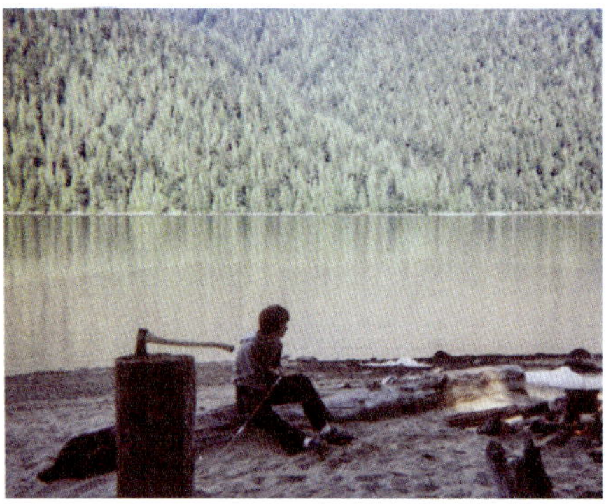

Brent at camp at Depot Creek

day to fish. My brother in-law, who was only 12 at the time, slipped on the rock and slid down into the lake. As he flailed in the water, I saw several red objects swimming around him. I managed to make my way down the rock and pulled him out, then quickly got him back to our campsite, soaking wet and freezing. I wrapped him in a blanket and started a large fire. I was scared that he was hypothermic and made him put on a wool toque to keep his body heat from escaping. Body heat escapes from your head and underarms when you are cold. He warmed up after a while and confirmed that he had been surrounded by large, red swimming objects while he was in the lake. We decided they must have been spawning salmon.

Later that day, a heavy mist enveloped the lake.

Several years later, two loggers were working their cedar claim on the south of the lake on a cold fall day and noticed a man in a canoe, fishing. After a while, the lake was covered in a heavy fog, and the two men heard yells and cries coming from the fog bank. They got into their small boat and set out to find the fisherman. They found his canoe floating upside down in the cold waters of the lake, but there was no sign of the man. Authorities were called and RCMP divers searched the waters for the body. Later they dragged the area and eventually even brought in a mini sub, to no avail. The missing fisherman's body was never found. He had become one of the mysteries of Chilliwack Lake.

One day in the fall of 1980, my brother in-law and I were fishing at the north end of the Chilliwack River. An old pickup truck approached and parked on the bank of the river. Two First Nations gentlemen got out of the truck, a young man and an elderly man with long, white hair. At first glance I thought he was Chief Dan George, the famous Coast Salish actor and advocate from North Vancouver. On looking again, I realized it wasn't him.

I had met the real Chief Dan George years before, in the summer of 1974, at the Cultus Lake Canoe Races. He arrived in a limousine, walked out onto the wharf at Main Beach, and played his guitar and sang to the crowd. He was wearing a powder-blue suit with a white belt and white shoes. Later he mingled with his fans, and I managed to meet him. I was enthralled to meet a man of his stature.

The two men invited us over to their campfire. The old gentleman said his name was Antoine and we sat and talked around his campfire for a while. We discussed many things. I told him of the fisherman who drowned and of the day my brother-in-law fell in the lake and was surrounded by salmon. It was then the old man told us the stories of the water babies. We sat around the fire a while longer and pondered those stories. Later, a thick fog rolled onto the lake. We said our goodbyes and left. The two men stood on the shore of the lake and vanished into the mist ....

Elk Mountain

Elk Mountain in the moonlight,
within Slesse's view.
Border Peaks pierce the sky,
the lunar orb is new.

Freshly fallen snowfall
upon the mountain shines.
Beneath the starlit universe,
where the moon and stars entwine.

Elk is always peaceful,
a place to hide away.
Enjoy the view forever,
among the spruce that sway.

Cheam in the distance,
her sisters all in line.
Elk Mountain in the moonlight,
forever for all time.

Chapter Nineteen

Elk Mountain And The Night Of The Cougar

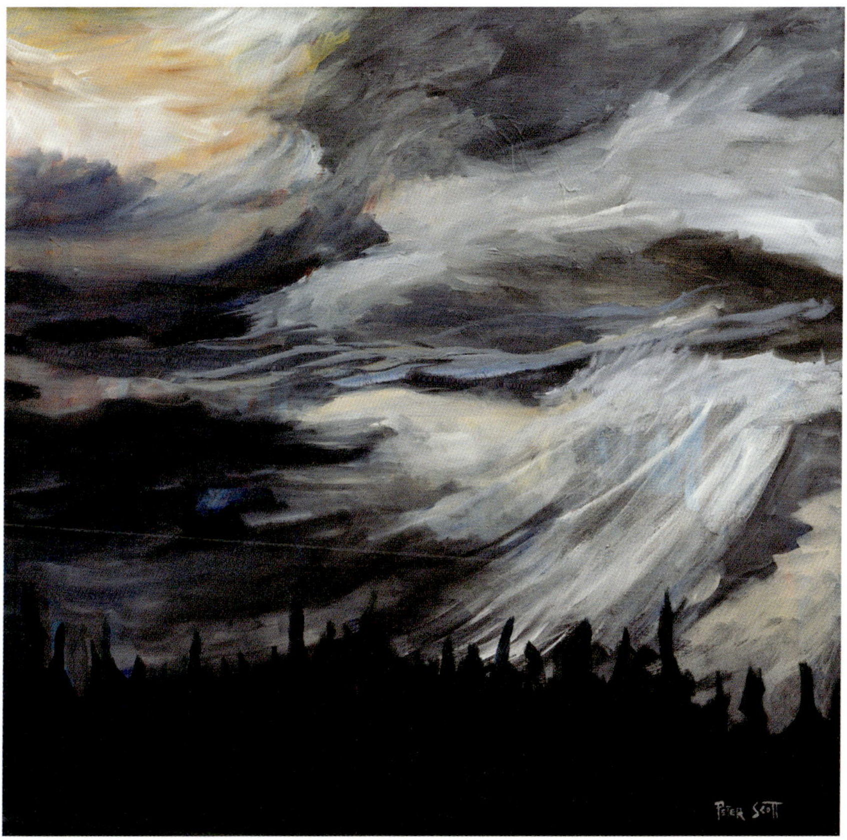

On the first day of spring in 1980, my brother, a friend, and I hiked up Elk Mountain to spend a few days in the bush. We expected the weather to be fair, so we didn't take snowshoes. Bad decision. Elk Mountain is a moderately easy hike, with great views of the mountains and the Fraser Valley below. We were making good time until we hit snow three-quarters of the way up. The snow was wet and heavy, and we sank in to our knees. It became a strenuous slog under our heavy packs.

Eventually we made it to the top, but the view of the surrounding scenery was obscured by clouds. We pitched our tent in the shelter of the trees, dug a fire pit, and gathered dry branches and lichen to start a fire. My friend Mike was a large, muscular man. He was a quiet guy, a man of few words. He was a great person to spend time in the mountains with, as he was an experienced woodsman. He would quietly set up camp and proceed to get meals ready while we gathered up wood. There was no need for talk; we worked in tandem, the three of us knowing what to do without wasting time discussing it. We called him "Man Mountain Mike," as he could effortlessly make his way up steep slopes while carrying a heavy pack. A good guy to have along on my trips into the mountains.

After supper, we sat around the fire and dried out. Then it hit. Strong winds and blowing snow. We retreated to our tent and bunked in for the night. Around 3 a.m., I awoke to hear something bashing around in our camp. When I opened the tent flap and turned on my flashlight, I found myself face to face with a serious-looking cougar. He let out a cry and proceeded to tear up our packs. He had already pulled down our food cache from the trees. After he destroyed our camp, he left. That was exciting. By now my brother and Man Mountain Mike were awake. We crawled out of the tent and surveyed the damage. Our supplies were scattered. The snow had quit falling, but the wind was still blowing, so we crawled back into our tent.

At daybreak we dug our tent out of the snowdrift, retrieved what was left of our supplies, had a cold breakfast and began our trip down. Now the snow started to come down again, and the wind began to howl. The top slope of Elk was windswept, and the snow was hard. As we were making our way across, my young brother lost his footing and began sliding down the slope. I dropped my pack and went after him, then slipped and was sliding after him when my jacket snagged on a branch sticking out of the snow. I grabbed my brother, and then his sleeping bag broke free from his pack, rolled down the slope and dropped off the edge to the valley below. Man Mountain Mike noticed us sliding down the mountain and, without uttering a word, made his way down, grabbed us and dragged us back to the top.

The blizzard started up again, with strong, howling winds and driving snow. We struggled through the whiteout and followed Man Mountain Mike down into the trees. The trail was obliterated by snow, and the trees hadn't been marked with tags yet. It took a while to find our route down, and then I noticed the tracks. Our friend the cougar had followed us down and then circled around us. This was concerning. We nervously continued down, keeping a firm grip on our axes. We made it down the mountain and our feline shadow disappeared. We arrived at our truck, dug it out of the snow and drove home.

That's one night I won't forget. It was still snowing in Sardis when we got back.

The first day of spring!

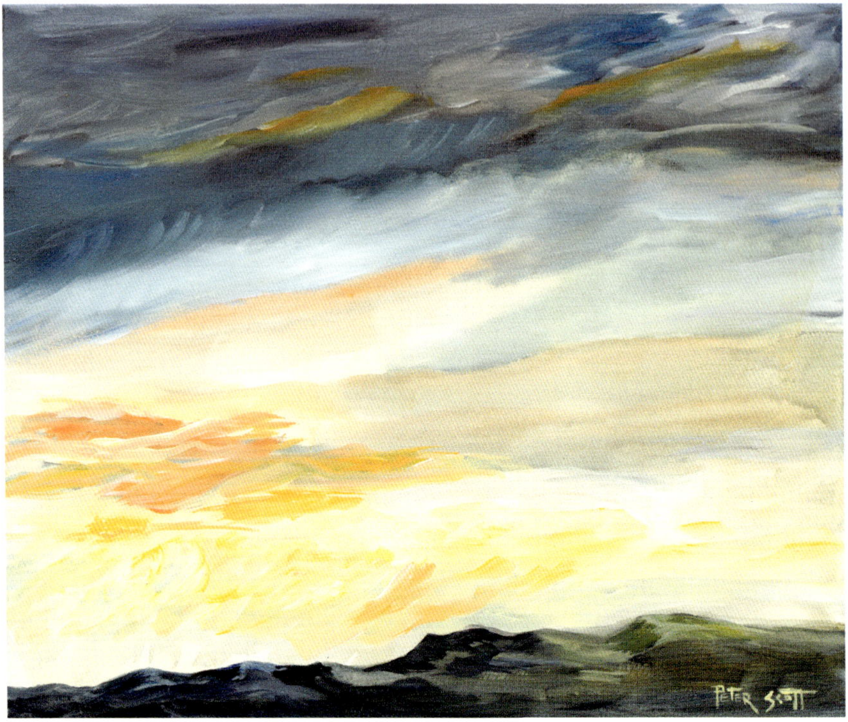

Fraser Valley Sky

The rains fall heavily
from the Fraser Valley sky
Giant Cedars swaying
in the mountains
to stay dry

Below the creeks
flow violently, from
the giant peaks so high
Deep within the forest
the Trickster Raven cries

From time immemorial
this sacred valley's thrived
Underneath the thunder
and the wonderous STAW-lo sky

Chapter Twenty

Creeks And Streams Of The Chilliwack River Valley

Chilliwack Lake "Sxótsaqel", "Sacred Lake", is ninety four kilometers in length and one kilometer wide. The Chilliwack River originates in the North Cascades National Park in Washington State, crosses the United States –Canadian border, then enters Chilliwack lake. The Chilliwack River exits the lake and flows forty kilometers west and changes it's name to Vedder River at Vedder Crossing.

Before 1875 the Chilliwack River flowed north from Vedder Crossing over a broad alluvial fan to the Fraser "STAW-lo" River. In 1875 heavy rains caused a log jam that diverted the river into two streams, Vedder Creek flowed West and Luckakuk Creek flowed North.

In 1882 a new log jam formed forcing the Chilliwack River to pour into Vedder Creek, this now became the Vedder River and it flowed into what was then Sumas lake, (now Sumas Prairie). In the early 1900's the river was dyked and the channel became the Sumas Canal.

The Vedder River and Sumas Canal convey water from the Chilliwack River to the Fraser River.

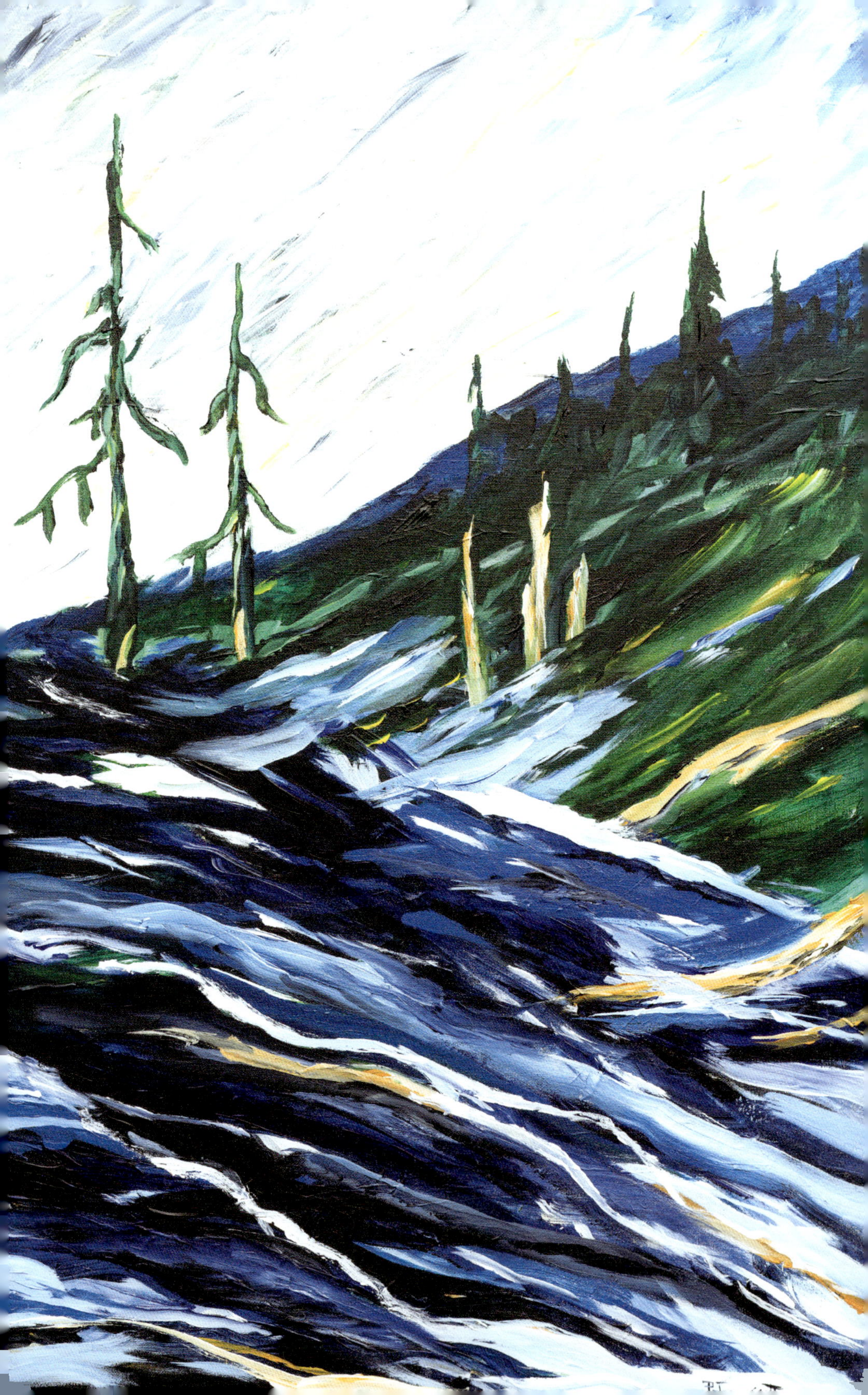

AIRPLANE CREEK serves as drainage from Knight Peak, Baby Munday, The Still, Mount Foley and Welch Peak. Its waters flow southeast into Foley Creek. The stream was named for the two aircraft that crashed into Knight Peak and Foley Peak in the 1940s.

BORDEN CREEK, originally called Silvery Creek, drains Spencer Peak, flowing west of Slesse Creek and north into the Chilliwack River. It was named in remembrance of Royal Canadian Artillery Private Russell Borden, a Langley boy who served with the Canadian Scottish Regiment. He died in action at Falaise Gap on August 11, 1944, at the age of 22.

CENTRE CREEK originates in the valley between Mount Rexford and Mount Corriveau, flowing north into the Chilliwack River. It was traditionally known as Stehiyoq, "place of fish trap."

CHILLIWACK RIVER, originally known as the Klabneh and Silliwak, begins in Washington State and flows northwest into Chilliwack Lake (Sxōtsaqel), at the lake's southerly end. This water exits at the northwestern end of the lake and flows the length of the valley to Vedder Crossing, where it becomes the Vedder River. The common use of the word Chilliwack meant 'heading back up to the head of the lake."

DEPOT CREEK, originally known as Kokanee or Brown Creek, begins in Washington State and flows northwest into Chilliwack Lake. Its name recalls a supply depot used by the international boundary survey team from 1858 to 1861. It was also referred to as Brown Creek after Michael Brown, a soldier in the 9th Infantry of the U.S. Army who drowned in Chilliwack Lake on Oct. 10, 1858, and is buried next to the creek. Its Stó:lō name is Chechexem, "slimy water."

FOLEY CREEK, once known as Ford's Creek, is the outlet of Foley Lake, which flows southwest to merge with the Chilliwack River west of the Chipmunk Caves, near Ford Mountain Correctional Centre. Its name was inspired by Timothy Foley, from St. Paul, Minnesota, one of the trio of Messrs. Foley, Welch, and Stewart, a contracting firm that built the Fraser Valley section of the Canadian Northern Railway, 1912-13. Its Stó:lō name, Xexitse, means "Little Lakes" or "washing something."

FRANCES CREEK flows southwest into the north end of Chilliwack Lake. It was named after Frances Webb, a pioneering resident in the valley.

LITTLE CREEK flows north to the Chilliwack River from the slopes of Church Mountain.

LIUMCHEN CREEK, originally known as Layomesin, Lithumptien, or Lihumitson, is the merger of two small creeks that begin in Washington State and flows into the Chilliwack River. Its Stó:lō name, Loyumthel, refers to "water swirling out in gushes."

NESAKWATCH CREEK, also known as Nesaquach (En-saw-Kwatch) originates in Washington State and flows north between Slesse Mountain and Mount Rexford to the Chilliwack River.

PALEFACE CREEK flows west into Chilliwack Lake and takes its name from the mountain at the head of the creek.

PIERCE CREEK flows out of Pierce Lake northwest into the Chilliwack River, east of Slesse Creek. It was named for G.O. Pierce, who prospected on the mountain.

POST CREEK, also known as the Silver and Koeholum, flows out of Lindeman Lake into the Chilliwack River. It was named after John Post, a prospector in the valley, but its Stó:lō name, Kwokelen, means "echo"—"You think somebody is talking back there, but it is your own voice."

RADIUM CREEK flows out of Radium Lake at the base of Mount Webb and runs north into the Chilliwack River.

RYDER CREEK flows south out of Ryder Lake into the Chilliwack River.

SLESSE CREEK begins in Washington State and flows west of Slesse Mountain into the Chilliwack River. The name was originally spelled as Selacee. In Stó:lō, it's Silisi (Sihilhets).

SWELTZER RIVER flows northwest from Cultus Lake into the Chilliwack River.

TAMAHI CREEK was originally known as Tamihey or Tummeahai Creek, from the Stó:lō name Támiyehó:y, which can refer to "hollering, the ones who are finished"; or the "place of cripples." It is known as "the place where deformed people were brought and left to die. From its beginnings in Washington State, it flows north into the Chilliwack River.

WILLIAMSON CREEK, an outlet of Williamson Lake on Welch Peak, flows southeast into Foley Lake. It is named after A.S. Williamson, who was in charge of mining operations during 1917 at the Lucky Four Mine, northwest of Foley Peak.

One weekend in the spring of 1979, my friends and I were camping at Tamahi Creek campsite, where the creek empties into the Chilliwack River. A group of teenagers from Vancouver arrived, set up their camp and proceeded to party for two days. On the second day, one inebriated teenager fell into the fast-flowing Tamahi Creek. My friends and I quickly made a human chain and jumped into the raging creek. I was at the head of the chain and strained against the current to grab the drowning teenager. My footing and grip were slipping. With much struggling and effort, my friends were able to pull us out of the creek and up the bank to safety.

During the spring, the waters of the streams and creeks are swollen with melt water and flow extremely fast and powerfully into the Chilliwack River.

The teen almost became an eternal part of the river.

The Chilliwack River Sts elxwiqw

Cedars cry into the river,
tears fall from the sky.
Water babies weeping,
sleeping giants lie.

Salmon swim forever
to their aquatic home.
Humpbacks, Sockeye, thrashing
among the river's foam.

Glistening in the waters,
below the river's roar.
Veins of quartz, golden dreams,
buried near the shore.

The river runs forever,
dancing on in rhyme.
Tumbling over boulders,
for an eternity of time...

Chapter Twenty-One

The Ford Mountain Lookout And The Two Brothers

During the spring and summer of 1960, the BC Forest Service built a lookout tower on top of Ford Mountain at an elevation of 4,760 feet (1451 metres). This would be the second forestry tower in the Chilliwack River Valley. Only a rugged trail led to the peak. The Forest Service needed to transport prefabricated sections of the 14-by-16- foot structure to the site. The rangers solved the problem by trucking the sections to an area near Slesse Creek, and from there a helicopter took them the rest of the way. The construction crew began at 10 a.m. and worked until 8 p.m. A crew loaded the sections onto the helicopter, and four other men unloaded the lumber at the site on the mountain peak. The mountain crew camped on the lookout site until the tower was completed during the summer.

The tower was in service throughout the 1960s and 1970s. The view from there was spectacular—a 360-degree, unimpeded view of the mountains that surrounded it. The tower had a cistern on the bottom level to collect rainwater, as there are no creeks on the top of the mountain. It also had a deck that went completely around the top level, giving the residing ranger a clear view of the forests. The tower was dismantled in 1980 because it was being vandalized.

My crew and I stayed at the tower off and on during the summers of 1978 and 1979. The tower had glass windows with plywood covers, going all the way around it. The lookout was perfectly equipped for one man to

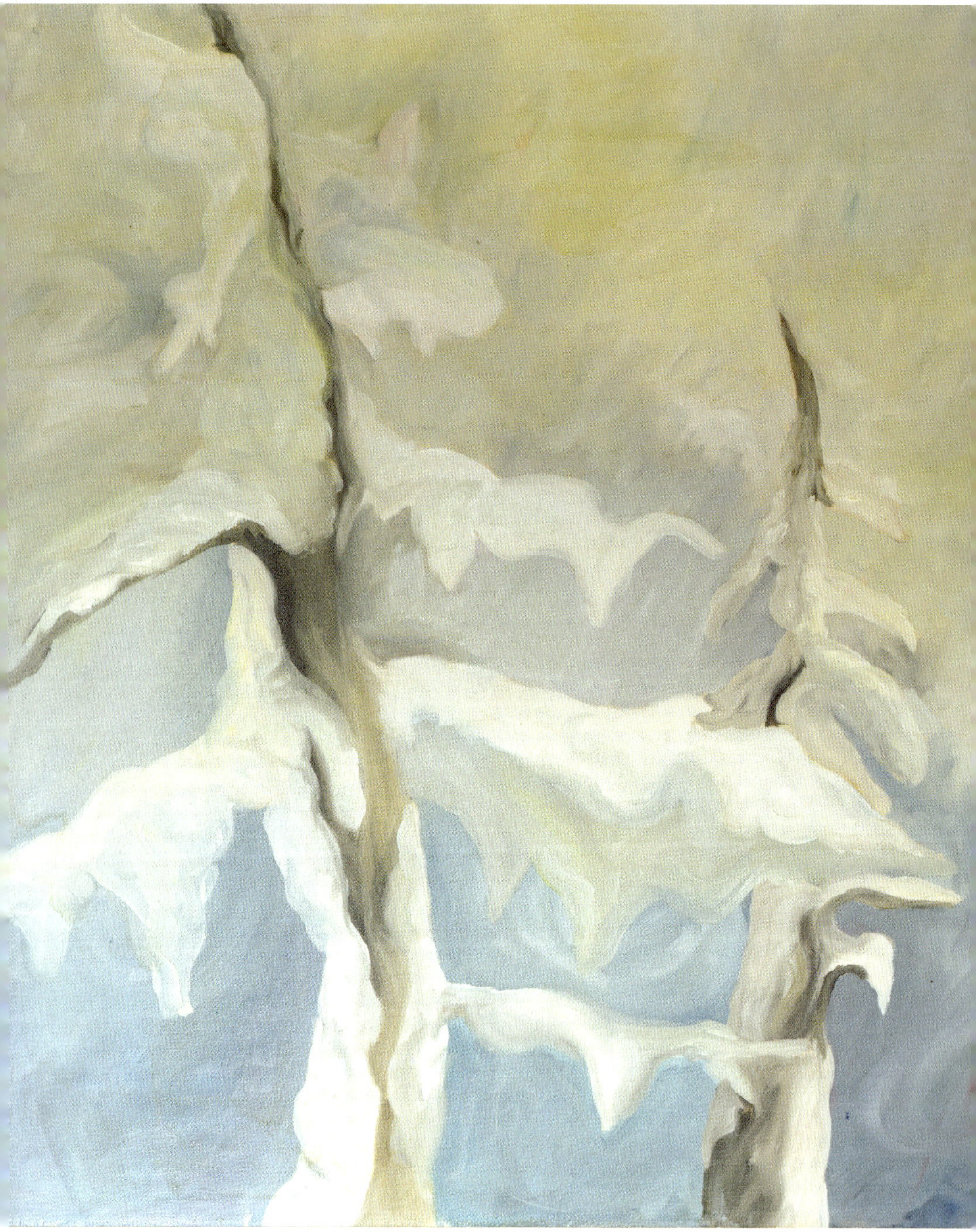

Trees on Ford Mountain

occupy. It had a metal cot, table and chairs, a potbelly stove, and cupboards for supplies. A lightning rod helped protect it from lightning. In 1980, I offered to live in it for a season. It would have made an exceptional art studio, however my request was denied.

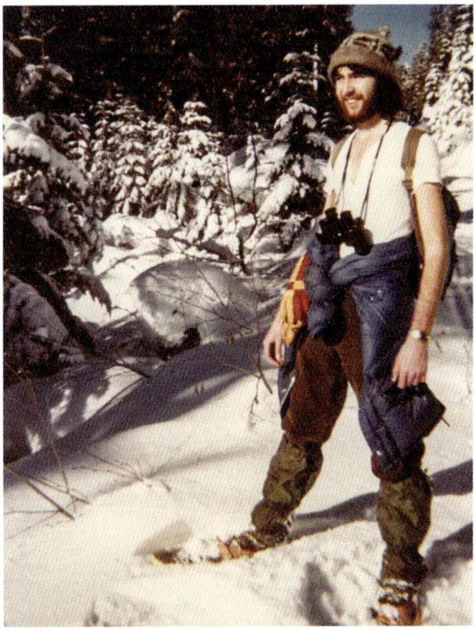

Snowshoeing on Ford Mountain

A few months before it was taken down, my brother and I decided to snowshoe up to the lookout and stay in it one last time. It was a beautiful, sunny day, with some clouds in the sky. We were able to drive our truck a quarter of the way up the Forest Service road before we hit snow. Then we donned our snowshoes and packs and, along with my brother's dog Bear, began the long trek up the road to the trailhead. The trail up to the summit in the summer is a 45-minute hike; it takes longer in the snow.

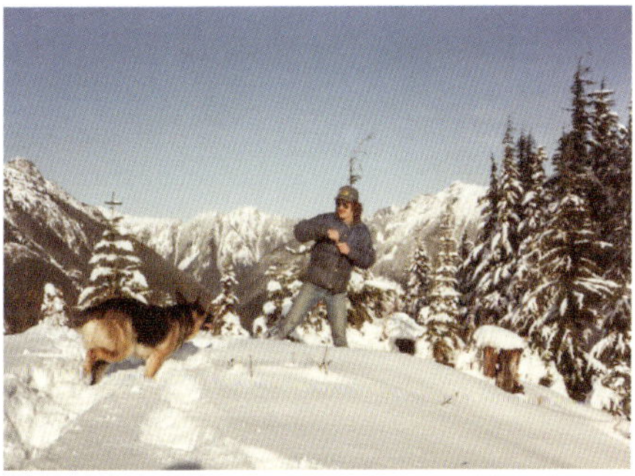

Brother and Bear on top of Ford Mountain

As we finally reached the trail, the strap on the harness of my brother's old, wooden, beaver-tail snowshoes snapped. Bad situation. He tried hopping on one shoe, using the other as a crutch. That didn't work so well. The snow was knee-deep and getting deeper the higher we went. Finally, after watching him struggle, I offered to help him. We tried sharing one shoe. It was an ordeal, but a funny one. It took us a long time to reach the summit. We had hopped and half-waded through the snow for most of the length of the trail. My brother even tried riding Bear, a large German shepherd. That hadn't worked, either.

By the time we reached the tower, we were exhausted from struggling in the snow and from laughing so hard. We had laughed all the way up, because the situation was ridiculous. We had never thought of taking a spare harness in our packs. Once we made it to the top, we stuck our large beaver-tail snowshoes in the snow, sat down, leaned against them and shared the contents of our thermos.

As we sat there, enjoying the view, the sun burst from behind a cloud and illuminated the tops of two old dead and bare alpine fir trees. The sight of that was inspiring, so I took out my old, tattered sketchbook and did several sketches.

We then spent the night in the old tower. The potbellied stove pumped out the heat. We cooked up some bacon and beans, and then spent the evening sitting out on the deck, taking in the spectacular star show.

Nights spent camped out on a mountain in winter are special. The moonlight sparkled off the snow. The night was cold, the sky clear, and the contents of the thermos kept us warm.

The next morning, we again donned our snowshoes. Well, I did. My brother strapped on his one shoe, and off we went, laughing all the way down as he hobbled on one leg in the snow. It was a weekend to remember.

When I arrived back at the studio the next day, I stretched out a 32-by-36-inch canvas, sized it with rhoplex and then did several sketches of the trees in charcoal on oatmeal paper to get the composition correct. After making several sketches, I taped them to the wall and painted two small panels in oils to get the idea of the painting. While I was finishing the small paintings, someone came in and bought them.

I then began the large painting. I sketched it out and focussed on the sunlight breaking through the clouds. To me, the two trees represented my brother and me. I felt like I had cut a piece out of that day and frozen it in time. I named it The Two Brothers. The painting effortlessly flowed out of my hand. I finished it in three hours.

Immediately afterwards, I began getting offers for the painting. It hung on display in the foyer of the Faculty of Education building at UBC for a year.

I have kept that painting for my personal collection. It reminds me of a wonderful day spent with my brother in the mountains.

Chapter Twenty-Two

Fishing On The Chilliwack River

There are many species of fish in the Chilliwack River watershed, Cutthroat trout, Rainbow trout, Whitefish, Dolly Varden and Salish Sucker among them.

The Chilliwack River system supports all five species of salmon. Fish runs in the spring for Chinook; summer for Chinook and Sockeye; fall, early winter, and spring for Steelhead. All salmon species have suffered population declines, but some are recovering better than others.

Pink salmon return to the river to spawn in every odd-numbered year (e.g. 2017, 2019, 2021, and 2023). Pink salmon numbers dropped off dramatically in the 1980s and 1990s but have been improving in the 2000s because of improved freshwater and ocean conditions. Sockeye salmon return to Chilliwack Lake between June and August.

The Chilliwack River hosts the largest recreational Steelhead and salmon fishery in British Columbia. Angling opportunities in the watershed are within a day trip from the largest population center in the province. An angler survey in 1998 discovered that more than 62 percent of anglers were from the Greater Vancouver region, 35 percent from the Fraser Valley, and just over one percent from outside of the country. Upwards of 60 percent of fishermen stayed overnight in the area or more than one night, contributing to the Chilliwack tourist industry. Fishing pressure on the Chilliwack River has increased dramatically over the past 45 years. A person used to be able to spend a day fishing in solitude; now, during peak runs, anglers stand nearly elbow to elbow on the banks of the river.

Fishing activity is higher in the months of October and November north of Vedder Crossing. From December to May, experienced anglers look for steelhead, the most sought-after freshwater gamefish, in the Chilliwack River. Many of the fish caught are offspring of the Chilliwack River Hatchery, which was built in 1981, upstream from Slesse Creek. The hatchery produces six million salmon smolts yearly of five salmon species: Chinook, Coho, Chum, Pink and Steelhead.

Chinook salmon within the Chilliwack River system are mainly hatchery stock, made up of both summer return (red-fleshed) and fall return (white-fleshed) Chinook. The summer-return fish originate from the upper Fraser River stock; the fall-return fish from the Harrison River stock. Chinook salmon native to the Chilliwack River are spring run and found in the upper portions of the watershed.

I used to live near Luckakuck Creek, a beautiful, clear stream that meandered along Vedder Road and through the hop yard at Sardis. Eden Bank Farm was built on Lukakuck Creek, which also hosted a bird sanctuary across the road from Sardis Elementary School. The stream used to run under Wells Road in Sardis, behind the Coquileetza Residential School and onward beyond the hop farm. We used to spend hours swimming and fishing in the creek. Now a large section of it flows through a culvert underneath pavement, concrete and subdivisions.

In the early 20th century, the diverted Chilliwack River was diked and channelized, and the river downstream of Vedder Crossing was permanently diverted westward into the Vedder Canal to drain Sumas Lake. The Chilliwack River below Vedder Crossing became known as the Vedder River.

Chapter Twenty-Three

The Making Of An Artist

Having worked with students for two summers, I discovered I enjoyed working with youths and decided to study to become a secondary school art and geography teacher. Everything was going according to plan. After three years at UBC, I was becoming accomplished as a painter and soon had another painting mentor, Don MacIntosh. Don was a legendary figure in the Education Faculty. His exploits were well known, far and wide. He was an established artist and a good teacher, as well as a hard-living character. He was in his fifties but looked to be in his eighties. He had been in a serious car accident the year before I met him and so was slightly crippled. He was somewhat hunched and walked with a cane.

He was also very accommodating and would allow me to take time off from classes, return to the mountains, and work as a tree planter in the fall and early spring. These trips back to my mountains were refreshing and recharged my creative juices.

I worked for a tree planting company from Victoria, and we would spend times planting in the Nesakwatch Valley. Every day was exciting. Our crew consisted of an array of characters who made the job enjoyable,and every day was spent in the shadow of Mount Slesse. The views were incredible and awe-inspiring.

Some days were cold, and sometimes the ground would be covered in early snow. I slept inside the canopy on my old truck, often on wet and cold nights. This sometimes inspired a beer run into Vedder Crossing, where I could warm up in the pub for a few hours. Driving back to camp in the mountains in the early morning hours was always an adventure. The work replenished my bank account and filled me with artistic energy.

At this time in my career as a student I was beginning to sell some of my work. My first sale was to a prestigious law firm where my girlfriend was employed. She convinced them to look at some of my paintings. I arrived at their office one afternoon with my paintings wrapped in green garbage bags. I was wearing a logging shirt, jeans that had 47 patches, old work boots, a thick black beard, and long hair. I heard the receptionist whisper to one of the girls there that I looked like Charlie Manson. When I walked into their office, my eyes fell off. Hanging on their walls were works by famous Canadian artists Toni Onley and Robert Genn (who I would later have the honour to meet). I was both impressed and intimidated. I was shown into a conference room and was soon joined by two of the firm's lawyers. They were educated in the arts. With shaking hands, I unwrapped my works and nervously showed them to the lawyers. They inspected my paintings, whispered some comments, and left the room.

Disheartened, I returned home to my one-room studio apartment and drank the last beer I had in my fridge to drown my sorrows. Then my girlfriend called to inform me her firm had purchased two of my paintings. I was ecstatic! When I delivered them the next day, I was told they were to be displayed in their conference room next to one of Toni Onley's originals. I felt like I had finally joined the big boys and took my girlfriend to dinner at the Four Seasons Hotel to celebrate. I was a selling artist at last.

Don Macintosh was impressed. Gordon was impressed. I was impressed that they were impressed. One of the paintings I sold was of Elk Mountain; the other of the Border Peaks. My mountains had come through for me! A few months later, several of my paintings sold at our class's year-end exhibition at the Sub Gallery at UBC. I was the only member of my art class to have sales. Don congratulated me and told me he was going to take me out on the town the next night to celebrate. Partying with the legendary artist was going to be an experience I didn't want to miss.

I had arrived at the UBC painting studio the next day with great excitement and expectations of a historic night when I discovered Don had been found unconscious on the floor of his office. The ambulance rushed him to St. Paul's Hospital, where he was declared dead. My mentor and hero had died of liver disease at the age of 51. I was devastated, as was the entire faculty.

I went to his wake, the wildest party I had ever attended. All of the Vancouver art community was there, along with prominent Vancouver doctors, musicians, and lawyers. After the wake, several of us returned to his house in

Point Grey, where his wife presented us with a delicious meal of chili, Don's own recipe. His living room had floor-to-ceiling bookcases stuffed with books on art and all the classics. I was impressed. This inspired me to start my own collection of books, and I now have a library.

A few days after the celebration of Don's life, reality set in. My friend was gone. And I was diagnosed with a serious eye disease, keratoconus, an ailment that warps the cornea of the eye until finally it ruptures. Glasses couldn't correct my vision. Luckily, the disease was affecting only one eye, but I was told by the specialist that eventually my other cornea would also warp and I would be legally blind by the time I was 35. I had noticed over the past few months that the vision in my left eye was distorted. The cornea couldn't control light entering my eye, so I saw long, multiple rays of light that totally obliterated my vision. I began wearing an eye patch while I painted, with one eye figuratively tied behind my back. Gordon Smith would sit next to me at my easel in the studio at UBC and cheer me on as I painted. I soon realized there was no demand for blind artists and went into a depression. I had hit artist's block. I hung up my brushes.

After our graduation ceremony, Gordon took me down to his office and gave me one of his drawings. Gordon never gave away his art to anyone, so I was greatly honoured. It hangs framed in my studio to this day.

Gordon Appelbe Smith was born in East Brighton, England, on June 18, 1929. He immigrated to Canada with his family in 1933 and later became one of Canada's most accomplished artists and teachers.

In 1937, he enrolled at the Winnipeg School of Art, ambitious to become a commercial artist or teacher. When war came, he enlisted in the Princess Patricia's Light Infantry and was sent to the Mediterranean in 1942 to participate in the invasion of Sicily. He was wounded on July 20, his right leg shattered. After recuperating in England, he returned to Vancouver, where he had married Marion Flemming before being stationed in Europe.

Gordon resumed his artistic career and soon became a leading figure in the art scene, along with his artist friends Jack Shadbolt and B.C. Binning, whose work he greatly admired. In 1955, he won first prize at the First Biennial Canadian Painters Exhibition at the National Gallery of Canada. By now he had become an abstract painter, deriving his inspiration from nature.

Gordon was a successful, accomplished artist and teacher in the Faculty of Education at UBC when I enrolled in his painting class and he became my mentor. He loved his teaching career, which he carried on for 26 years, influencing thousands of teachers. His enthusiasm was immense and contagious.

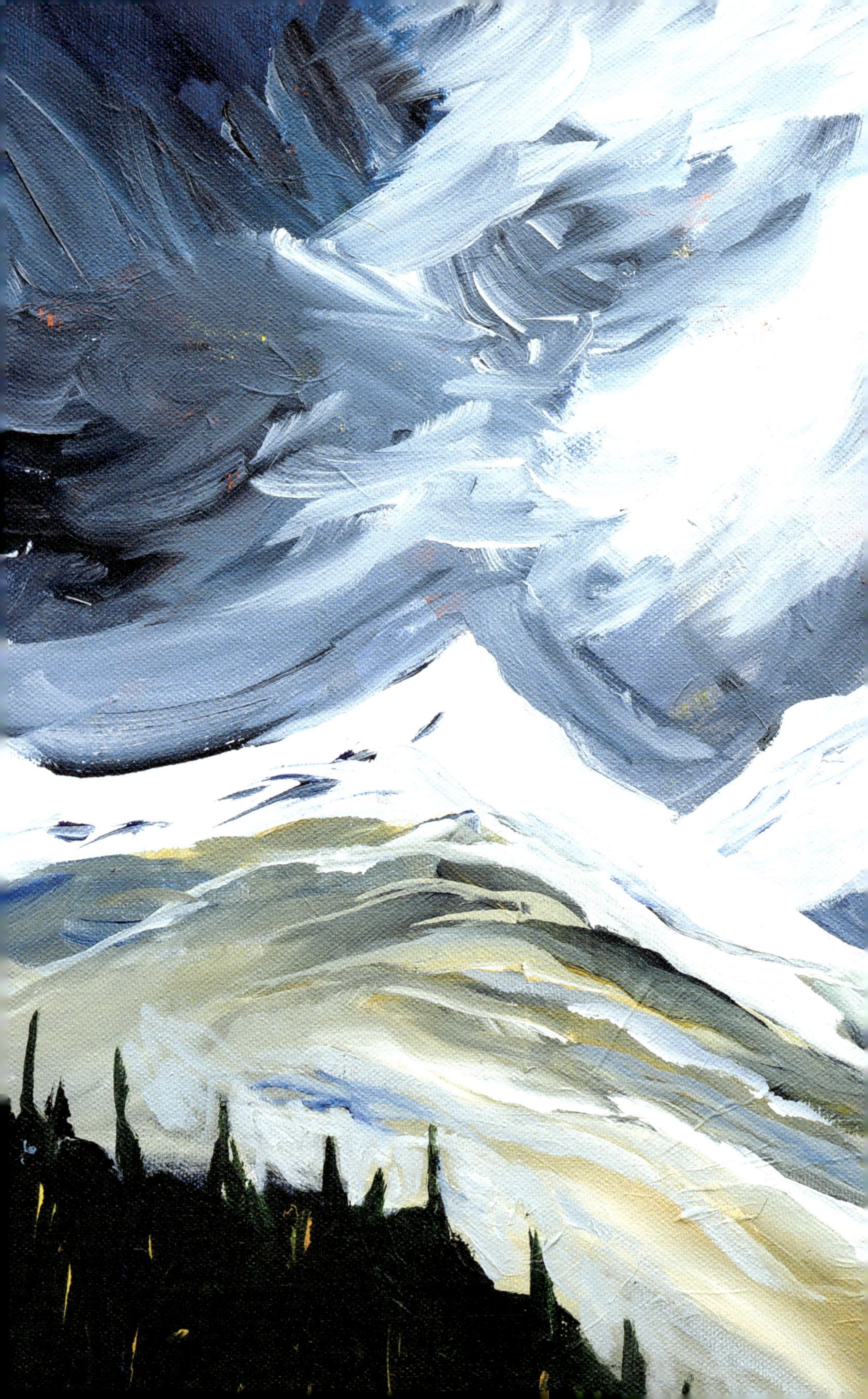

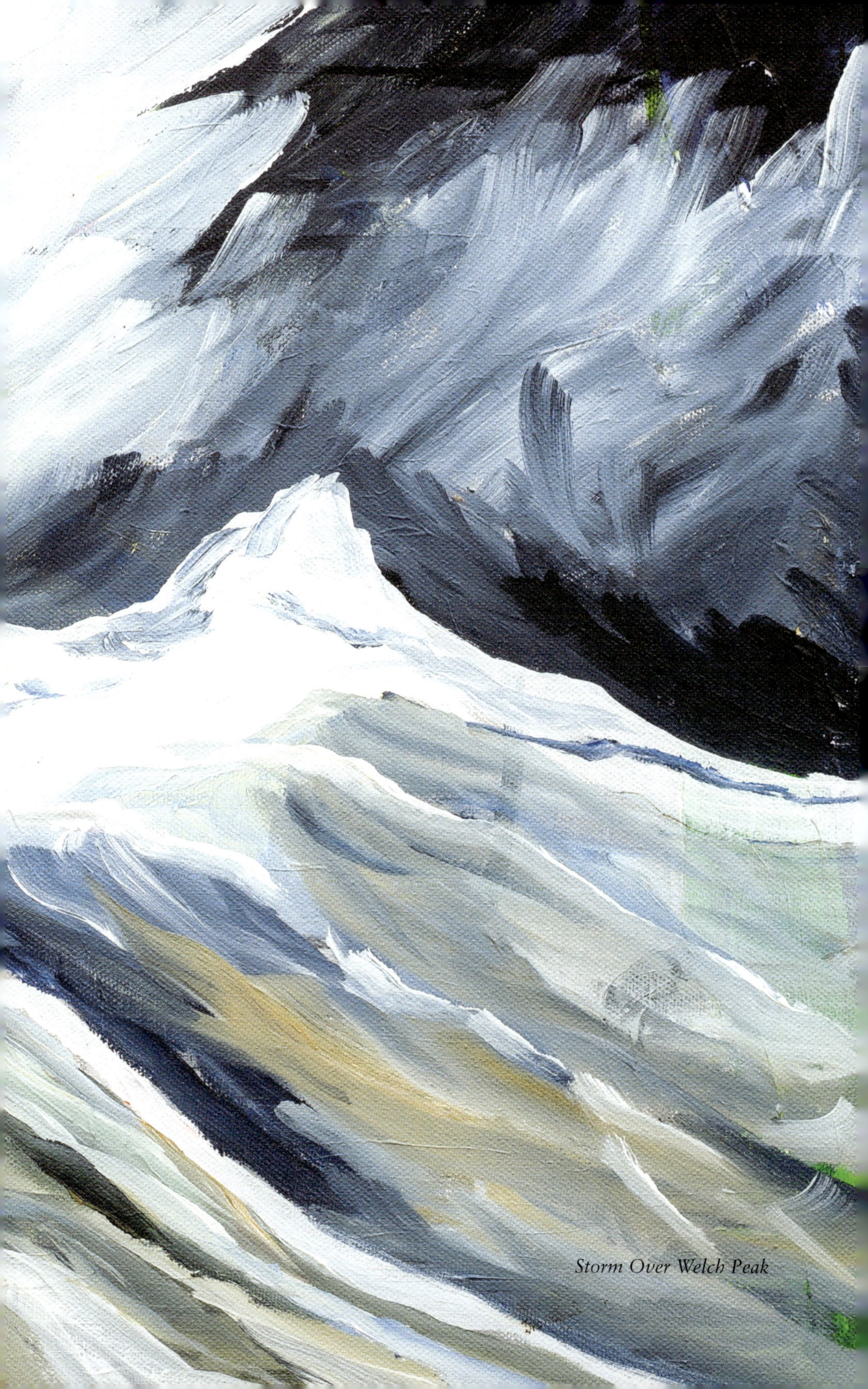

Storm Over Welch Peak

He made his students feel important. He once said that "creativity and art and all the meaning it can give to people to enrich their lives was a gift."

Gordon was also one of the nicest people I have ever had the pleasure to know.

One afternoon in 1982, he invited myself and some classmates to his home in West Vancouver. He had a beautiful house on the shores of the Pacific designed by the famous Canadian architect Arthur Erickson. It was built around a pond, with walls of glass supported by cedar beams. His home was stunning.

Attached to the house was a massive painting studio, painted white and pristine. His canvases and supplies were all carefully organized.

Gordon had become friends with Lawren Harris, leader of the Group of Seven, in Lawren's later years. Gordon would visit Lawren at his Point Grey home on Saturday nights and watch Hockey Night in Canada. He recalled that Lawren watched the hockey game while standing, painting at his easel, always dressed in a suit and tie—on Saturday nights.

While we were in his studio, Gordon called me over and showed me one of Lawren Harris's original sketchbooks, which he had left to Gordon after his passing. The sketchbook contained a rough drawing of Lawren's famous painting, Mount Lefroy. I was stunned. I was holding an original sketchbook of the great Canadian painter, Lawren Harris! Gordon then gave me some tubes of paint and brushes. What a day.

In 2019, shortly before Gordon died, I sent him a letter congratulating him on the successful one-man show he'd recently held at a gallery in Toronto, which sold out in a single night. One of his paintings sold for $217,250! Incredible, and at the time he was 98 years old. Gordon wrote back, congratulating me on my 30-year teaching career. He said he was proud of me and what I had accomplished as an artist and teacher. He invited me to visit him at his house and show him some of my work. I never made the trip, and Gordon passed away at his home on January 18, 2020, at the age of 100. He had continued painting to the end.

Gordon used to tell me that artists get better with age. At his age, he was a remarkable artist with a distinguished career. Among his many awards was the Order of Canada Medal.

I am so fortunate to have had him as a mentor.

Chapter Twenty-Four

Back To The Mountains

After graduation, I went back to the Chilliwack Mountains. I trained with the BC Forestry to become a juvenile spacer. We were given chain saws, fallers' pants, helmets, cork boots, and a tool kit. We were driven up the Neskawatch Valley and taught how to use our saws, falling techniques, and species identification. The main purpose of juvenile spacing is to go into an overcrowded timber stand, identify healthy trees, leave one standing every eight feet, and cut down everything else. The trees we cut were left to decay on the hillside. The trees we left standing were usually 24 inches in diameter; the ones we felled were much smaller. The main rule of juvenile spacing is to let the healthy trees grow to optimum size and don't get killed doing it.

The work was difficult but energizing. I soon forgot my troubles and revelled in being back among the Cascades. The fresh mountain air and sounds of cascading waterfalls and rumbles of the surrounding glaciers filled my lungs and spirit. Each morning, we would get up at 5 a.m., drive for an hour in the crew truck back up the valley and then up the steep logging roads to our work site. It usually took another half an hour hiking through the slash with our gas and oil jugs slung over our shoulders, our saws, tool kit and pack, to get back to where we had left off cutting the day before. As we cut higher and higher up the slopes, our hikes became longer and longer each morning. We would race each other, running uphill along the lengths of the fallen trees, carefully balancing so not to fall into the slash and be skewered by a dead branch. Once we arrived at our spot, the first thing was to sharpen our saws, have a coffee and take in the view. Then it was time to don the helmet, pull down the visor, fire up my 032 Stihl and start to drop trees. Time was a major factor; we were paid by the hectare, so the faster and more we cut, the more we got paid. By the end of the day, we were exhausted.

Early one morning, we were introduced to a new crew member. We were told he was an experienced faller and would be a great addition to our team. He was a huge man. Introductions were made, and then we headed up through the deep slash to start to work. "Mac" was working in the section next to me. Soon after we started cutting, I heard his whistle blow. I shut off my saw, made my way over to Mac's section, and there he was, standing with a shocked expression on his face and blood gushing out of his leg.

"I have a boo-boo," he said.

"No kidding," said I. I quickly laid him on his back and lifted his leg. Our forestry crew chief heard the whistle and rushed up to help. Seeing the gaping, gushing wound, he proceeded to vomit, and one of the other guys on our crew passed out. I grabbed the first-aid kit and tied a tourniquet around Mac's upper leg. The bar of his saw had bounced off a tree and cut him across the leg just above the safety padding in his fallers' pants. Bad luck.

Luckily, Mac was a big man, and his legs were thick. The saw cut through a lot of muscle and fat before it hit the bone. I wrapped bandages around his leg to close the wound, and then Big Mac passed out. Great. Now I and my two partners, who had recovered by then, had to get Mac down the mountain. He regained consciousness, and with much effort we carried and dragged him through the trees back to the truck. Then we had to load him into the back of the truck and drive him down to the Chilliwack Hospital. Somehow, he survived—missing several pints of blood, but alive.

Another fun day in the bush.

After four months of falling trees in the Nesakwatch valley, our crew was sent up to Anderson Creek, near Yale, to work on a cut block there. We were bunked in at a logging camp; the trailers were warm and dry, and the grub was incredible. Our camp cook was a master chef. Every morning we were served stacks of hot cakes, bacon, ham and eggs, and steaming coffee. For dinner we had our choice of thick steaks, pork chops, or roast beef. Life was good, and the pay wasn't bad. Occasionally, my roommate, Bob, and I would jump into his old truck after supper and make a journey down the steep roads to Yale to wet our whistle for a while at the local hotel. Driving back to camp at one in the morning was always an adventure; luckily it was dark, so I could never see how close we came to the edge of the road, and it was a long way down.

After a month our contract was finished. We packed up our gear, and our crew decided to celebrate. After much celebrating at the Yale Hotel,

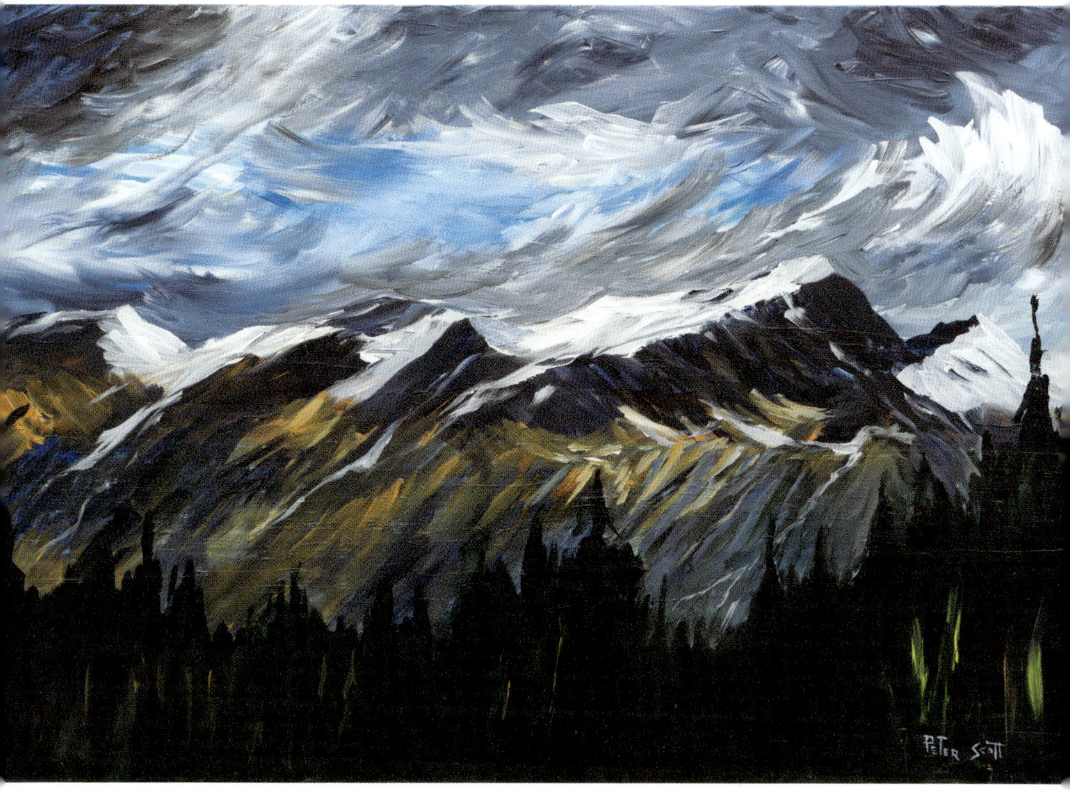

Nesakwatch Valley

Bob and I jumped back in his truck and headed for Hope. Unfortunately, Bob decided to fall asleep at the wheel just as we hit the Hope Bridge. We literally hit the bridge, careening into the path of an oncoming semi truck. I managed to grab the wheel to avoid the semi, and we bounced off the railings before finally coming to a stop. By then, Bob woke up. The truck had blown a tire and stalled, so we had to quickly jump out and push the truck off the bridge. Then I had to run back and pick up our gear, which was scattered all over the highway. The party was over. I decided then that my career as a woodsman was also over.

The last time I saw Bob, he was changing a tire. I hitchhiked back to Bushwack (Chilliwack). I also decided to return to Vancouver and be a one-eyed artist all over again.

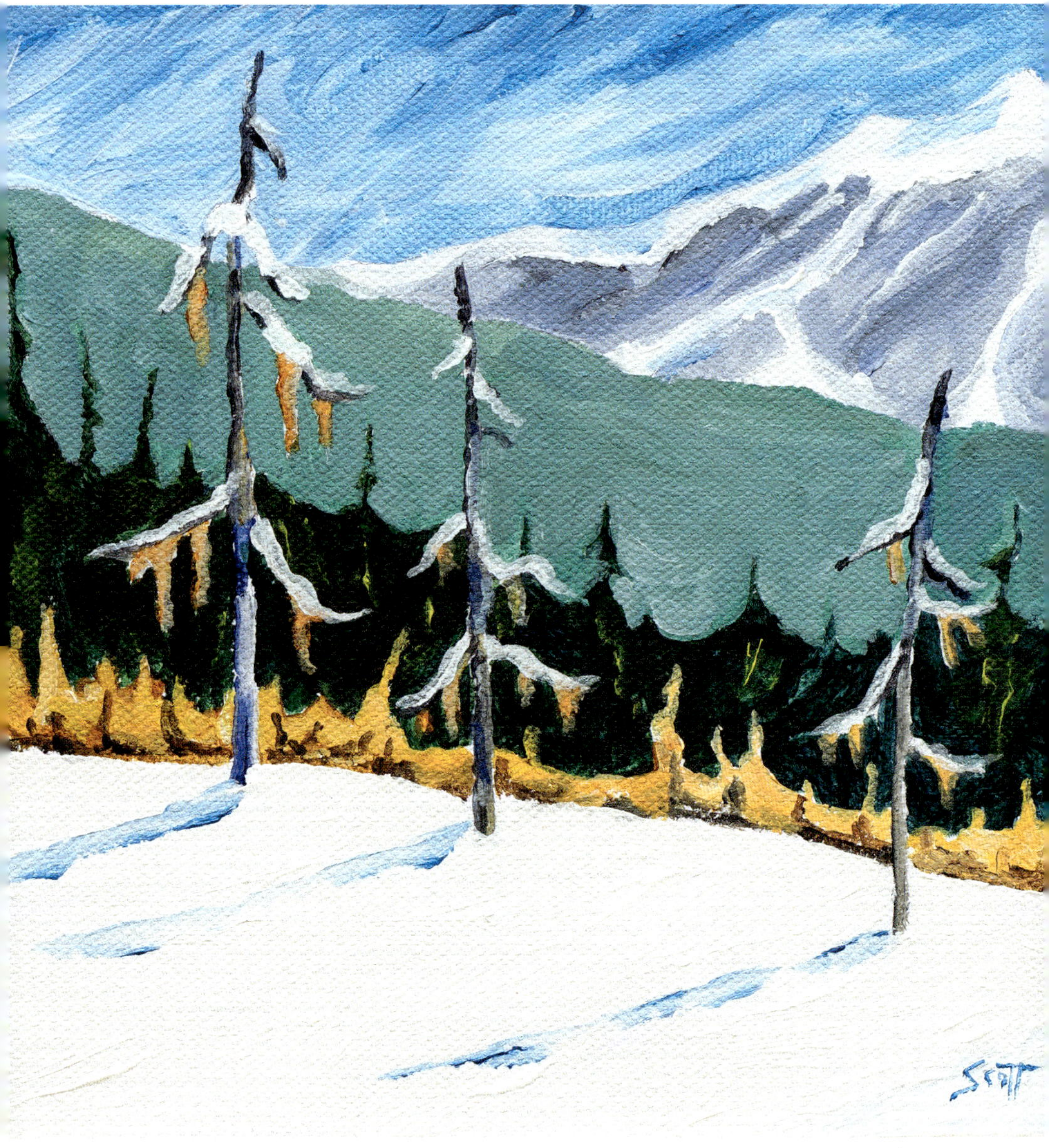

Alpine

Chapter Twenty-Five

The Cabin Fire, "Chuck The Truck," And Mud

Once upon a time, in mid-October, my brother Colin, cousin Andrew, Man Mountain Mike and I decided to make a trip up to an old, abandoned prospector's cabin, far up the slopes above Nesakwatch Valley.

We packed up my old, half-ton, gold-coloured pickup, dubbed Chuck the Truck, and headed up the Chilliwack River Valley in a heavy rain. We arrived at the trail far up the Nesakwatch Creek Forest Service Road. Mount Rexford loomed over the valley, enshrouded in cloud. We donned our packs and began the long, steep, muddy hike up the trail.

The creek was swollen, the trail extremely slippery, and it was difficult to keep up with Man Mountain Mike. After three hours, it began to get dark. The overhanging branches of the cedars dripped with water, and so did we. Wet and tired, we had to make several crossings on slimy logs across the raging creek. We had forgotten to bring headlamps. My Tyrol hiking boots were supposed to repel water, but my feet and wool socks were soaking wet anyway, from stepping into the creek.

Finally, we arrived at the cabin. It looked cold and lonely standing there, abandoned in the forest. Exhausted, cold, and drenched, we immediately fired up the old potbellied stove, changed into dry clothes and hung our wet woolen underwear around the stove to dry.

The cabin became warm and cozy and smelled of stinky, sweaty wool socks. We ignored the smell and cooked up a hearty dinner of wieners, beans,

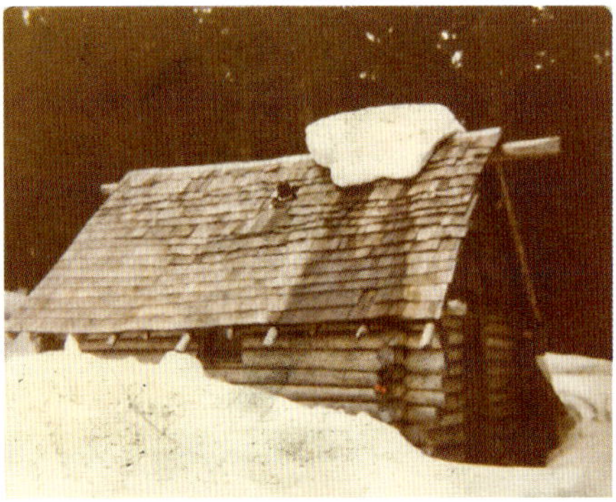

Trapper's Cabin

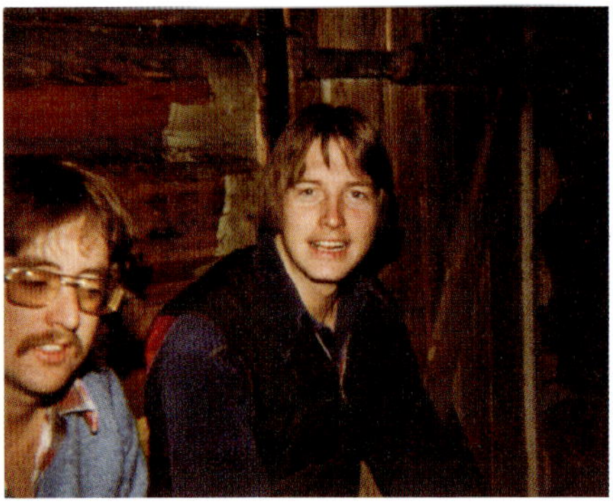

High Stakes Black Jack

and sourdough bread, then began a game of five- card stud sitting around the worn, wooden table. Liquid refreshments were brought out, and soon we were revitalized.

As we played poker late into the night, it became apparent that the cabin was extremely hot and smoky. Man Mountain Mike made a trip to the outhouse, came back and informed us the cabin was on fire. Being a man of few words, he failed to elaborate, took his seat back at the table, and dealt out a hand of cards.

After a while, I made a trip outdoors. As I stood in the rain, I looked up to see flames dancing along the roofline. I ran inside and opened the attic door. The attic was a raging inferno. Flames lashed out at my face. By now, the cabin was full of smoke and my friends were stuffing their clothes into their packs and heading for the door. Once we got outside, we realized my brother was missing. He had gone to bed and was oblivious to the falling ash and timbers. We ran back into the fire, rescued him, and threw him out into the rain. He was not happy we'd disturbed his slumber.

We had barely escaped with our lives. The cabin was fully engulfed in flames, a firestorm from Hell. Even the escaping pack rats were on fire. Luckily the rain was still coming down in buckets, so the forest didn't catch on fire.

We were in shock, half toasted and soaking wet at the same time. Our eyes burned from the smoke. Then Mountain Man Mike finally uttered some words: "That was close. Why didn't you guys listen to me?" As we stood and watched the cabin burn to the ground, we realized how lucky we were. The next time Man Mountain Mike gives us a warning, I'm going to listen to him, I told myself.

We gathered our gear, spread a tarp across the branches of some large cedars, and bivouacked in the rain for the night. Then it started to snow.

My sleeping bag was already damp and uncomfortable when the heavy snow weighing down the tarp made it collapse on us. We were definitely not having fun.

It would have been a wise idea to bring a tent for backup. On our next trip, we promised ourselves, we would pack a tent and headlamps.

The clouds lifted the next morning. That's when I noticed I was sleeping next to the grave of the old prospector. A faded, wooden cross stood crookedly in the ground.

This trip couldn't get any worse.

All that was left of the cabin was a large, black, smoking, burned square on the landscape. Pieces of stovepipe lay scattered on the ground, and the scorched potbelly stove stood forlornly in the corner of the black square. The roasted corpses of a couple of pack rats lay nearby.

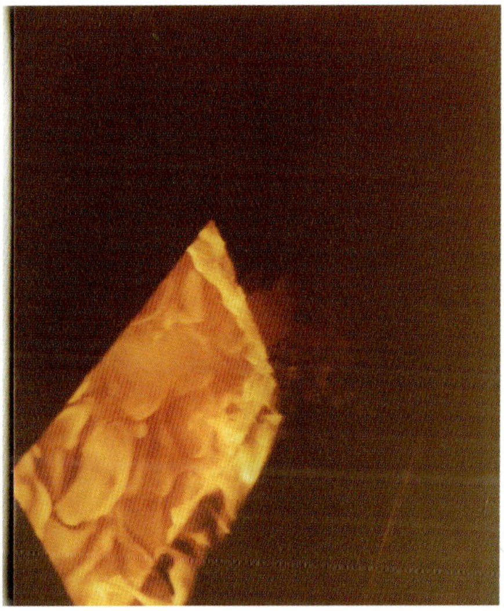

Attic Fire

We paid our respects to the deceased cabin and the buried prospector. Then, fighting off hypothermia, we tried to warm ourselves around our small Primus camp stoves and cooked up a breakfast of more wieners and beans. After drinking a pot of hot coffee, we felt better, packed up our gear and made the long hike through the wet snow to our truck.

Just when we thought things couldn't get worse, Chuck the Truck got stuck in the snow and mud. Unfortunately, we had forgotten to bring a shovel. One more thing to add to our list of what to bring on our next excursion. We cut some cedar limbs and stuffed them behind the mud-stuck tires.

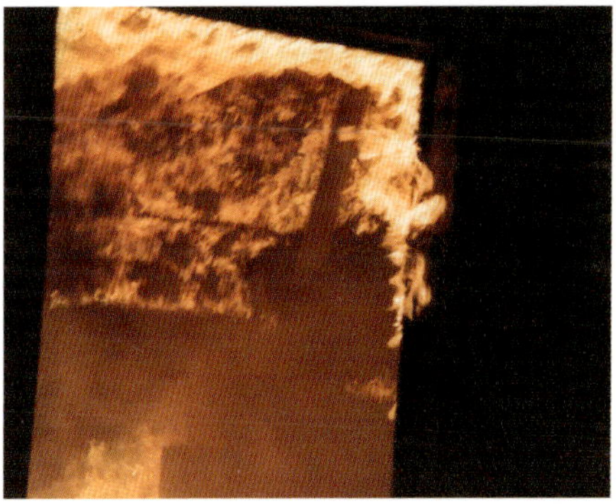

The Cabin Fire

Then it began to snow again. With much pushing, swearing, and falling in mud, we extracted the truck. We thought the day was starting to improve until we rounded a curve in the road and discovered the road had become part of Nesakwatch Creek.

I backed up Chuck and made an attempt to drive through the rapidly flowing stream. The stream was deeper than it looked. Chuck got stuck again. This time, it seemed like he had decided to become a permanent resident of the valley. My brother decided to drive the truck, and as we tried to push Chuck out of the water and mud, I fell into the creek. Then the snow turned to rain again.

By now we were wet, muddy, cold, and decidedly unhappy campers. Luckily, I had a spare bottle of refreshment in my pack that lifted our spirits, though not the truck. So we began a long walk back down Nesakwatch Valley to Chilliwack Lake Road, hoping to hitch a ride home before it got dark. While we waited for a ride, the Centre Creek prison guards pulled up. They asked to see our ID. Then I got arrested again and taken back to the Centre Creek prison camp, where I explained my story about the "other" Peter Douglas Scott, who was still wanted on a Canada-wide warrant. It became a long night.

Finally, they received information on the computer that I was not the guy, and I was released from my cell. Then I had to hitchhike back to Sardis, where I rejoined my friends.

When I got home, I made a list of what to take on our next adventure: headlamps, shovels, a jack, a come-along, chains, a cake with a file in it. And a fire extinguisher.

But first, I had to go back and rescue Chuck.

Chapter Twenty-Six

Huckleberry And The River Runs Forever

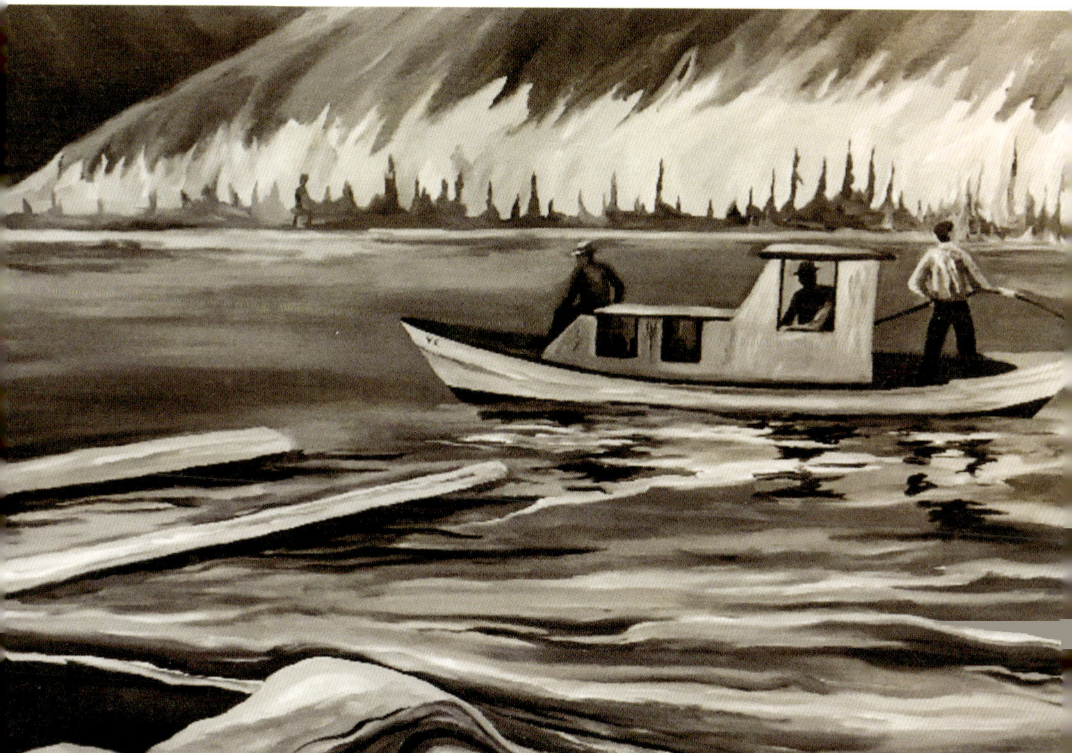

The River Runs Forever

The Fraser River, the STAW-lo, carries the life blood of the province of British Columbia and the Stó:lō, the "People of the River."

My uncle Bob Cromarty is of Stó:lō heritage. His great-great-grandmother was the daughter of a Stó:lō chief. Uncle Bob's great-great-grandfather worked at the Hudson's Bay Company fort at Langley as a cooper. Uncle Bob and his family have lived and worked on the Great River for thousands of years. The river was in his DNA.

Uncle Bob met my father, Vern Scott, in the early 1940s. They were both fishing on the banks of the river. My dad was 14 and had just moved from the prairies to Chilliwack with his family. Uncle Bob was 16. He grew up on Dancing Island, situated in the Fraser River, just off Fairfield Island.

Uncle Bob lived an idyllic life on Dancing Island. He and his six brothers and sisters swam, rowed, and sailed around the island. Uncle Bob's father, Sam Cromarty, farmed the land on their island and also worked as a logger. Uncle Bob told me his dad once caught two steelhead right off the front porch!

My dad and Uncle Bob became fast friends, and became family later when Dad's sister, Helen Scott, married Bob.

As a teenager, Dad spent much of his time staying with the Cromarty family on the island. Dad and Uncle Bob spent their days exploring the river in Uncle Bob's dugout canoe. The two of them were a 20th century Tom Sawyer and Huckleberry Finn. I used to call Dad Huckleberry; in response, he called me Charlie Crow, as I had long, jet-black hair and used to get dive-bombed regularly by a murder of crows.

Together they paddled the old dugout canoe from Dancing Island to Fairfield Island to classes at Strathcona School. Dad retired from school after Grade 10 and, with Uncle Bob and my grandfather, worked at a sawmill to raise money to buy a boat. They planned on beachcombing logs off the shores of the Fraser.

Uncle Bob and Dad were incredibly happy and fun-loving characters, carefree and mischievous. Uncle Bob always had a twinkle in his eye, and his good nature was contagious. They were also strong men. My dad stood at 6 feet 2 inches, had forearms thicker than Popeye's, and hands as large as hams. Uncle Bob once told me a story about Dad. He was 16 then, and milking a cow. The cow kicked him. Dad stood up, faced the cow, and punched her between the eyes. The cow dropped to her knees. I admired and respected my dad after that, and made sure I never kicked him …

As teenagers, Dad and Uncle Bob became blood brothers to seal their friendship. They took their hunting knives and cut the backs of their hands, then pressed the backs of their hands together until their blood mingled. Dad carried a large scar on the back of his hand for the rest of his life.

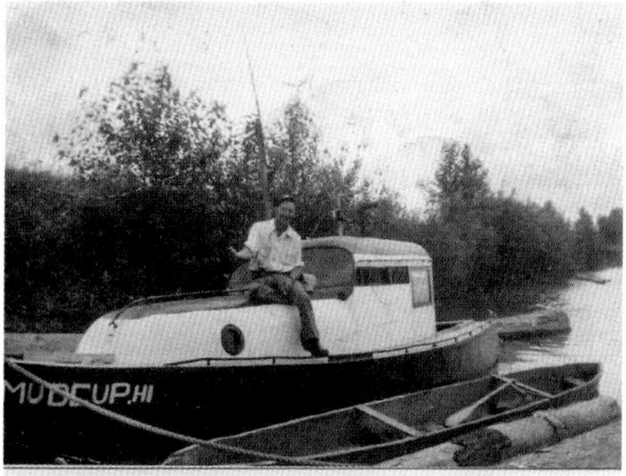

Skipper of the Mad Cap

When Dad was 17 and Uncle Bob 19, they bought an old scow they named the V.B., for Vern/Bob, and set out on their new enterprise as beachcombers.

My grandfather, Alexander Scott, and uncle Lorne Scott joined on as crew. The four of them spent long days hauling logs to sawmills at Chilliwack and Mission. During their time off, they fished.

Uncle Bob told them the Stó:lō story of the Salmon, told to him by his father. A long time ago, a powerful Transformer travelled the world. He carried Salmon bones in his hand. When he came to a river, he would drop the bones into the water. He told them they would become the Humpback and there would be many of them. Then the Transformer came to the Great River (the Fraser) and dropped Salmon bones in the streams and small rivers; they became the Sockeye. He then dropped bones in other lakes and streams, and they became Steelhead and Trout.

Uncle Bob told Dad and my grandfather that only humans and Sockeye possess a soul. The Transformer sent the souls of birds and animals back to the Creator.

He told them the Sockeye possess a soul because in their home out in the ocean, they are human beings.

He then told them the Stó:lō names for the Salmon. The Sockeye are traditionally Sthéqi. The Humpback and Pinks are Holiya, the Coho are Kwóxweth, and the Chinook, "Springs," are Tl'élxel.

After my dad taught me the names of these fish, I got a pen and wrote the names on the lid of my tackle box. Who can remember that stuff?

After two years of beachcombing with the V.B., Dad and Uncle Bob took their savings and bought a 30-foot, steel-hulled tug. They named her the Mad Cap. Now they were real tugboat operators, river pirates! Dad used to get angry when their friends would sneak to the Mad Cap at night and paint out the a's in the name so the boat became the Mud Cup.

Uncle Bob and Dad would sail to Port Douglas and tow booms down the length of Harrison Lake to the Harrison River and then to the mills at Mission. According to Uncle Bob, there was a Stó:lō legend that an Old Woman lived in Harrison Lake. She had long white hair and hid in the water. For thousands of years, people would smear black ash on their faces when they travelled on the lake so she couldn't see them and drown them. They would leave gifts of tobacco on a rock at Sasquatch Island so the Old Woman wouldn't create howling winds and squalls that would capsize their canoes and boats.

One day, while leaning over the starboard rail of the Mad Cap to place a tin of tobacco on the rock, Dad's new watch fell off his wrist and into the lake. He guessed they had probably brought Old Woman the wrong brand of tobacco.

When we were kids, my brother, many cousins, and I swam in the Fraser River. We would jump and dive off the log booms.

There was a swimming area in a back eddy of the Hope Slough called Dayton's Pool. Log barriers made a swimming area. When I was four years old, I nearly drowned in Dayton's Pool. My mother had told me to stay in the shallow end of the eddy. Being an obedient child, I immediately headed to the deep end. The water was up to my chin. Four teenagers sitting on the log barrier decided to dunk me. They were overzealous and held me under the water until I no longer had breath. To this day, I can see their laughing faces looking down at me through the bubbles escaping my lungs. As I was thrashing and passing out, my pregnant mother dived in and rescued me. Then she tanned my posterior.

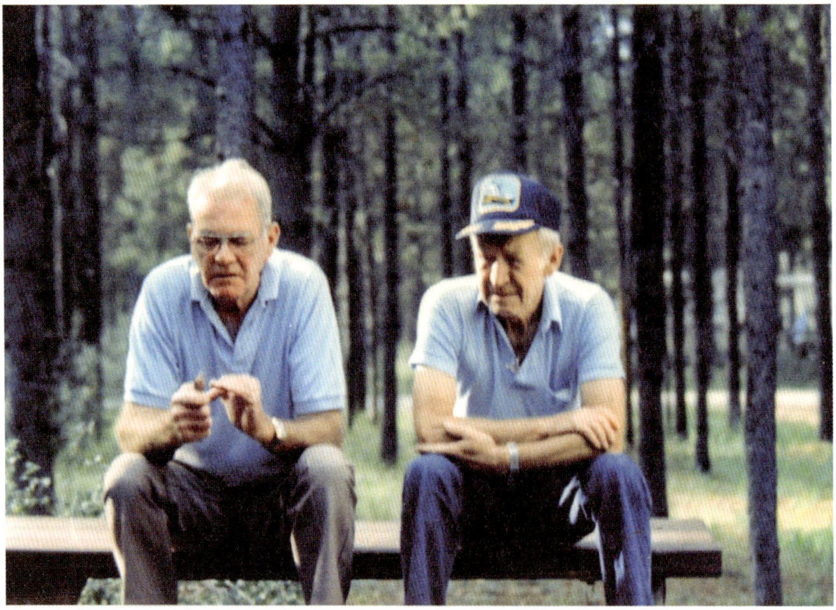

Vern Scott (Huckleberry) and Bob Cromarty (Old Man River)

Chapter Twenty-Seven

Princesses, Voyageurs, Fur Traders And Old Man River

My uncle Bob Cromarty's family history reads like a book of classic Canadiana, beginning in Scotland and weaving its way to intertwine with the very soul of Western Canada and its original inhabitants.

Uncle Bob's great-great-grandfather, William Magnus Cromarty, was born in 1825 in the small town of Cromarty on the Orkney Islands, off the coast of northeastern Scotland.

He apprenticed at a young age as a cooper (barrel maker). Everything was packaged and shipped in barrels during the early 19th century. He joined the world-famous Hudson's Bay Company when he was 18 years old. Fur traders in North America traded with the Indigenous people to acquire fur pelts that were shipped to Europe and converted into fur coats and beaver-felt top hats, the height of men's fashion in the 1700s and 1800s. He sailed from the port of Stromness, Scotland, aboard the Company's tall ship Prince Rupert on June 23, 1843. He arrived at York Factory on Hudson Bay on Aug. 10, 1843. William Magnus Cromarty was recorded in the Company's journal as Cromartie the cooper.

The Hudson's Bay Company (HBC) is the oldest corporation in North America. Some people sarcastically refer to the company as "Here Before Christ." The HBC controlled the fur trade throughout much of British-controlled North America for two centuries. Its trappers and traders created a working relationship with many First Nations and built a network of trading posts across the continent.

William Cromarty worked at the Company's northern department at York Factory until July 1844. At the age of 19, William Magnus Cromarty joined a fur-trading brigade and set out in a large voyageur canoe for the distant shore of the Pacific Ocean. He travelled alongside strong, seasoned voyageurs, men who spent their lives travelling in 36-foot canoes constructed of birch bark. Each canoe carried 12 to 14 paddlers, along with their camping, cooking gear and food. The canoes were stable, seaworthy, and easy to paddle. Their destination was Fort Vancouver, at the mouth of the Fraser River in the land now known as British Columbia.

I have had the pleasure to ride in one of these massive vessels. It takes much practice to paddle in unison with so many other people. When I lived in Quesnel, B.C., our local canoeing club owned a voyageur canoe named the Black Water Dancer. Watching them paddle down the Fraser River was a majestic sight. Seeing a brigade of these magnificent craft would have been awe-inspiring.

Voyageurs generally wore a white cotton shirt for protection from the sun and mosquitoes. They also wore breeches with leather leggings, leather moccasins, a red toque, and a sash around their waist. Voyageurs had to be extremely strong and physically fit, as they would pack their supplies, freight and canoes on long portages across and through muskeg, hills, and forests. Each canoe could carry up to 3500 pounds of freight, including up to 30 bales of furs. These canoes also carried transferring Company officers and large sacks of mail containing important correspondence for the forts along the routes.

According to family lore, William's favourite saying throughout his life was "go with the flow and portage when necessary"—wise words for a 19-year-old.

Because their packs were so heavy, voyageurs used tumplines to ease the strain on their backs. A tumpline is a strap that crosses the forehead and is attached to your pack. A tumpline transfers the weight from the load directly to your forehead and down your spine, relieving stress on your shoulders. My crew and I often used these when we were packing our supplies and heavy trail-building equipment up the steep trails of the Cascades.

William and his crew of adventurers travelled to Lake Winnipeg, along the North Saskatchewan River, across the Rocky Mountains and down the Columbia River, finally arriving at Fort Vancouver, the headquarters of the company's western department. The voyageurs travelled up to 50 miles (80 kilometres) a day, completing a journey of approximately 2,600 miles (4184 kilometres).

Uncle Bob's great-great-grandfather was assigned the position of cooper at Fort Vancouver when he arrived at the mouth of the Great River in 1845. He worked at Fort Vancouver until 1847 and was then assigned to Fort Langley, where he was given the position of foreman in the cooper's shop. He had four assistants working under his supervision.

William and his men were responsible for building barrels that were used to ship cured salmon to markets as far away as the Sandwich Islands (Hawaii) and Australia. During this period, Fort Langley supplied all the salt-cured salmon needed by the Company's outposts west of the Rocky Mountains.

The fort produced potatoes, barley, peas, and wheat, and supported a stock of 200 pigs and 500 head of cattle on its 2,000 acres (809 hectares). The fort itself enclosed an area 630 by 240 feet (192 by 73 metres). The walls were constructed with logs placed vertically around the perimeter of that area, and each corner of the walls had a bastion. The fort also had 15 buildings to accommodate barracks, storehouses, offices, a general store, blacksmith shop, cooper shop and various others.

The Factor of Fort Langley, James Murray Yale, had a policy of arranging marriages of his men to local Indigenous women to help in acquiring land. The men married daughters of local chiefs, with the eldest daughter of a chief deemed a princess. William Magnus Cromarty married a young girl named Salum'mia, the eldest daughter of a Stó:lō chief of Matsqui. William was now married to a princess!

William built a cabin next to the fort for his young wife, and they soon had a daughter. Unfortunately I could find no information on her from my family. Their second child was a boy named William, who grew up and married a Stó:lō girl, Lucie, daughter of Cheam Chief Philippe.

Their second son, James, was a legendary character. He grew to 6 feet, 4 inches, a giant of a man in those days. He was known from Cheam to Fort Langley and was famous for his strength. One story passed down from my uncle's family was that James was a skilled boxer and once killed his opponent in a prizefight. Another time, he won a weightlifting contest in Moody Ville, setting a record by lifting 1300 pounds. Other family lore is that he walked ashore from a river steamer at Fort Langley carrying 13 sacks of flour, each bag weighing 50 pounds. He carried two bags under each arm and nine bags in a pack on his back. He lived a long life, never married, and died at the age of 83.

Their next daughter, Mary, was born when Fort Langley became famous. Gold had been discovered upriver at Yale. During the Cariboo Gold Rush, some 30,000 prospectors passed through the fort. She married a Cariboo prospector, and they had two boys.

On July 30, 1869, William Magnus Cromarty and his wife Salum'mia, now called Mary, had a son named Samuel Ephraim Cromarty, my uncle Bob's grandfather. Sam grew up at Fort Langley and married a Stó:lō girl named Gussie Garner. Her father was an American from the Southern states who married a Stó:lō princess named Alice from the upper Fraser Valley and with her opened the very first store and post office in Chilliwack!

Sam and Gussie had 12 children, who were affectionately called The Dirty Dozen by family members. Sam followed the gold trail to Dawson City, Yukon, and worked as a river pilot on the sternwheelers. As he could not read or write, he was unable to get his captain's papers, however his incredible skill at navigating the Yukon River made him legendary. After a year, he returned home and spent six months with his family. His boys all eventually joined him working on the Yukon River sternwheelers.

During the 1970s, my Uncle Bob and his brothers visited Dawson City, and checked out the large display in the Dawson City Museum dedicated to Samuel Ephraim Cromarty. My uncle told me he and his brothers were supplied with free drinks from the locals for the entire week they were there!

Sam and Gussie Cromarty's first child was named William Henry, though he was called Bill. According to family history he was a gentle, kind man who often brought home unemployed men during the Depression. He married Marie Stranger on April 8, 1915. They had one daughter.

Sam and Gussie's second son, born May 27, 1895, was named Samuel Ephraim after his father. He was my Uncle Bob's father. The tallest of the two boys, at 6 feet, he was full of fun, loved to tease his relatives, played guitar and sang. He joined the army in World War I, along with his older brother Bill and his mother's two brothers, Samuel Roy and Joe Garner. Samuel Roy was killed in action.

Before he was sent overseas, Sam Cromarty garnered the title of Heavyweight Boxing Champion for the army. While in England, he met the love of his life, Emily May Jelley. When the war ended, she came to Canada, and they were married on May 19, 1919.

I have a letter written to the editor of the Kelowna newspaper on June 26, 1968, by one of Sam Cromarty's comrades in arms, Don Ellis, from his World War I unit. It reads like this: "Sam was a Battalion scout, and I was a Battalion sniper. Sam was a hero and a big brother to me as I was only seventeen when I met Sam in the trenches at Paschendale. From then on I saw lots of him. Sam was a real soldier and many a battle patrol we were on together. If ever the Brass wanted a prisoner for information, Sam was the man they asked to lead the raid, he was Lieutenant W.D. Graham's right-hand man who was our scout officer. They say old soldiers never die they just fade away, believe me the memory of Big Sam Cromarty will never fade away from me."

A real testament to a real man.

After the war was over, Sam Cromarty returned to Chilliwack, lived on Dancing Island with his family, worked as a logger, and worked on the river, keeping it clear of debris and log jams.

My dad loved Ol' Sam Cromarty. He said Sam was the nicest man he ever met. Samuel Ephraim passed away on June 6, 1968, his widow Emily joining him four years later on Sept. 3, 1972.

Sam and Emily had five sons and a daughter. Uncle Bob was born on Dec. 29, 1929, and married my dad's sister Helen Scott, with whom he raised five boys and two girls—my cousins Linda, Robert, Donald, Karen, Doug, Sam, and Dwayne. They lived on a farm in Flood, B.C., upriver from Chilliwack.

Uncle Bob was always linked to the mighty Fraser, having been born and raised on the turbulent river. He spent 35 years skippering his tug Red

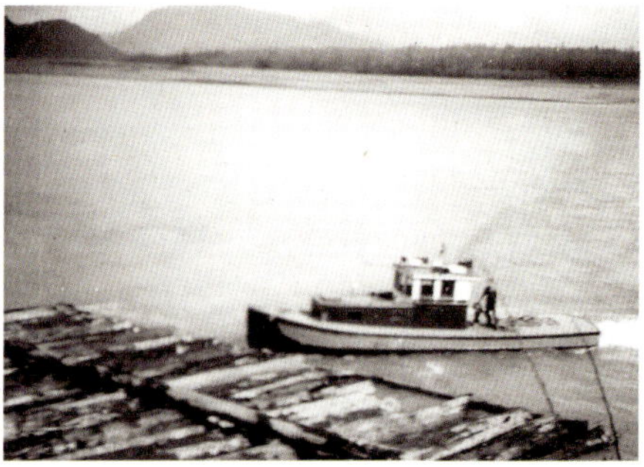

Red Fir One

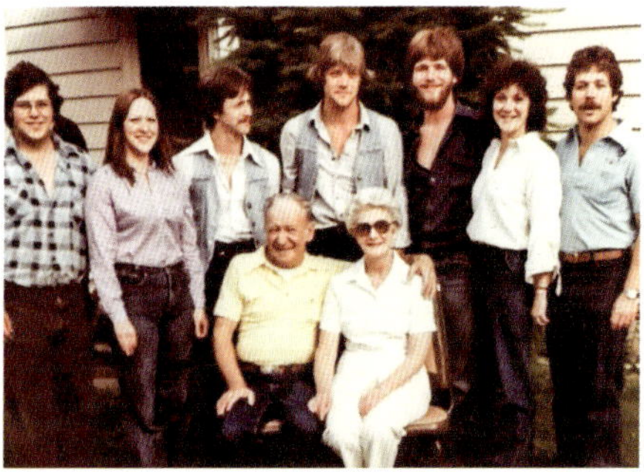

The Cromarty Clan

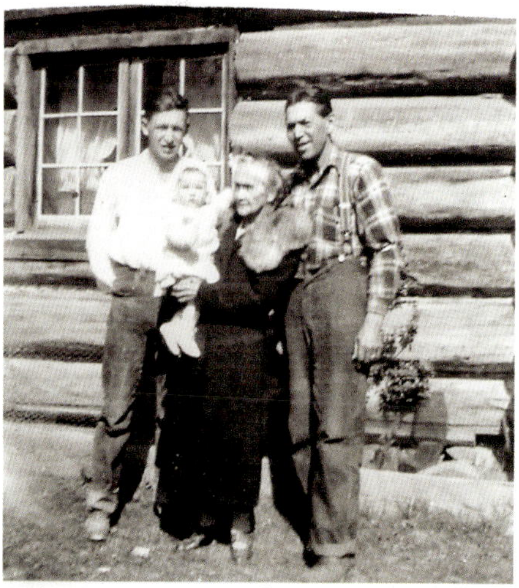

The Cromarty Family - Four Generations

Fir 1, which pulled log booms from Yale to Sumas. He always told me, "You have to respect the river; if you don't, it will kill you."

He told me of a whirlpool below Yale called Hémq'eleq, which means "getting swallowed." He said there was a tunnel leading to a cave at Yale near Franklin Rock called Tekwóthel, meaning "where things pile up." The tunnel transports driftwood swallowed by the whirlpool into the cave. According to ancient lore, a young man fell into the whirlpool and was transported underground to the cave and survived.

Uncle Bob also told me there was a mythical tunnel running underground from Spuzzum to Yale, but he didn't know anything else about it or why it was there.

On one occasion, Uncle Bob was trying to negotiate a corner with his tug and the log boom became jammed. He tried to pass between the logs and the mountain wall, but the boom came at him at a furious speed. He narrowly escaped by opening up his throttle.

Uncle Bob's fame as a river skipper came when his tug became the first power boat to make it past Franklin Rock since the days of the sternwheelers. This involved passing the whirlpool, Hémq'eleq. His tug got sucked down by the powerful, swirling water, and he spun around the whirlpool three times before, pushing hard on the throttle, he managed to pull out. He nearly sank in the harrowing incident; he told me it was the first time he ever put on a life jacket!

Uncle Bob worried about the river. Before he joined his ancestors on April 1, 1997, he lamented that the beautiful river he grew up on and knew so well was dying. When he was a kid, he said, fish were everywhere, but "now there are hardly none." Life on the river was hard, but he loved it. The Fraser, STAW- lo, was in his blood.

I miss him greatly.

The Cromarty clan belong to the Skwah First Nation in Chilliwack. Since time immemorial, their people have lived, worked, played, and fished on the traditional, ancestral, unceded territory of the Stó:lō Coast Salish.

In 1946, the Cromarty family tree began to branch out from Dancing Island when one of the Dirty Dozen, David Craig Cromarty, and his wife, Mary Mang, moved their young family upriver to the north Cariboo wilderness. Like his forefathers, David Cromarty was a brave, adventurous son of the river.

They settled in the old gold-rush town of Quesnel, located at the mouth of the Quesnel River where it spills into the Fraser River. David Craig Cromarty soon convinced the northern lumber barons that he could drive booms of logs down the Fraser River from Prince George to Quesnel. From there, the logs would be transported by train to the mills in Vancouver. No one had been successful at this before.

Below are portions of a story written by David Craig Cromarty's son Dave. He wrote about his dad's exploits on those first early runs of hauling log booms down the Fraser River to Quesnel. Keep in mind Dave Junior was only ten years old while working on the boat with his father.

Patriarch's Legacy

By Dave Cromarty

"A logging camp and booming grounds were built north of the Cottonwood Canyon, which is approximately 32 km north of Quesnel. The idea was to ship logs to New Westminster. There was no problem building a logging camp and booming ground, but there were three other major problems.

"Firstly, could he tow a boom of logs through the Cottonwood Canyon without it breaking up? Secondly, upon arriving at Quesnel, could he pilot the boom between the piers of the old bridge? The distance between the riverbank and the first pier was only 65 feet, and the distance between [that and] the second pier was 175 feet. This limited the boom to a width of 100 to 125 feet. The last problem was, how do you get a boom of logs into a boom yard from the fast-flowing river?

"To move a boom of logs against the pull of the river's current was extremely difficult. Immediately upon passing through the piers, we would cut loose of the boom and run the boat onto shore near a buried post. One man would jump ashore with the rope and run up to the post that had been planted and wrap the rope around the post. As the rope tightened, the current would pull the boat towards the boom yard. If the rope was tied too short, the boom would wreck on the riverbank; too long, and the boom would miss the yard and be long gone down the river. Skill and timing were required to swing the boom around and push the boom into the boom yard.

"The main memory I have of my time on the river was driving the boat. My dad would sleep upon the roof over the operator and engine. The boat did six miles an hour; it was tedious to pilot the boat hour after hour. I was only ten years old when I piloted that boat on the Fraser, hour after hour, day after day. The river would rise at times and fall three feet overnight. On one trip you would be driving over clear water and on the next trip rocks were a foot under water. Sand bars came and went day by day. Dad would wake up from time to time and make waving motions that meant I was too close to shore. How many ten-year-olds get to pilot a river boat!

"No one ever noticed the impact my dad had on the tugboat industry in Northern B.C. To this day I have a particular affinity for the Fraser River and nostalgic memories of the river and my dad. Captain David Craig Cromarty was a true pioneer."

David Craig Cromarty was more than a riverboat skipper. He was an artist. He was a talented painter and carver and a founding member of the Quesnel Arts Club. He was instrumental in bringing the famous Group of Seven painter A.Y. Jackson to the Cariboo, particularly to the Barkerville area, where two of A.Y. Jackson's original paintings are on display at the Barkerville Museum.

Granddad "Dave" Cromarty inspired his daughter Yvonne and sons Don and Dave to also pursue the arts. His granddaughters Andrea Williams and Brenda Bonin and their brother Joel are all talented artists in their own right.

Granddad "Dave" passed away in 1953, but he is remembered through his historic deeds on the river and through his art.

The Cromarty family have come a long way from the town of Cromarty on the Orkney Islands and have left their mark in the history of this province.

Chapter Twenty-Eight

Father John Patrick And The Pirate Convention

After I returned to Vancouver, my fiancée and I decided to get married. We wanted a small ceremony with only our immediate families attending. We hoped to be married at my fiancée's parents' home. I knew of an Anglican minister who was of an open mind, and we hoped he would agree to come to their house and perform the ceremony. One evening, I went to his house to discuss this with him. My friends had told me he was very accommodating. He met me at the door and led me into his house to talk. He then asked if I would like a glass of wine. I said yes, and he immediately brought a jug, not a bottle, of homemade red wine to the table. I noticed he tossed away the cap. This was going to be an interesting evening.

I began asking if he would come to the house and marry us. He said no. We would have to have the ceremony in his church, which he designed. He was the architect of the chapel, presiding minister, and janitor. As we drank our wine, I noticed all the beautiful paintings on his walls. I asked him who the artist was, and he explained that the art was his own and that he had a bachelor's degree in fine arts. I was impressed. I was beginning to really like this man. He was an interesting character, a bachelor in his late fifties who seemed to have a lifetime of varied experiences.

He then informed me that after his career as a professional artist he had moved to northern B.C. and become a bush pilot. After a few years, his plane crashed and he lost his left arm. He wore an artificial arm with a claw.

By now, we had started into a second jug of homemade red wine, and once again he tossed away the cap. By now I was increasingly liking this man. Sometimes in life you meet someone and immediately feel as though you have been friends forever. This was a case of like at first sight. He then told me that after his accident he had studied theology and had become a minister. He then proceeded to tell me that he was a poet. I questioned this, as many people consider themselves poets. Then he showed me a book of his poetry and informed me the well-known firm of McClelland and Stewart were his publishers. He was also a friend and drinking buddy of the famous Canadian writer Farley Mowat. Now I really liked this guy.

He asked me what I did for employment, and I told him I was an unemployed, partially blind artist. He told me he a had a friend, a Scottish tradesman, who painted classic million-dollar yachts at the Vancouver Yacht Club and was looking for an assistant. Father John believed he could get me the job.

Now I really, really, really liked this man. As he staggered over to his cupboard to bring out another jug of homemade red wine, I heard a knock at the door. I looked up at the clock and it was well past midnight. Father John opened the door, and there stood my fiancée. She said it looked like a pirate convention—an old guy with a hook and a long-haired, bearded guy wearing an eye patch, along with two empty jugs of wine on the table. Introductions were made, and then my fiancée carried me home.

We were to be married the next Friday evening, Nov. 7, at Father John's parish.

I was hired by Wilson Youngson, a crusty, Scottish yacht painter, as a painter's helper. I began the job by scrubbing the decks of beautiful power yachts. The upcoming weekend was Remembrance Day, so my soon-to-be wife and I planned to take a four-day honeymoon by train to Banff. We were looking forward to seeing the Rocky Mountains. I had to work the day of my wedding. It was a cold, dark, rainy Vancouver day, and I anxiously awaited the end of the workday so I could rush home, get dressed and get to the church on time.

When I arrived at the church, our families were there. My brother was best man and my fiancée's sister was maid of honour. My soon-to-be wife looked beautiful in her white dress as she walked down the aisle. We said our I do's, exchanged rings, Father John pronounced us husband and wife—and voila, we were married.

As we went into the side room to sign the register, Father John Patrick came in carrying a box full of art supplies, books, frames, and a roll of canvas. I was dumbfounded and grateful. This minister had become my friend. He then announced he had been honoured with a literary prize for his poetry and showed us his beautiful award. He wished us well and then picked up his broom and began his janitorial duties, sweeping up the confetti.

We were taken to the train station, boarded the train, and headed for the Rocky Mountains as we embarked on a new life together.

After we moved to the Cariboo, I kept track of Father John and his literary career by reading and collecting the newspaper and magazine articles written about him. He had become an established, leading Canadian literary figure, and I was proud to know him. When he passed away in the late 1980s, his name was etched in glass on the main window of the new Vancouver Library, along with other notable Canadian authors. He had made himself a successful career as a poet, and I was beginning my career as a secondary school art educator and professional artist. I still use the brushes he gave me on my wedding day, and they possess a divine magic.

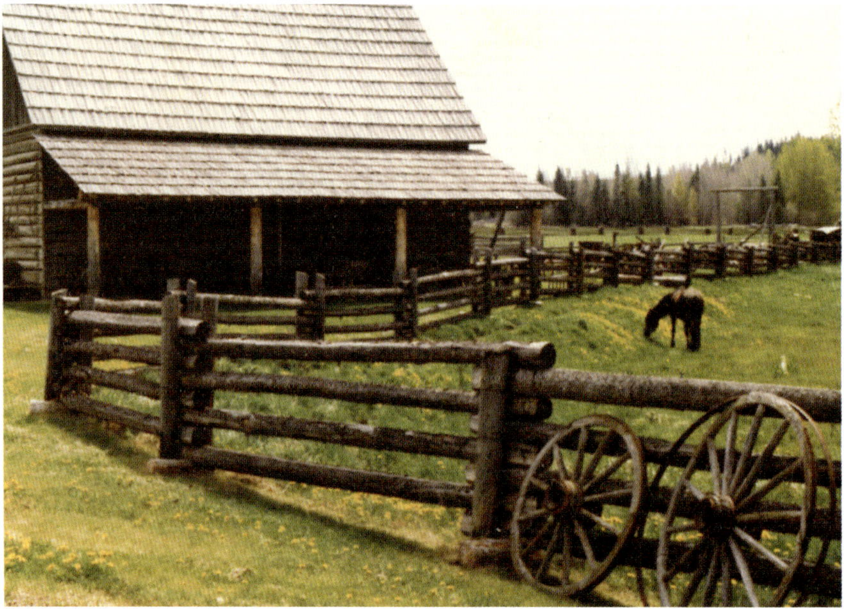

Cottonwood, B.C.

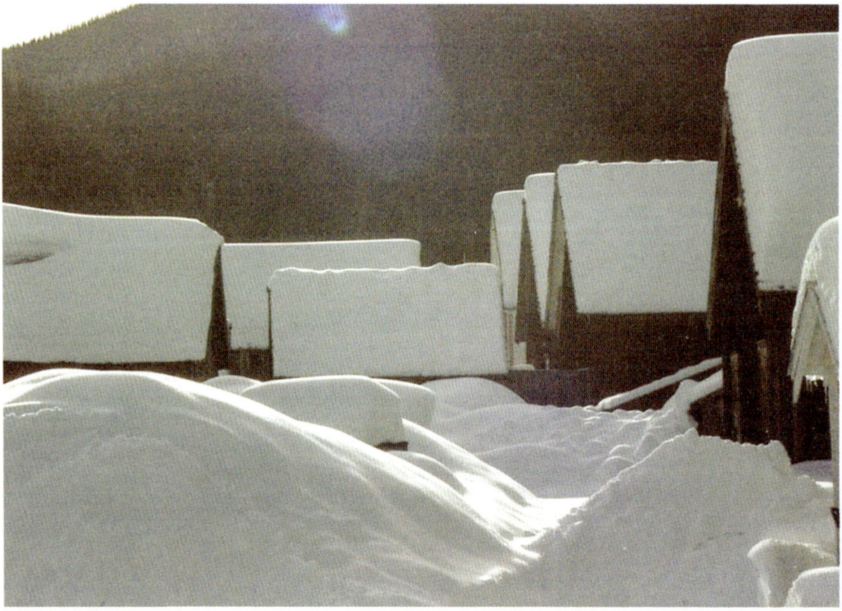

Barkerville Winter, Forty Below

Chapter Twenty-Nine

Move To The Cariboo

After our marriage in November 1980, I hung up my brushes, oil paints, sketchbook, pencils, and put my easel in storage. I was dealing with one blind eye and depression.

For a year I had worked as an apprentice yacht painter at the Vancouver Yacht Club. My boss was an old, cantankerous, Scottish master tradesman, and my work partner was his journeyman. John was two years older than me, a large, strong Norwegian lad.

One cold, wet, rainy, grey Vancouver morning in February, John and I were walking down the dock to scrub and bleach the teak decks of the Sundowner, a beautiful 80-foot power yacht—the plaything of kings.

I had a roll of hose over my shoulder, a bucket and long-handled scrub brush in my hands, and was wearing hip waders. As I stepped towards the stern of the yacht, my foot missed the transom and I fell into the chuck. My hip waders immediately filled with seawater. I was dropping like an anchor. John the big Norwegian quickly reached down with both hands and strong arms and hauled me up onto the wharf. I was swearing and thrashing around on the dock like a wet salmon when John informed me it was my lucky day. The Vancouver Yacht Club had a policy that if a tradesman fell into the water, the guard at the gatehouse would give him a bottle of rum and the rest of the day off.

That caught my attention, and I quickly proceeded to the gatehouse. I fell in the chuck twice more that month, and the club changed their policy.

Soon after the "rum" incident, I accepted a one-year, temporary art teaching position at a junior secondary school in the north Cariboo region of British Columbia. My wife resigned from her position at the law firm, and we moved upriver from the overcrowded city of Vancouver.

We moved to Quesnel for one year and stayed for 30.

Quesnel in 1980 was a step back in time, a small town locked in the 1930s. It was still the Wild West. As we approached the little Cariboo town late in the twilight evening of a long nine-hour drive, we nearly hit a moose.

We rounded a bend in the highway, and there he was, a massive beast. I don't know who was the most surprised, the moose on the loose or us. My wife was excitedly pointing and jumping up and down in her seat, as this was her first moose experience. I was frantically trying to avoid hitting Bullwinkle.

Fortunately, the moose made a lifesaving decision and fled the scene, crashing like a thousand-pound linebacker into the bush!

Cariboo Lesson #1: Avoid moose.

We soon found that Quesnel was an extremely friendly town. Many of its citizens were Chilliwack transplants who, like us, had moved farther up the Fraser River to avoid the fast-growing masses of the Lower Mainland.

You had to be careful, though. Folks in the Cariboo keep rifles in their trucks, and their homes. If you trespass on their property, they will shoot you.

My first plan upon arriving in this beautiful old gold-rush area was to stake claims for my family. According to mining law, section one, page five, of the Prospector's Manual, individuals are allowed to stake two claims per family member. As there were four in our small family—my wife, me, our two-year-old daughter and four-year-old son—that meant we were good for eight claims!

Unfortunately for us, every inch of river and creek frontage in the Cariboo had been staked and claimed since gold was first discovered in Antler Creek by two grizzled prospectors, Ned Stout and One-Eyed Jack, back in 1858.

Fortunately for us, according to section one, page two of the

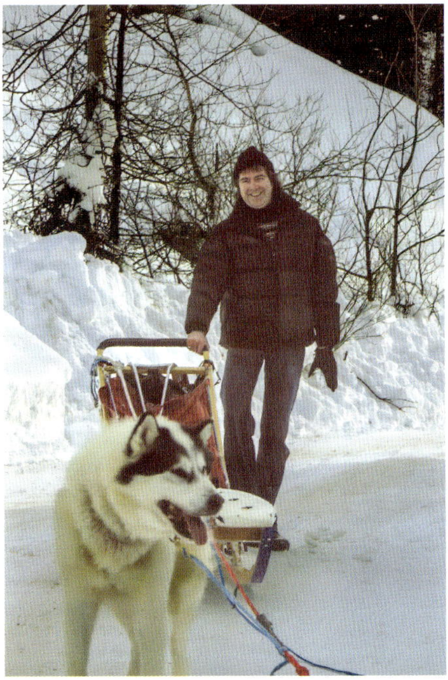

Author and Dog Sled Team

Prospector's Manual, individuals were allowed by law to pan for gold on other miner's claims as long as you weren't digging holes or altering the landscape of the claim. Gotta love placer mining.

Although my children were only two and four years old, they could hold gold pans, so like any other gold-crazed father/prospector, I took them gold panning. We hiked below Quesnel Canyon on the Quesnel River and chose a quiet back eddy where we hoped nuggets would have settled. Then I looked up and saw a scary old crazy-eyed prospector peering at us from behind a tree across the river. He was holding a rifle.

Cariboo Lesson #2: Never rub another man's rhubarb. Meaning, don't pan for gold on some crazy old wild-eyed prospector's claim. My Cariboo motto for the next 30 years was, "When in danger, run away, and live to run another day."

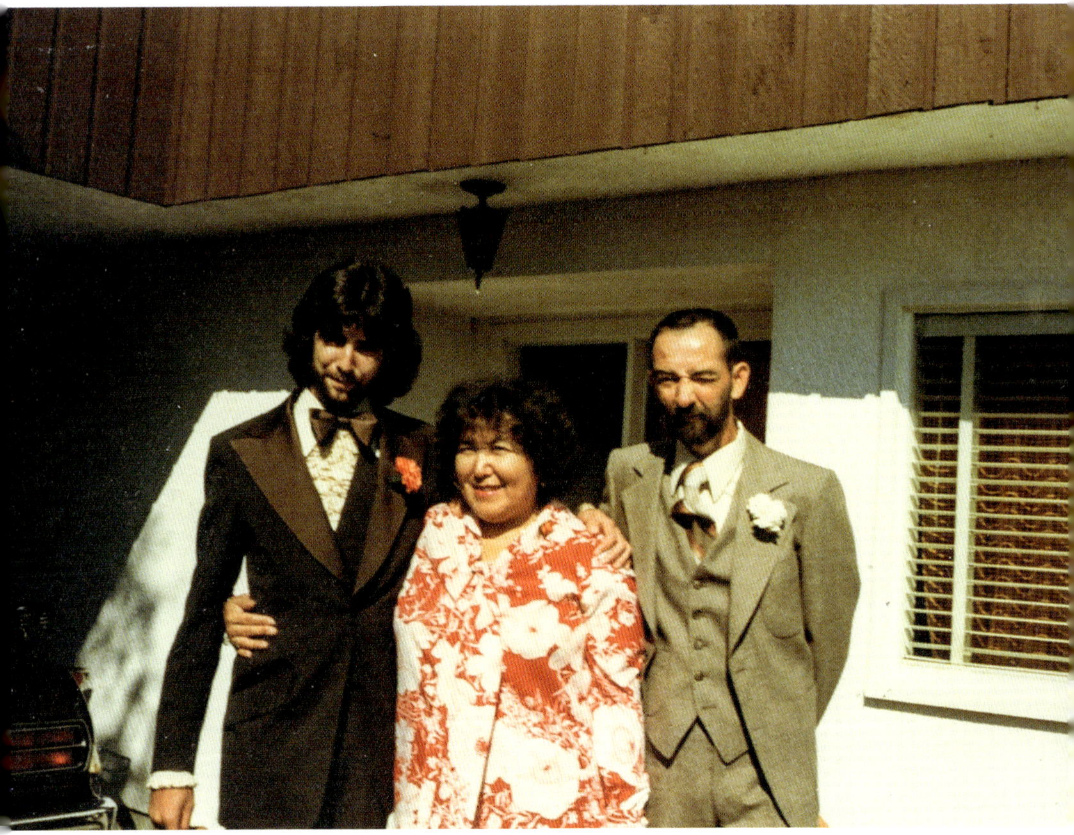

Author, Xwanquamaat and The Woodsman

Chapter Thirty

Xwanquamaat And The Woodsman

This chapter is dedicated to my Aunt Jessie and Uncle "Sandy." Aunt Jessie inspired me to become a teacher and mentor, and Uncle Sandy was my inspiration to become an artist and outdoorsman.

Jessie (Reid) Demerse

Aunt Jessie was a member of the Qualicum First Nation on Vancouver Island. She was Coast Salish. In the distant past, all the women and children from her tribe were kidnapped by the Haida and taken to Haida Gwaii as slaves. Eventually, after many generations, descendants of these slaves made their way back to Vancouver Island and the tribe was regenerated. My Aunt Jessie was a distant cousin of the famous Haida artist Bill Reid.

My aunt met my Uncle Sandy in the early 1960s in Qualicum, where he worked for the BC Forest Service. It was in Tofino that my aunt met Group Of Seven artist Arthur Lismer while walking on a beach one morning. The artist was sitting on a log, painting a scene of the wild Pacific Ocean waves crashing against the beach. Aunt Jessie visited with the famous Canadian painter and was given a tour of his studio and recent West Coast paintings.

My aunt and uncle moved to Port Alberni, where my uncle worked for MacMillan Bloedel as a forest engineer, designing logging roads for the company, and my aunt worked as a teacher at the alternate school.

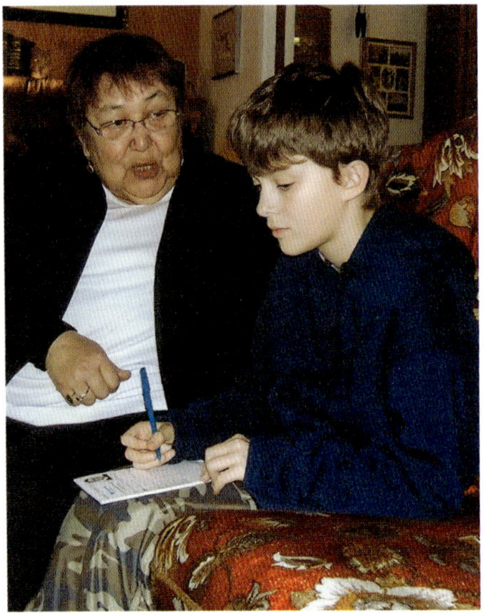

Xwanquamaat and Carson

After raising a family, they moved to Qualicum and Aunt Jessie became Elder-in-Residence for the Parksville/Qualicum School District First Nations Program, where she taught well into her seventies. She said she always felt more like an elder-in-training and had no desire to retire from working with First Nations youth.

During these years, I was living in Quesnel and teaching a First Nations art program. Aunt Jessie helped make my program a success. She was only a phone call away, and often supplied me with lesson plans and ideas for my students. She was a natural-born mentor and confidant. Whenever life became overwhelming, my aunt Jessie was there to guide me through the turmoil. She had a calming, assuring voice and manner.

After a long-distance phone conversation with Aunt Jessie, life became brighter again. Because we lived so far apart, we only saw each other at family reunions and visits at my parents' home in Chilliwack, when my aunt and uncle would make the voyage over from Vancouver Island.

Aunt Jessie's Hulquiminum name was Xwanquamaat, "One who is always busy, never catches up to herself." She had a seemingly limitless supply of energy, compassion and humour. Aunt Jessie's teaching position gave her the opportunity to go into all the district schools, Grades 1 to 12, and write their hands-on curriculum. Her assistance with my First Nations program was invaluable. Always the center of calm, she had a talent for slowing things down and making life enjoyable again.

Fifteen years ago, when my father was at home dying of lung cancer, Aunt Jessie came and performed a Cedar Sweeping ceremony for my family. She went to our creek and cut several branches from a large cedar tree and then individually swept the branches around each of us to sweep away our sorrow.

When the ceremony was over, she returned the branches to a place under that large cedar tree. The next morning, all the branches she had used were gone from under that tree, meaning the sweeping ceremony was successful.

I suddenly had a surge of strength and confidence that helped me deal with my father's agonizing death.

She also taught us that owls are "shadow trackers" and that an owl in your yard was a messenger of death. Four days before my dad passed away, a large Great Horned owl appeared in a tree next to my dad's bedroom window. The owl stayed there until my dad passed, and then it disappeared. Aunt Jessie's cedar sweeping helped us all survive a sad situation. It was mystical.

My aunt taught her students hands-on, practical life skills. She was always sending me lessons I could teach my students that would help them acquire "real life" skills, too.

Below is my aunt's recipe for Fry Bread (Bannock), my favourite delicacy:

4 cups flour

4 tbsp. sugar

1 tsp. salt

4 tbsp. oil

2 pkg. rapid yeast or sourdough starter 2 cups warm water

Deep-fry for 6 or 7 minutes in oil or wrap around a stick and cook over a campfire until done.

Alexander 'Sandy' Demerse

My uncle Sandy was an artist as well as a woodsman. He loved to create oil paintings of logging trucks, mountains and forests. For decades, one of his paintings hung on the wall of my grandparents' living room. As a young child, I marvelled at that painting of the yellow logging truck carrying a load of logs down a winding mountain road through a forest of tall Douglas firs. I could see the brush strokes and the gloss of the lush oil paint. That painting inspired me to become an artist and devote my life to painting landscapes.

He also taught me to love the forests and mountains. My uncle was a slender man, but he was part mountain goat. No one could keep up with him on a mountain trail. He was born and raised in Chilliwack and spent his youth exploring and camping in the local Cascades. He passed his passion for the outdoors and painting to me. I have that painting of the yellow logging truck hanging in my studio, and I think of him every day.

I was blessed to have these two wonderful people in my life.

Mount Tomyhoi

Reaching skyward
from the valley
Her mighty steeple rise
Commanding glacier hanging
over cliffs and ravines high.

Sparkling in the sunlight
a monument she stands
prominent from the valley
towering o'er our lands

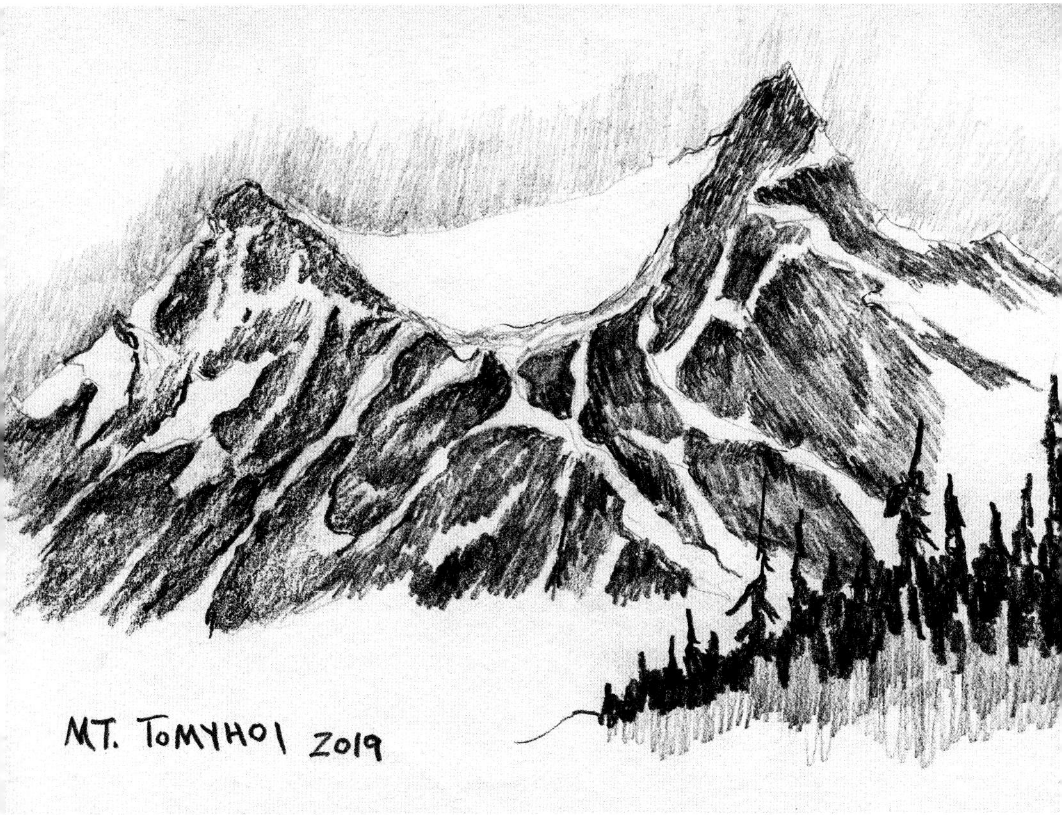

Chapter Thirty-One:

Artists Who Inspired Me

Bill Reid

During the summer of 1983, I attended classes at the Emily Carr School of Art and Design on Granville Island in Vancouver. I was taking printmaking courses, learning the intricate techniques of screen- printing and lithography.

Next door to the art school was the studio of British Columbia's famous Haida artist, Bill Reid. I made the discovery one noon hour while I was out for a break. The shop door to his studio was open, and there was the master artist, working on a scale plaster model of a killer whale.

I nervously approached his studio, said hello, and was offered a chair by the door. I was in shock; one of Canada's pre-eminent artists had invited me into his shop! I accepted his invitation, sat on the chair, and began quietly eating my sandwich while watching his every move.

His hands shook until he picked up his tools and began to sculpt. His genius lay in the design of his sculptures. As I watched him work on the plaster model, I noticed he had assistants working quietly on his larger-scale plaster models. It reminded me of the Renaissance period, when master artists oversaw their apprentices painting and sculpting to the artist's designs.

I was a fly on the wall, never really speaking to the artist, just observing the master at work. I marvelled at his dexterity and level of concentration as he skillfully maneuvered his sculpting tool on the plaster whale. It was both fascinating and inspirational.

He was in his sixties and battling Parkinson's disease, however it didn't seem to deter him from sculpting. The model he was working on later became the iconic Killer Whale bronze sculpture that resides in front of the Vancouver Aquarium. I felt fortunate to spend my noon hours observing a Canadian legend perform his artistry.

Bill Reid was made an Officer of the Order of Canada for reviving Haida art and bridging two cultures. He passed away on March 13, 1998, at the age of 78.

Toni Onley

During the late 1970s, B.C. artist Toni Onley was teaching in the Fine Art Department of the University of British Columbia in Vancouver, at the time I was taking painting courses with the esteemed Gordon Smith in the art studios of the Education Faculty Building. On occasion, Gordon would invite his friend Toni to come to our studio and participate in our class critiques. He was harsh but honest and accurate. Several times, some of my classmates were brought to tears by his astute evaluations.

Toni Onley was a master watercolour painter, and I greatly admired his work. I took advantage of his visits and gleaned as much information as I could on his painting techniques and colour palette.

In August of 1980, he sold 800 watercolours to Peter Brown and the Canarim Corporation for an outstanding sum of $900,000. This allowed Toni to cease teaching at the university and focus fully on his painting career. He purchased an amphibious airplane and began flying to remote mountains and lakes in British Columbia.

He told me at one of his exhibitions that he did this to escape the tourists who were always watching him when he painted in popular areas such as Whistler and Blackcomb. He also told me he would tear four 11-by-15-inch sections of 140-pound watercolour paper from a sheet of 22-by-30-inch Rives paper and then tape them to the wing of his airplane. Using the wing as an easel and his homemade paint box, he would complete four paintings a day of mountain glaciers and lakes and sell each of them in galleries for $3000.

In the winter of 2004, my wife and I were fortunate to purchase two of his works from a set of ten that were being exhibited in a local art gallery. Several days later, the Lloyd Gallery in Penticton burned to the ground. The remaining eight paintings of that collection perished in the fire. We were so thankful we'd had the insight to purchase our two paintings one week before the gallery and its art was destroyed.

Two months later, on March 2, 2004, Toni Onley was killed at the age of 75 when his plane crashed into the Fraser River.

Toni Onley was made an Officer of the Order of Canada in 1999.

Robert Genn

I first became aware of Robert Genn in 1978, when I saw two of his paintings hanging in the law office of DuMoulin and Black in Vancouver. At the time, my girlfriend worked there as a secretary. When I walked into their reception area, I noticed two original Onley paintings, and next to them two landscape paintings by an artist named Robert Genn. I had never heard of him but was immediately impressed by his impressionist style. His paintings were in the vein of the Canadian artists in the Group of Seven.

I wanted to know more of this artist and searched through Vancouver's art galleries to find his landscapes, a stylized representation of the Canadian landscape. I soon discovered he was based close by, in White Rock. I loved his work, however, being a starving art student, could not afford to own an original Robert Genn. I was able, however, to purchase his book In Praise of Painting, which included his life story and many of his paintings. That book became one of my favourites.

Years later, when I was a high school art teacher in Quesnel, Robert Genn came to our area to teach a one-day workshop. I immediately registered for his session. The workshop was held in the small town of Wells, B.C., partway between Quesnel and the historic gold-rush town of Barkerville. Wells had originally been a gold-mining town during the 1930s and 1940s. The town became an artists' community during the 1960s and by the 1980s had established the Wells School of Arts. Music and art workshops were held every summer and on various weekends during the winter.

One day in July 2006, I finally met Robert Genn. By then he was in his sixties, internationally known, and at the height of his career. We spent the day discussing his career, marketing strategies, art schools, and how to become represented by art dealers and galleries. He was humorous and straightforward.

"To become an artist, lock yourself in your studio and paint!" He quoted Winston Churchill: "To be a painter, you need a heightened sense of observation." Robert's advice to us was: Look three times and try to understand. Think twice about what it is you are seeing. Paint once, with economy and audacity.

After our day's workshop, Robert and the folks from our class came to the Wells Art Gallery to view my one-man show. The gallery is a beautiful building in downtown Wells, which, with a population of about 200, is in a unique setting for an artists' community. Most of the town's houses have been renovated and decorated in an eclectic array of colours. The town sits on the edge of a large meadow and forested mountains.

Robert and my classmates looked at my landscape paintings, and Robert gave me a very positive critique. I was ecstatic! Robert Genn, the famous Canadian artist, liked my work!

We then drove the eight miles to Barkerville and had dinner at the Lung Duck Tong Chinese restaurant. I couldn't believe I was sitting at the same table as Robert Genn. Over dinner we discussed art, artists, and my style of painting. An artist I long admired was having a meal with me. I couldn't believe my good fortune. I learned so much from my day with Robert. He gave me his private phone number and told me to call any time. What a privilege!

Robert and I corresponded over the next few years. In September 2011, I had a one-man show at the Woodside Gallery in Harrison Mills, B.C. Robert critiqued my exhibition and said he was impressed with my watercolours, which I took as high praise from such a renowned Canadian artist.

Robert Genn passed away from pancreatic cancer in May 2014. He had gained international recognition for his landscapes of Canada's West Coast, and his death was a major loss to the art world.

Emily Carr

Unfortunately, I was born too late to meet the legendary B.C. artist, who passed away 11 years before I was born. Although I was unable to meet her in real life, I met her spirit. She taught me so much while I drew from her original paintings at the Vancouver Art Gallery in 1978. She taught me how to paint the forests of British Columbia. As I sketched from her paintings, I could feel her guiding my hand and sketching pencil.

I read and researched everything I could on Emily Carr. During the 1930s, Emily made a painting trip to the Cariboo region and on the way home stopped at Sardis and sketched my grandfather's barns at the hop yard. At an exhibition of her works at the Heffel Gallery in Vancouver in 1982, I found that pen and ink sketch of my grandfather's barns. It was a small drawing titled Hop Barns at Sardis. The price for the small drawing was $4000. Being a poor art student in 1982, I couldn't afford to purchase it. For years I have been trying to locate it. To own an original Emily Carr drawing of my grandfather's barns would be extremely special.

I greatly admire her for her eccentric personality and the fact she could create such original, inspiring work. Although she was chastised and treated as an outcast by Victoria's elite, she continued to pursue her artistic vision despite their ignorance.

Emily Carr became a legendary Canadian artist and the reason I became a landscape painter. I wish I could have known her.

Creatures in the Night

Screeching in the moonlight
Howling to the air
Stomping through the forests
in the dark without a care

Giant shadows lurking
in the darkness of the trees
Stláleqm or Sasquatch
Ghosts that no one sees

Mystery in legends
Subjects of tall tales
Only those believe
who have heard
the creature's wails...

Chapter Thirty-Two

Stl'áleqm, Sasquatch And Cries In The Night

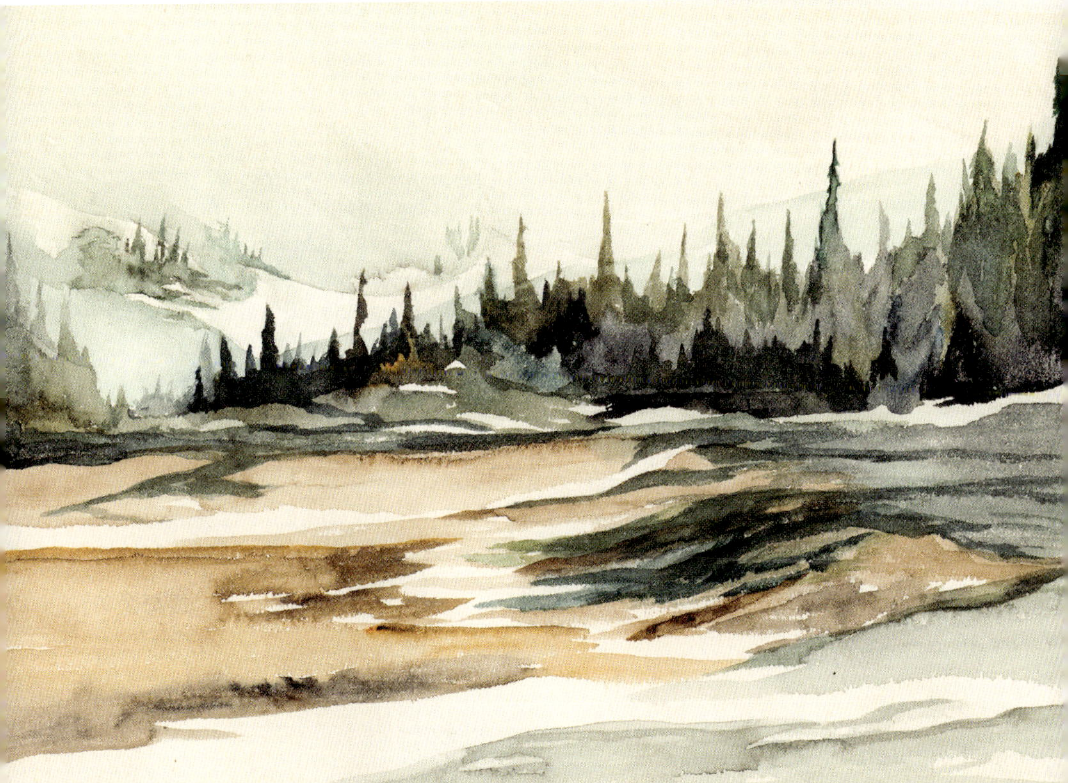

Early Spring on Elk Mountain

According to my Stó:lō uncle, Stl'áleqm, in the Halq'eméylem language, means supernatural creature. There are many supernatural creatures in the Stó:lō culture.

Beings such as slollicums in Cultus Lake, water babies in Chilliwack Lake, the Giant Maggot, the Two-Headed Snake, Salmon people, Plant People, the Cannibal Woman, the Ghost Woman of Harrison Lake, and the S'l:lhqey (SEEL-KEE) of the Chilliwack River.

According to John Wallace, in the book Being Ts'elxwéyeqw, "There was a large animal living in a deep pond near Semiault, where the Chilliwack Airport is now. It travelled along the river into the Cultus Lake area and in the olden days had been seen as far up as Chilliwack Lake. It was called SEEL-KEE

(S'l:Lhqey)".

In Oliver Wells' 1970 compilation book Myths and Legends of the STAW-loh Indians of South Western British Columbia, Richard Malloway discusses a double-headed serpent, Yeqwyeqwíiws (Yook-Yohk-WHAY-oo.s), that in ancient times was the protecting "power" that dominated the entrance to the family home, known as a WHIL-muh-QWELTH. When ceremonial gatherings were held, no one entered without first washing in a special "medicine" bowl provided for such purpose. This cleansing ritual freed one from the power of the SEEL-KEE. The bald eagles, regarded as guardians of the Ch.ilhl-kway-uhk tribe, "keep watch over the abandoned home site and returning SEEL-KEE serpent."

According to Gwen Point, in the same book, "Stl'áleqem are spiritual beings." When you move into higher levels of spirituality or enlightenment, "Everything has its place. You have spiritual people, you have elders, you have plant people; well, these Stl'áleqem have their place as well. They are messengers and teachers, just to be used to maintain balance in a good way."

Sasquatch

Some people believe that the Sasquatch is not a Stl'áleqm, but a real being. This is an excerpt from Lisa Kadane's July 21, 2022, article for BBC Travel, "The True Origin of Sasquatch"1:

"There have been 37 notable Sasquatch sightings near the town of Harrison Hot Springs, B.C., since 1900. The Sasquatch is sacred to West Coast First Nations. Particularly the Sts'ailes (Sta-hay-lis) who have lived in the Harrison River Valley for at least 10,000 years. The Sts'ailes people believe the Sasquatch is a caretaker of the people. The Sts'ailes have passed down songs and stories about 'Sasq'ets,' a shape-shifter that protects the land and people. Sasq'ets (sas-kets) means 'hairy man' in Halq'eméylem. The word comes from a mountain that's called Sasq'ets Tel, 'the place where the Sasquatch gather.' Sts'ailes tradition holds that the creature can change from its physical form to a rock, tree, or even another animal. The Sasquatch is believed to be able to walk in two realms, the spiritual and the physical; that's why they've never been caught."

Cries In The Night

In the late spring of 1980, Man Mountain Mike, my brother and cousin and I went camping on the top of Elk Mountain. There were still remnants of snowdrifts in the shady areas; otherwise the weather was clear and warm. We chose a campsite in a gully below the top of the mountain, in a sheltered, treed area.

My 16-year-old cousin was from Victoria, B.C., and had never camped in the bush. He was a mountain virgin. We were going to show him a good time, camp on Elk, then hike the ridge to Cheam.

We set up both tents after the day's hike, started a campfire and made supper. We sat around the fire until late in the night. I had camped on Elk Mountain many, many times over the years and during all seasons. We retired to our tents at 1 a.m. My cousin shared a tent with my brother, and I bunked in with Mike.

1 https://www.bbc.com/travel/article/20220720-the-true-origin-of-sasquatch

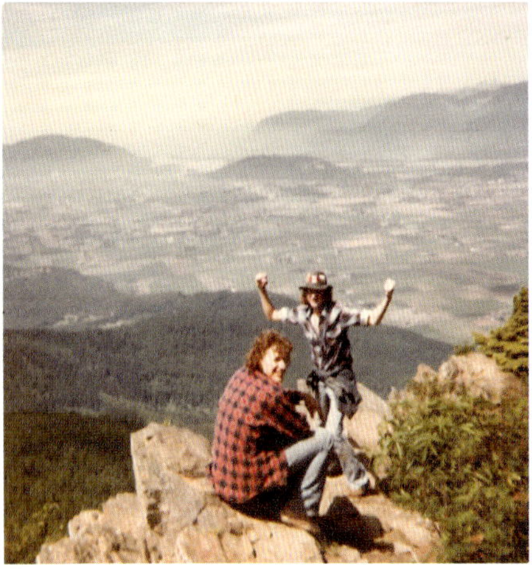

Brother on Elk Mountain

We were awoken two hours later by a blood-curdling scream from far out in the bush. It wasn't a cougar, coyote, or wolf. The loud cry sounded human; however, we hadn't seen anyone else camping up there. The cries went on sporadically for an hour and then stopped. The cries seemed to have come from a distance away, over the rise from where we were.

The four of us stoked the fire and tried to decide what it was that was making those unnerving screams. We could not come up with a rational reason, so returned to our tents. Our city-dwelling cousin was quite nervous, but we assured him it was nothing sinister, probably just a screech owl.

The rest of the night was quiet, and we awoke rested in the morning. After an early breakfast we gathered our daypacks and set out on the trail that followed the ridge to Mount Cheam. We looked for prints on the ground to identify what kind of animal had disturbed our sleep. We found no prints but made our way to the ridge and had a good hike above the Chipmunk Valley, with great views of the Fraser Valley to our left. We eventually made it to the peak of Cheam. Our cousin was tired but impressed. The view of the surrounding mountains and the valley floor was stunning. We made it back to camp quite late, gathered dead branches and dry lichen, and started a roaring fire. We started up our Primus stoves and made supper. There is no water on Elk, so we melted snow from the old snow drifts (which is a long process) for our cooking water and coffee. There was no discussion of the cries from the previous night. We sat around the fire late into the night and then retired to our tents.

A few hours later, we were again suddenly awoken by loud cries. This time they seemed to come from both sides of our camp, and they were close. The screams were not human, nor animal. The hairs on the backs of our necks stood on end. Stl'áleqm!

The cries were getting closer and louder. My cousin packed his gear and ran for the trail. Man Mountain Mike was right behind him, and in an instant they had both left camp and vanished into the darkness. My brother and I were experienced outdoorsmen and convinced ourselves the screams were coming from some sort of wounded animal, but the cries came closer and louder and seemed to encircle our position.

We quickly extinguished the fire with snow and dirt, tore down our tents, rolled up our sleeping bags, donned our packs and ran for the trail. Neither of us had heard such sounds in the woods, after all our years and trips into the bush. The farther we got from camp, the closer came the cries. They were following us down the mountain and getting closer, giving out shrill screeches as they pursued us. It wasn't a wolf pack or coyotes. They moved quickly and stealthily through the trees. We were now running desperately and dangerously down the dark trail, dodging tree trunks, thrashing through branches and stumbling over rocks. Halfway down the mountain the pursuit ended, the cries stopped, and we suddenly felt safe.

Elk Mountain is a civilized, popular mountain, with many visitors. We weren't deep in the bush in a remote part of the Chilliwack River Valley. What had we heard? What was chasing us? We quickly made it the rest of the way down to Chuck the Truck, where we found Man Mountain Mike and my cousin, locked inside the cab. Man Mountain Mike was usually an unflappable, practical, brave outdoorsman, but this time he had fear in his eyes. My cousin had soiled himself. We fired up Chuck the Truck and put the pedal to the metal.

Was it Stl'álqem, supernatural creatures, or the legendary Sasquatch? One thing we knew for sure: we would never camp on Elk Mountain again!

The Mountaineers

Intrigued by nature's steeples
that reach up to the sky
Immense in size and granite
who stand to thwart
man's tries

Of those who strain
to climb them
the question always why?
Because they're there
to conquer
among the clouds so high

Nylon ropes and courage
the climber struggles on
over crevices and obstacles
only for the strong

Once upon the summit
in the warm sun rays that gleam
alone with Mother Nature
another realized dream...

Chapter Thirty-Three

Modern Day Mountain Man

For as long as there have been mountains, there have been brave souls who climbed them. Legendary climbers who have scaled our Chilliwack Cascades are men and women such as Phyllis and Don Munday, Elfrida Pigou, and Fred Becky. During the 1970s and 1980s, local climbers Jack Bryceland and Neil Grainger climbed our local peaks. Neil Grainger is an Honorary Lifetime Member of the Chilliwack Outdoor Club and author of The Mountain Project. He is a respected local mountaineer and my former employer when I worked for the Chilliwack Search and Rescue mapping project in the late 1970s. Neil introduced me to the wonderful world of hiking and exploring our majestic local Cascades.

The torch has been passed to a new generation of climbers. Men and women from the Lower Mainland and beyond have now been lured by the challenges of our Chilliwack Mountains. One such mountaineer is an East Coast transplant who fell in love with our awe-inspiring granite towers. He moved out west and has now become a local Peak Bagger. The young gentleman's name is Lukas Mann, and this is his story:

"British Columbia became my home roughly two years ago, in 2021. It's now my eighth home, having grown up in three different Canadian provinces (Ontario, Nova Scotia, and P.E.I.) as well as a stint in Indonesia for my middle school and high school years.

"The mountains have always fascinated me from a young age. I first strapped on a snowboard when I was seven years old, and it quickly became my sport of choice. I spent many, many hours watching and downloading all the cutting-edge snowboard films put out by riders on the West Coast of the continent. Man alive, I was hooked. Mountains of that scale seemed like a pipe dream to me, and belonging to a family of eight on a single income meant that big vacations weren't commonplace.

"Fast-forward a decade, and I ended up in Vancouver, B.C., for university. From the moment my plane touched down in YVR, my eyes were constantly glued to the peaks that tempted me daily.

"My first real outing into the B.C. mountains was an all-night push through three feet of snow to the summit of Panorama Ridge with a few new friends from school. We made it to the top in time to witness the most incredible sunrise I've ever witnessed in my life. I was hooked.

"Within a few weeks, I had reached out via Facebook to a number of local mountaineers and had started to make regular forays into the mountain ranges surrounding the Fraser Valley. The Chilliwack Cascades quickly became an area of particular interest to me. The North Shore Mountains and the Duffey are stunning, but they tend to be highly trafficked and a fair bit further afield as well. The Chilliwack River Valley, on the other hand, is much more appealing. Jagged peaks, verdant valleys, turquoise alpine lakes—the Cascades are a special place.

"It is not uncommon to find a trail in a guidebook and plan a good overnight trip, only to show up and find the trail ceases to exist. The Chilliwack Cascades seem to be the only range that has become more inaccessible as time passes, due to the deterioration of logging roads and a general lack of tourism. It's wild, remote, and unforgiving. It's no joke. But it's also incredibly appealing.

"This past summer, I ticked off a few climbs that had been on my list for a while.

"Foremost on that list was the Fang of the River Valley, Mount Slesse. Slesse is one of those mountains that doesn't just have a local reputation—it's known the world over for its ragged profile and world-class climbing. The Northeast Buttress route up Slesse earned a spot on the Top 50 Classic Climbs of North America, and any alpine climber worth his salt has either made an attempt on the buttress or plans to at some point. Needless to say, Slesse has a reputation that precedes itself. A summit of the Fang would be quite the prize, and I was set on making it happen, one way or another.

"Not being a particularly confident climber, I settled on the southwest face route, which isn't nearly as technical as the Northeast Buttress. That being said, it still involves a long, steep approach and a great deal of exposed scrambling, with one or two pitches of roped-up climbing. I had bounced the idea off a few friends, and it eventually got the go-ahead in early August 2022.

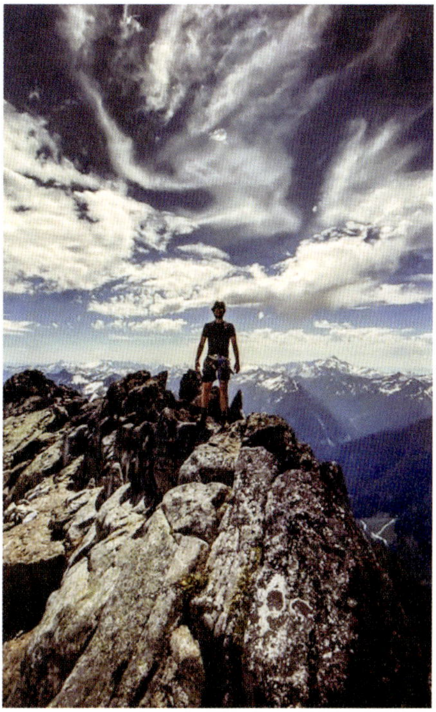

Lukas Mann on Top of Mount Slesse

"We left the trailhead at 4 a.m. and started the long trudge up the decommissioned logging road before veering straight up the steepest trail I've ever been on in my life. Three hours later, we found ourselves at the high knoll, with the imposing rock face looming above our heads. Another hour later, and we were donning helmets and harnesses at the base of the first of three third-class gullies.

"The southwest face route isn't terribly technical, but it is uber-exposed and known for requiring a high degree of route finding. There are three gullies, a few ledge traverses, a pitch or two of roped-in 5th class climbing, and then some more exposed 4th class to the summit.

"Thankfully, our leader, Ben Hall, had climbed this route the previous summer, and he remembered the route well enough to keep us well on track the whole day. We moved relatively slowly, more due to the fact that I was out of shape than anything else. (Sometimes it's good to be humbled in the mountains, and this was one of those days.)

"By 12:30 p.m., our party of four was standing on the knife-edge summit, taking in the panoramic vista. Views deep into the American Alps as well as north into the Coastal Mountains were more than enough to keep us satisfied for over an hour on the summit, before we packed up and started to retrace our route back off the summit block.

"Down climbing is always a bit more precarious than the way up, and we ended up making five rappels. A few of those could've been avoided, but when you haul a rope and gear that high up, it always feels good to make as much use of it as possible. We finally breathed a sigh of relief once we dropped out of the last gully, and were back on the actual trail. Looking back up at the craggy ramparts of Slesse felt pretty darn good now, knowing I had finally knocked it off my list, thanks to a solid effort with a great team.

"The rest of my summer was spent almost exclusively in the Chilliwack Cascades. Rexford, Welch, Flora, and a number of other peaks fell off my list before the first snowfall of the year. Waking up to six bears in the alpine meadow below Welch was a particularly memorable moment, as was the fiery sunset below the Nesakwatch Spires. But alas, if I told every story I had from the mountains, this chapter would drag on far too long.

"The Chilliwack Cascades are a special place, and any time I have the chance to spend time in that blessed place I jump on it. It's not always a summit, and it is not always epic ... but it's what I love, and I wouldn't trade it for the world."

Chapter Thirty-Four

Radium Lake And The Attack Of The Killer Pack Rats

In early June of 1980, I was asked by two friends from Vancouver to lead them to Radium Lake, above Chilliwack Lake. It was early spring, so I told them to wear proper hiking boots and bring warm clothes and jackets, as there would still be snow at that elevation.

They arrived in Sardis early on the designated day. We packed our gear into the back of Chuck the Truck and made the drive to the trailhead near Chilliwack Lake. It was a fairly hot spring morning when we arrived. The two guys were wearing shorts, t-shirts, and running shoes. First, I laughed, then told them I wouldn't take them on the hike dressed like that, as they would get extremely cold and their shoes would get soaked as we gained elevation and reached snow.

They put on their jeans, had only brought running shoes, and insisted it was too hot to wear jackets. I was wearing my Tyrol waterproof hiking boots, gaiters, and water-repellent hiking pants, and had brought my down-filled ski jacket, gloves, and wool toque.

My survey crew had marked and mapped the route to Radium Lake two years previous. Since then, I had made the trip several times and always enjoyed staying in the old cabin at the lake. The cabin had a wood stove, counter and cupboards to store our grub. It came equipped with plates, utensils, pots and pans. It had been built by inmates from the Ford Mountain Camp in the early 1960s and was a well-built log cabin with a shake roof.

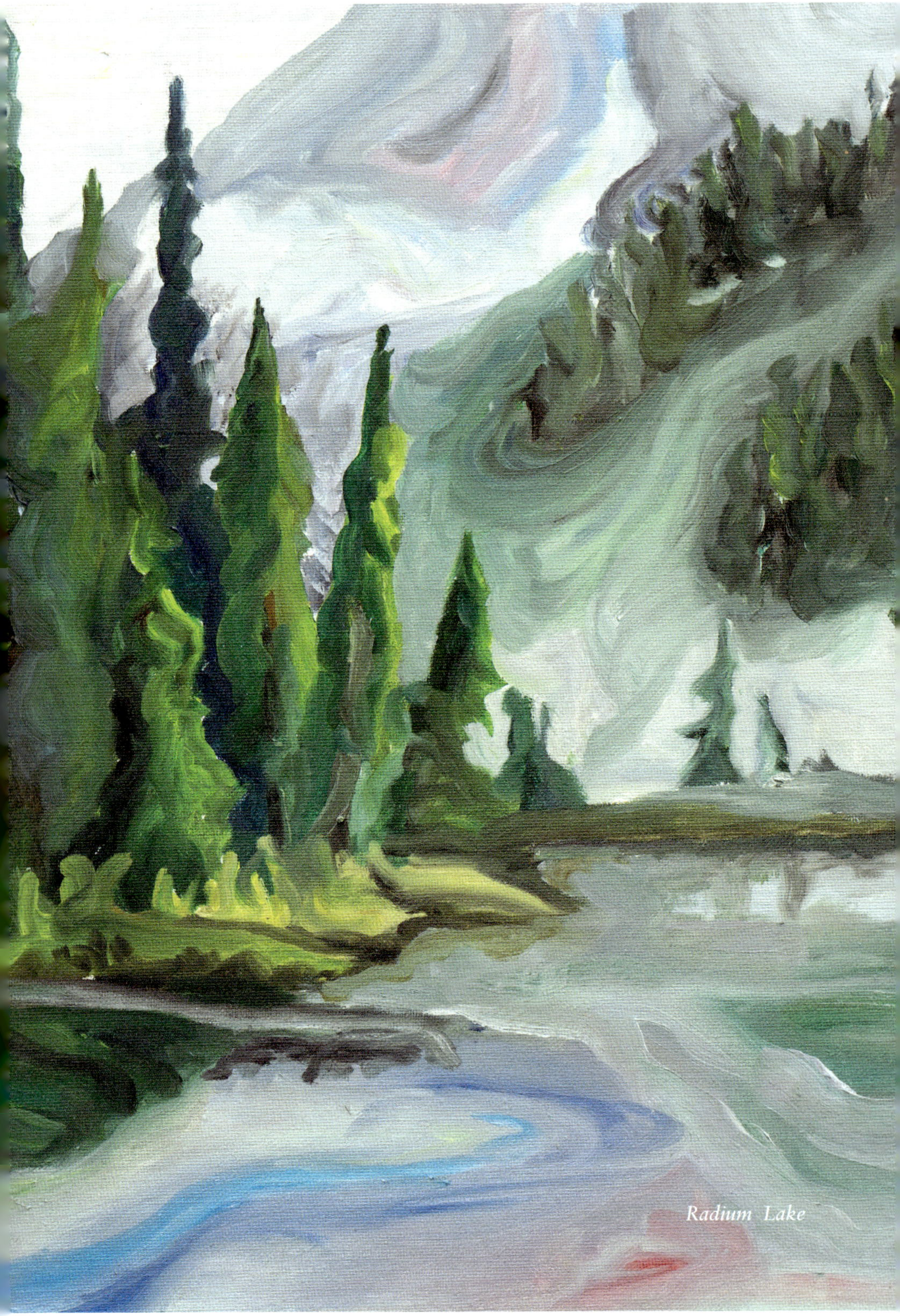

Radium Lake

The lake was a good size, and the view of Mount Webb was beautiful.

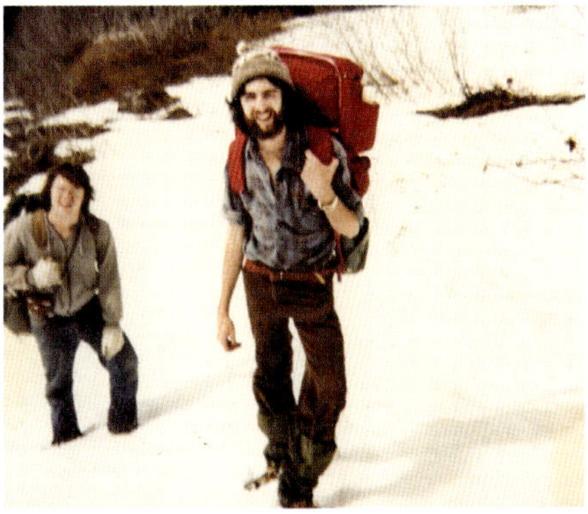

Author as tour guide

I was under the impression my two acquaintances were experienced hikers. Two hours into the trip, I realized they weren't. They had bottles of beer inside their packs, along with many other unnecessary items: cast iron frying pan, cans of beans and other heavy foodstuffs. I should have checked their packs before we left. Packing bottles of beer up a steep, long trail was definitely a rookie mistake. I didn't realize they had brought their Black Label refreshments until they stopped and cracked open a couple cold ones. I should have turned them around and made them camp at the Chilliwack Lake campsite, however they insisted they could manage their heavy packs. After they'd drained their first beer, we continued up the trail. The trail was in good condition, however after two hours I could see they were straining under the weight of their packs. I had them stash some of their beer in the creek and left their frying pan behind. The trail started getting slippery, and they had no traction with their running shoes.

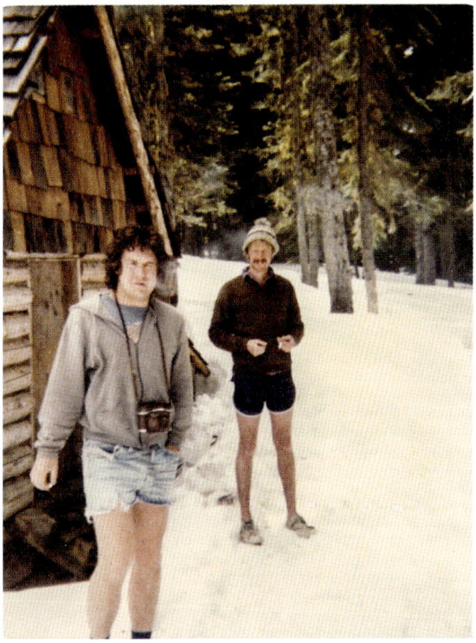

Rookie Hikers at the Cabin

Watching them try to balance while crossing the creek on the old mossy logs was entertaining. The farther we got up the trail, the cooler it was getting. Soon they were donning sweatshirts and complaining of sore feet. We were only a third of the way there. Then we started to run into snow, then more snow, then more snow, and then the trail became completely covered. Now their feet were wet and cold, but they resisted advice to turn back. After four hours, they were exhausted, and the snow was getting deeper. They were not having fun. The trail to Radium Lake is steep and long. By the time we reached the lake they were stunned. The snow was knee-deep, and the old cabin was buried. The lake sat frozen under a foot of snow.

Before we set out on our journey, my adventurers had insisted I was joking about the lake being frozen. They expected to be swimming in the lake once they arrived. Reality soon set in when we reached the cabin. We had to dig down through the snow to get to the door. It was cold. I was warm and dry but starting to worry about my hypothermic companions.

The woodshed was full, so I split some kindling and fired up the stove. The rookies hung their wet jeans above the stove and set out their runners and socks to dry. I had packed dehydrated meals and a small Primus stove and was soon enjoying my dinner, along with a pot of hot coffee. Fortunately for the city boys, there was a can opener in the cabin so they could cook their cans of beans. I was astounded to see one of the guys pull a small hibachi out of his pack, along with a small bag of briquettes. They took their mini barbecue outdoors and cooked their steaks.

After dinner, they cracked open their remaining bottles of beer and we played poker until midnight. I bunked up in the loft. One of the guys slept on the cot next to the counter, and the other guy took the cot along the other side of the room. Unfortunately, my weary travellers had neglected to wash their plates and cooking utensils. Empty food containers were also left on the counter.

I was awoken a couple of hours after we crawled inside our sleeping bags by screams from my travellers. Pack rats had emerged to snack on my friend's leftover food scraps, and the rats were jumping down off the counter onto the guy sleeping next to it. He was screaming in terror. The other adventurer turned on his flashlight, grabbed the pellet rifle that was leaning against the cabin wall, and began shooting at rats. Unfortunately for his friend, he was a poor aim and in the semi-darkness shot his friend several times while they jumped around inside the cabin.

Up in the loft, I was safe from the attacking pack rats and ricocheting pellets. I turned on my lantern, and the rats vanished back into the shadows. My two shell-shocked companions were loading their packs. It was the middle of the night, and the temperature was far below zero, so I convinced them to stay. We stoked the fire, and I went back to sleep. The unhappy campers sat up all night with the lantern on and at the crack of dawn were ready to leave.

Unfortunately for them, it had snowed overnight so we weren't going anywhere for a while. They spent the day splitting wood and searching the cabin for rats. The victim of the shooting session was nursing his wounds and removing pellets from his body. That night they scrubbed their plates clean and stashed away their food supplies. Again, they sat up all night with the lantern on and the pellet rifle loaded.

It warmed up overnight, so we set out on our return trip early the next morning. There had been no further casualties that evening. The boys were tired, wounded, covered in pellet wounds and a few rat bites. I was thoroughly enjoying the trip. It had been an extremely entertaining two days watching these amateur outdoorsmen suffer after having not taken my advice to prepare properly.

We arrived back at Chuck the Truck after a long hike down. My two compadres swore never to go camping again and no doubt carried a fear of rats for the rest of their lives!

Survival

Call out to me in morning
Call out to me in night
The sentry in the tree tops
is heard but out of sight

Soaring in the daybreak
His kingdom at his claws
Black feathers hold his magic
and echos out his cause

Where do you go at day's end?
Where do you go to rest?
Survival of the strongest
is Mother Nature's test.

Chapter Thirty-Five

Cornea Transplant, Heart Surgery And The Girl In My Bed

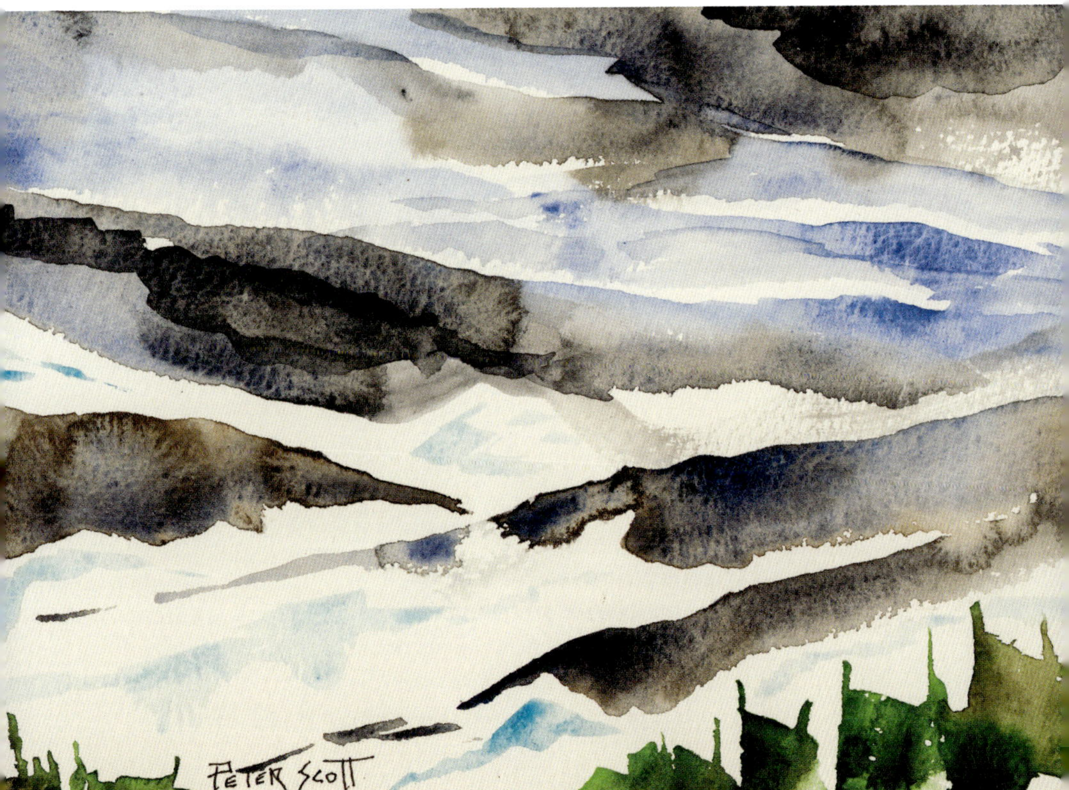

My Cascades

I moved to Quesnel in 1983 to teach art and graphics at Maple Drive Junior Secondary School. My painting career had been put on hold because of the blindness in my left eye. Fortunately I had 20/20 vision in my right eye, and so far it had not developed keratoconus. I was put on a waiting list for a corneal transplant. The eye surgeon wanted to wait until my cornea was ready to rupture before operating. In the meantime, I taught school, painted, coached, and played hockey with one eye.

We played teachers' hockey at midnight on Friday nights. One-eyed goalies were not in great demand. I used one eye looking at the puck and my blind eye looking for it! I also helped coach my son's hockey team, daughter's soccer team, and the junior girls basketball team at MDJS. I drove teams all over the north, usually during snowstorms and always with one eye tied behind my back.

I noticed at the beginning of the hockey season I was feeling exhausted, nauseous, and shaky-legged at the end of every game. On Oct. 12, I received a call from my eye specialist saying they had a cornea for me. I had to get to St. Paul's Hospital in Vancouver within 24 hours. I stood outside the bus depot in the freezing cold, waiting for the midnight bus to Vancouver, wearing my old ski jacket and my eye patch.

I arrived at the hospital in time for the operation. My bed was in a ward with three other patients also waiting for eye surgery. They were all diabetics, missing appendages and extremely nervous of their upcoming procedures. I told them to quit worrying, that it wasn't heart surgery, and each of us had two eyes. Then they wheeled me into the operating room.

The anesthesiologist looked at me while preparing to put me under and asked how tall I was. I told him 6 foot 1. He asked my weight. I told him 130 pounds. Then he marvelled at how long my arms and fingers were. Then the lights went out.

When I came to, I touched my bandaged eye and asked the doctor how my eye was. He said my eye was fine but I needed a heart operation. The guys in my room burst out in laughter.

"Tough room," stated the doctor. I told him it was a private joke. The cardiologist asked me if I was aware of a condition called Marfan's Syndrome. It is a rare connective-tissue disease that weakens the heart and causes people with Marfan's to be extremely tall and thin, with disproportionately long appendages. Undiagnosed, people with this condition often die by the time they are 30. I was 37.

My eye surgery had just saved my life. Without undergoing a cornea transplant, I would have died of heart failure while playing hockey.

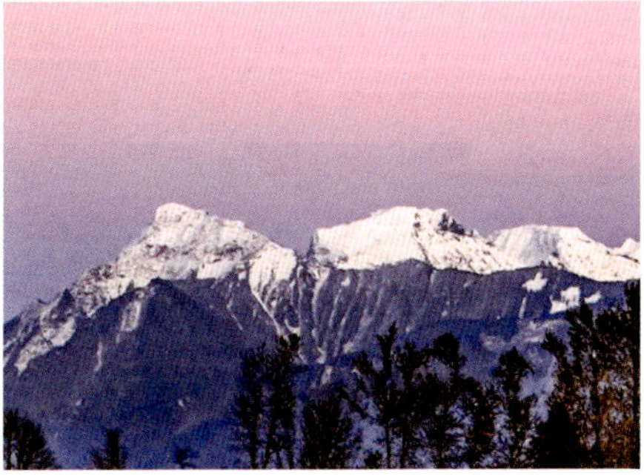

Sunset Over Mount Cheam

The doctor told me I eventually would need an artificial mitral valve, as the anesthetic and strain of the surgery had shredded my own valve and it was now leaking severely.

After I heard this uplifting news, Dr. Dubord, my eye surgeon, paid me a visit. He walked me down the hall to his examination room, had me look into a scope, and checked my new cornea. I repeatedly asked him whose cornea I had. He told me it was unethical to divulge that information. After many, many requests, he relented and told me I received the cornea from a deceased 81-year-old Asian gentleman, and the woman down the hall had received his other one. He told me the age of the cornea didn't matter as long as the tissue was healthy. I was ecstatic! Now I was part Asian as well as of Scottish, French Canadian, and Moroccan heritage! (At the time of this writing, 2023, my cornea is 111 years old!)

I dubbed my new eye Kwon Luck and returned to my ward. As I approached my room, I noticed an elderly Asian woman sleeping in my bed. My roommates were delirious with laughter. I asked, "What the heck? First, they gave me his eye, now they gave me his wife?" The woman had wandered over from the psych ward and crawled into the first available bed.

What a day.

In addition to the disproportionate limbs, I learned that people with Marfan's Syndrome usually have a sunken chest, high palate and long face. The connective tissue of a Marfoid is constructed like a spider web, whereas healthy people have connective tissue constructed like rope fibres. People with Marfan's Syndrome have a high metabolism, are extremely thin and find it difficult to gain weight. They also have loose joints, and this results in frequent injuries such as sprained ankles and wrists. The disease also affects bone mass and causes bone fractures.

My cardiologists and genetics team were astonished at how I had been able to hike and climb steep mountains for years without having experienced an aortic dissection, which typically results in death by the early thirties. (Born lucky, I guess.)

Ironically, people with Marfan's Syndrome are well designed for sports such as basketball and track due to their height and long appendages. There are stories of famous athletes who seemed in superb physical health but suddenly collapsed and died of a ruptured aorta due to undiagnosed Marfan's disease.

After my corneal graft and Marfan's diagnosis, I was forced to stop playing hockey, and because of my severely leaking mitral valve, I could no longer hike mountains. Once again, I slid into a deep, dark depression.

After six weeks of healing, I drove to Vancouver with one eye to have Dr. Dubord remove the first set of stitches from my eye. As he was cutting the stitches with his scalpel and removing them with tweezers, I suddenly felt excruciating pain. It felt like I had been stabbed in the eye with a knife. Dr. Dubord looked shocked and immediately left the room. Not a good sign. My new cornea had separated from my eye. He returned and placed a special contact lens on my eye to heal the wound. He then told me I was the first of over 2,000 patients to have that occur. (The joys of being a Marfoid.) A healthy person's cornea after surgery would heal in six months; I had stitches holding my eye together for three years before it healed.

I continued to teach art at the high school with a pirate patch. On two separate occasions, while bending over to lift a box of clay, my stitches snapped and punctured my cornea. This was not enjoyable. None of the optometrists in Quesnel nor the doctors would attempt to remove the broken stitch, so on both occasions I had to drive my rusty old 4x4 pickup truck a hundred miles to Prince George (usually during a blizzard) to have an eye specialist remove the stitch and save my eye. During these events, it felt like I had a burning cigarette in my eye, a sensation that usually lasted for several weeks. (Brought a tear to my eye.)

During the three years my eye was healing, my mitral valve was continuing to shred and stretch and leak, causing me extreme fatigue. Over those three years, my wife and I made many, many, many road trips to Vancouver from Quesnel to interview heart surgeons, hoping to find one who was knowledgeable about Marfan's Syndrome, as it was a rare condition 30 years ago. None of the heart surgeons we interviewed could assure me the tissue around my heart would be able to support the stitches needed to hold an artificial valve in place, due to my connective tissue disorder. My depression was not improving, time was running out, and I was incapable of running.

In July 1996, three years after my cornea transplant, my eye had healed and Dr. Dubord was able to remove the last of my stitches. I could see to paint again.

My father travelled to Vancouver with me, as I also had an appointment with another heart surgeon. This time I was fortunate to meet Dr. Hilton Ling, an extremely accomplished heart surgeon. He had trained in South

Africa with Dr. Christian Bernard, the famous surgeon who performed the first human heart transplant. Dr. Ling assured me he could replace my damaged valve with a mechanical, carbide steel valve. It looked like the top of an old-fashioned carburetor. He had successfully performed this operation on another Marfan patient.

My dad and I were ecstatic. Finally, after three years, I could see again, and now I had hope that my heart could be repaired. We celebrated over a meal of fish and chips and beer.

The operation was scheduled for Valentine's Day, February 1997, at St. Paul's Hospital in Vancouver.

By now I was extremely weak and tired. I could barely make it through the school day or pick up a paintbrush. I continued to teach until Feb. 10, four days before my scheduled surgery.

I said goodbye to my kids and then boarded the Greyhound bus to Vancouver with my wife. I was not certain I would be returning to my children.

The day arrived, and I was wheeled into the operating room. My wife, parents, and siblings wished me luck and said goodbye. I was more and more sure it was the last time I would see them. I was 40 years old.

I awoke the next morning with an elephant sitting on my chest and tubes down my throat. I couldn't breathe easily, but I was ALIVE! A playboy cardiologist waltzed into the room, flirted with the nurses and then, with a Cheshire cat's smile, ripped the tubes out of my throat. Unfortunately, I had wires protruding from my stomach and connected to a machine, or I would have ripped his throat out.

I was wheeled to a ward, feeling dazed and confused. I had a 14-inch-long incision on my chest. My sternum had been cut with a saw and my ribs had been cracked open. However, I no longer had a broken heart.

Dr. Ling told my father my valve had been far too stretched to accommodate the mechanical valve they had prepared for me, and they had sent someone down to the storeroom to find a larger one. I lay on the operating table cracked wide open for half an hour before they found a valve that would suffice. The surgeon told him I was extremely fortunate, as the new valve barely fit. They triple-stitched it and crossed their fingers it would hold in place.

It has held in place now for 26 years, which stupefies my current cardiologists.

I was placed in a ward with three other heart patients. One was a tough, 70-year-old miner I nicknamed "Hard Rock." One was a golf pro I called "Arnold" and the other an 87-year-old World War II veteran who had also had a valve replacement.

I couldn't understand what the constant clanking sound was in my head. The nurse informed me that it was the new metal, mechanical valve in my heart. It sounded like an old alarm clock. I asked how long the sound would last, and she informed me, forever. If it stopped clanking, I would have five seconds before I fell dead to the floor.

Good to know. I love that clanking sound. Now I sound like the crocodile in the Peter Pan story. When I'm in a quiet elevator with someone and they tell me I have a loud watch, I tell them no, what you hear is my mechanical carbide steel heart. That usually makes them shut up.

The World War II veteran was a character. He had been an intelligence officer in the British Air Force. His job was to fly into enemy territory and photograph their gun emplacements before an Allied bomber strike. I called him "007."

It took several days before I could sit up. There was a screen on the wall in the hallway, where the patients would gather around and watch the numbers. I thought it was a Keno machine and was disappointed when my numbers didn't come up. I found out later it was monitoring our vitals. During the two weeks I was in the hospital there were several Code Blues, which meant someone had bought the farm.

"007" regaled me with stories of his war exploits. "Hard Rock" visited with his miner buddies, and "Arnold" told me boring stories of his talents on the fairway. I'm not a golfer. One week, 007 went several days without a bowel movement. The nurses plied him with laxatives. I hadn't been able to eat for several days, and finally I was hungry and the nurse brought me a bowl of oatmeal. Meanwhile, Hard Rock locked himself in our bathroom for half an hour. 007 suddenly had to go and danced around the room, panicking that he was going to stain himself. Finally Hard Rock emerged from the bathroom, grumbling that after all that time he had only passed gas. At that point, 007 exploded! There was diarrhea flying across the floor, up the walls, and some even landed in my oatmeal! It was a disaster. I laughed so hard my ribs hurt.

Later that morning a nurse came and removed the staples from my chest with a pair of pliers and then pulled the copper wires from my stomach and disconnected me from my friendly monitoring machine.

After 14 days, I was released. I lay on my bed at home in Quesnel waiting for my ribs to heal. Every night, I saw a green outline of three figures standing guard by my bed. My doctor couldn't explain this phenomenon. I believe they were my spirit guides.

My dad came to Quesnel and drove me back to Sardis in a blizzard so that I could recuperate at my parents' house and be back with my mountains. Lying in their front room, staring out the window at Mount Cheam, Lady Peak, Welch Peak, Foley and Mount Slesse rejuvenated me. I began to heal. The power of my mountains restored my strength, and soon I was able to go outside on short walks.

I had survived, and in time lived to hike another day.

Constant Change

Something in the wind
is telling me
Somethings going to change
Nothing stays forever
Things get rearranged

My soul lives
in these mountains
forever, for all days
A spirit in the shadows
Here is where I'll stay...

Chapter Thirty-Six

My Soul Lives In These Mountains

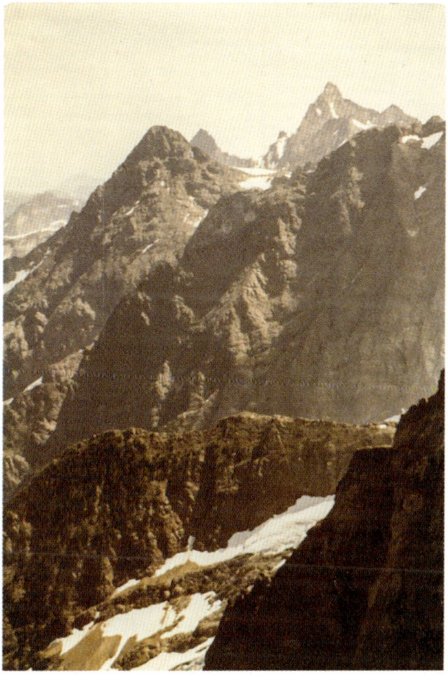
The Cascades

For over 67 years, the Chilliwack Mountains have been a source of inspiration and strength for me. These monuments of granite have withstood time. Their permanence has given me the resolve to struggle on, overcoming obstacles along life's path while trying to reach the summit.

Steep inclines, boulder fields, roaring streams, and cascading waterfalls have not stopped me as I strained under the weight of a heavy pack, attempting to reach the top. Along the way I stopped to marvel at their beauty and grandeur, as they always gave me a sense of peace.

These majestic peaks have made me want to capture their image on film and paint on canvas and in water color, forever freezing them in time.

The Chilliwack Cascades have healed me when I was ill and strengthened me when I was healthy. Making my way to the top after a long hike always filled me with a sense of accomplishment.

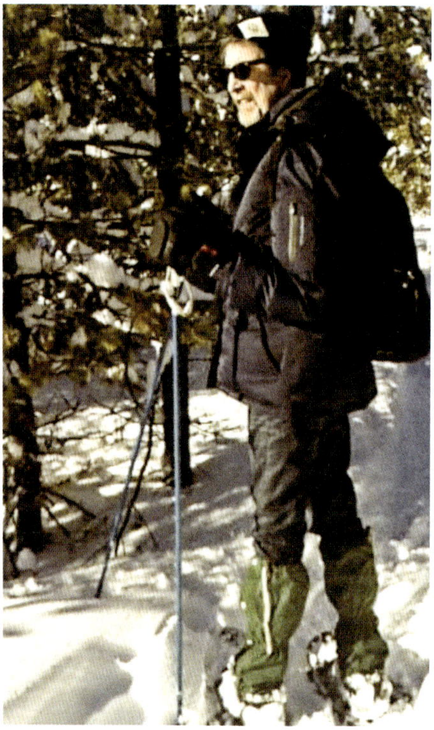

Author snowshoeing, winter 2023

Standing on them overlooking the valley was a euphoric feeling as I stood in awe of their majesty.

Over the years, people have discovered "my mountains." Thousands of hikers travel the trails enjoying the Chilliwack area. I hope they continue to respect our great outdoors and keep the trails, campsites and lakes pristine, so future generations can experience them.

Within the last few decades, the population of Chilliwack has exploded. When I was born in 1956 and lived in Sardis, the Chilliwack region had approximately 16,000 residents. As of 2023 that population stands at nearly 103,000, an increase of 87,000 over 67 years.

The geography of Chilliwack has also changed. Hop yards and farms have transformed into subdivisions, condos, malls, and big-box stores. Every year, more and more houses climb the slopes of the surrounding mountains, but still Mount Cheam, "Lhileqey," Lady Peak, "Sqwema:y," Mount McGuire, "Támiyehó:y," and Mount Slesse, "Suh-LEE-see," stand defiant and proud.

I always head home to these mountains for solace and calm. My soul lives in these mountains, and always will.

Acknowledgements

In writing this book I would like to acknowledge and thank several people who have assisted me in a variety of ways. I have used an assortment of books and source material for this project.

I thank Yvonne Way and her family for providing me with the book In The Arms Of The Mountains, A History of the Chilliwack River Valley, written by the Chilliwack River Valley Historical Society, authors David Lamson, Carol Murray, Don and Gloria Parker, Frank and Bev Sobkowich, Eileen Way and David Way. Their book was published by The Chilliwack River Valley Historical Society, 48151 Auchenway Road, Chilliwack, B.C. V4Z 1B8, 2006. This book was a great source of information for me. Meeting Yvonne during my research for this book and discovering our families were intertwined decades ago in the early days of settlement of the Chilliwack River Valley was an extremely pleasant surprise. Her family's unselfish gift of the last copy of their parents' book to me was an extremely generous and greatly appreciated present. Thank you from the bottom of my stitched-up heart!

The Chilliwack River Watershed – Fish, p.6 and p.7.

The Chilliwacks and the River Valley, p.21 and p.22

Mountains Within the Chilliwack River Valley, p.209, p.210, p.211, p.212, p.213

Creeks Within the Chilliwack River Valley, p.214, p.215, p.216, p.217, p.218.

Aircraft Crashes, p.229, p.230.

The book Being Ts'elxwéyeqw, First People's Voices and History from the Chilliwack-Fraser Valley, British Columbia, edited by David M. Shaepe, written and produced by the Ts'elxwéyeqw Tribe. Published by Harbour Publishing Co. Ltd. P.O. Box 219 Madeira Park, British Columbia, Canada, V0N 2H0

The following pages were used for reference material: The Meaning of Ts'elxwéyeqw Place and People, Albert Louie, p.26.

History of a People, Bob Joe, p.50, p.51

The Origin of Swiltcha (Cultus lake), Bob Joe and John Wallace, p.148, p.149.

The St'áleqm of Cultus lake, Billy Sepass, Bob Joe, John Wallace and Ken Malloway. p.152

S'ó:lmexw and Sxótsaqel ('Babies lake'/Chilliwack lake), John Wallace, Dan Milo, Diamond Jenness, Frank Malloway, p.154, p.156

Lhilheqey, Mount Cheam, Amy Cooper, Legend Of Mt. Cheam, p.244

Lhilheqey, Albert (Sonny) McHalsie, p.244

I am gratefully indebted to the publishers and the Ts'elxwéyeqw Tribe for the use of such an informative and valuable resource.

Neil Grainger and his book *The Mountain Project*. Neil gave me the opportunity to explore these mountains, and his book gave me extremely valuable reference material. Author Neil Grainger, published by Neil Grainger, 1998.

Jane Cromarty, for her research and documentation of the Cromarty family history. I could not have completed this book without her unfathomable research.

Dave Cromarty and his recollections of his father.

Brenda Bonin and the entire Cromarty clan for their assistance and permission to document their fascinating family history.

Indian Myths and Legends of the North Pacific Coast of America by Randy Bouchard and Dorothy Kennedy.

The Chilliwack Story, by Ron Denman.

Disaster on Mount Slesse, the Story of Western Canada's Worst Air Crash, by Betty O'Keefe and Ian MacDonald. An in-depth story of the fatal crash of TCA Flight 810.

"In the Face of Disaster, True Stories of Canadian Heroism from the Archives of Maclean's", edited by Michael Benedict. Published by Penguin Books Canada Ltd.

"The Strange Legacy of Flight 810's Crash on Mount Slesse" by Fred Clement, July 14, 1962. pages 278, 279, 281, 285, 287.

Gordon Smith The Art of Painting, by Ian M. Thom and Andrew Hunter.

British Columbia, A natural History of it's Origins, Ecology, and Diversity with a New Look at Climate Change by Richard Cannings and Sydney Cannings

Article by Lisa Kadane – "The True Origin of Sasquatch," for BBC Travel, July 21, 2022

Bradley Peters – "Making the Invisible Visible: Discovering Deep Stó:lō History of the Fraser Valley."

Greg Reely, photographer, who spent a huge amount of time

and energy photographing and documenting all my paintings included in this book. This book would not have been completed without Greg's generous use of his enormous talent. Thanks, Greg!

Photographers Skipper Fisher and Ivan Harris for contributing their photographs of the mountains for this project.

Lukas Mann, for his in-depth look at his climbing experiences in the Cascades.

My brother Colin Scott, for his technological skills and for assisting me in putting this book together.

My sister Janet Scott, for guiding me through this journey.

Sandra Albo and Andrew Bitcon, for reviewing my work and providing insight to my career.

To my family Lori, Brandon, Clare, Loren, Chris and Rumi.

To everyone who provided me with assistance, thank you for making this an enjoyable venture.

RELATED TITLES

Hiking Mt Baker & the North Cascades

D'ONOFRIO, JOHN

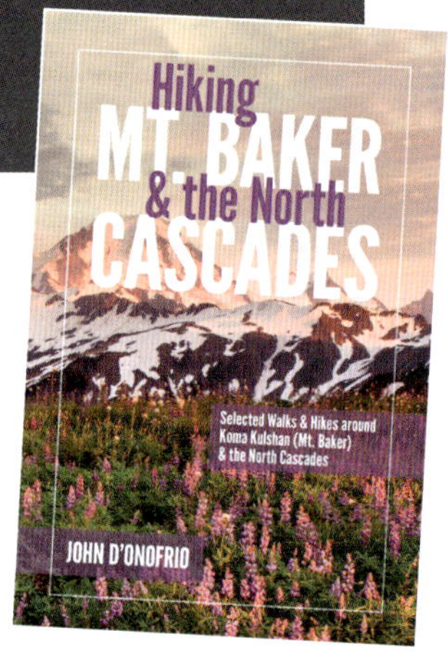

Selected Walks & Hikes Around Koma Kulshan

Complete with all the maps, access and local information you might need to navigate the trails, this book focuses on the inspiring beauty to be found on these extraordinary footpaths around Mt. Baker and the surrounding area. Lavishly illustrated with beautiful photographs and detailed topographic maps, each hike is presented with an eye toward the exceptional scenic splendor of these carefully-selected destinations, allowing you to maximize your aesthetic experience in these glorious mountains.

978-0-88839-760-7 [paperback] 978-0-88839-761-4 [epub]	5½ x 8½, sc, 304pp	$34.95

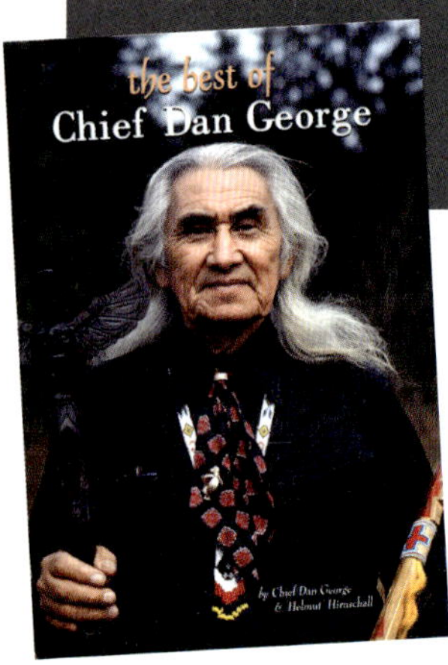

The best of Chief Dan George

CHIEF DAN GEORGE & HELMUT HIRNSCHALL

My years living & working with the Dene of the Northwest Territories

This collection brings together the most resonant and profound works of Chief Dan George, a distinguished Tsleil-Waututh chief, actor, and poet. This book combines his previously published works "My Heart Soars" and "My Spirit Soars" into a single volume, providing a comprehensive view of his poetic expression and spiritual insights. Central to this collection is "Lament for Confederation," a poignant piece that has become a cornerstone of Indigenous literature in Canada.

978-0-88839-544-3 [paperback] 978-0-88839-190-2 [epub]	5½ x 8½, sc, 128pp	$12.95